WHAT ARE ARCHIVES?

To the Walrus

What are Archives?
Cultural and Theoretical Perspectives: A Reader

Edited by
LOUISE CRAVEN
The National Archives, UK

ASHGATE

Published by
Ashgate Publishing Limited
Wey Court East
Union Road
Farnham
Surrey
GU9 7PT

Ashgate Publishing Company
Suite 420
101 Cherry Street
Burlington, VT 05401-4405
USA

Reprinted 2010

www.ashgate.com

British Library Cataloguing in Publication Data
What are archives? : cultural and theoretical perspectives
   : a reader
   1. Archives
   I. Craven, Louise
   027

Library of Congress Cataloging-in-Publication Data
What are archives? : cultural and theoretical perspectives : a reader / [edited] by Louise Craven.
      p. cm.
   Includes index.
   ISBN 978-0-7546-7310-1 (hardback : alk. paper) 1. Archives. 2. Archives--Social aspects. 3. Archives--Philosophy. 4. Archives--Automation. 5. Archival materials--Digitization. 6. Archivists. I. Craven, Louise, 1952-

   CD971.W48 2008
   027--dc22

2008022326

ISBN 978 0 7546 7310 1

Mixed Sources
Product group from well-managed forests and other controlled sources
www.fsc.org Cert no. SGS-COC-2482
© 1996 Forest Stewardship Council
FSC

Printed and bound in Great Britain by
TJ International Ltd, Padstow, Cornwall

Contents

THEME III   THE IMPACT OF COMMUNITY ARCHIVES

THEME IV   ARCHIVAL USE AND USERS

List of Figures

About the Contributors

Gerard Collis – better known as Paddy – is a librarian. Paddy is data and website editor for the Archives Hub, a gateway to descriptions of archives held in UK universities and institutions of higher and further education. The Archives Hub is supported by JISC, and is a service provided by MIMAS at the University of Manchester. Paddy's research interests include subject indexing, science fiction and surrealism.

Louise Craven is Head of Cataloguing at The National Archives of England and Wales and the UK (TNA). Prior to her post at TNA she worked as an archivist for the Historical Manuscripts Commission and for the Greater London Record Office (now London Metropolitan Archives), and as a teacher for the Open University, the Roehampton Institute and Thames Polytechnic. She has contributed actively to conferences concerned with archives and society and has published on a variety of archival and historical topics, most recently in *Archives* (XXXII (117), October 2007) on the role of epic and heroic narrative in archives and society today.

Andrew Flinn is Programme Director of the Archives and Records Management M.A. programme at University College London, chair of the Forum for Archives and Records Management Education and Research (FARMER) and editor of the *Journal of the Society of Archivists*. He is principal investigator on the AHRC-funded 'Community Archives and Identities' project which will examine community archive and heritage initiatives amongst black and minority ethnic groups. Andrew was previously archivist of the Labour and Communist party archives held at the National Museum of Labour History at the University of Manchester. Recent publications include 'Community histories, community archives: some opportunities and challenges' in the *Journal of the Society of Archivists* (28 (2), 2007) and (with Morgan and Cohen) *Communists and British Society 1920–1991* (London: Rivers Oram), 2007.

Andrea Johnson is a Ph.D. computer science student at University College Cork, Ireland. Her research interests include the use of digital archives, the information-seeking patterns of digital archive users, user modelling, contextual inquiry, evaluation methodology and discourse analysis. She is a project management consultant specializing in the areas of project specification and development and user-centred evaluations. She has recently undertaken several commissions for the Archives and Records Council of Wales, including 'Ask the People', which consulted the people of Wales regarding 21st-century archive provision.

Andrea is a member of AX-SNET, the international research partnership, and of the IDEAS research group at University College Cork. Recent papers include '"Lost in Translation": Users and Digital Archives' (for the COST 298 conference in Moscow, May 2007) and '"Why Do They Do That"? Modelling Contextual Interaction in the Digital Archive Domain' (for the Chicago Colloquium on Digital Humanities and Computer Science, 2006).

Michael Moss is Research Professor in Archival Studies in the Humanities Advanced Technology and Information Institute (HATII) at the University of Glasgow. He is a member of the board of the National Trust for Scotland, a non-executive director of The National Archives of Scotland and a member of the Lord Chancellor's Advisory Council on National Records and Archives. His recent publications included 'Choreographed encounter – the archive and public history', *Archives* (XXXII (116), 41–57, 2007); with Alistair Tough (as editors) *Record Keeping in a Hybrid Environment – Managing the Creation, Use and Disposal of Unpublished Information Objects in Context* (London: Chandos Press, 2006); and with Laurence Brockliss (as editors) *Advancing with the Army: Medicine, the Professions and Social Mobility in the British Isles 1790–1850* (Oxford: Oxford University Press, 2006).

Andrew Prescott was from 1979 to 1999 a curator in the Department of Manuscripts of the British Library. He was the principal British Library contact for the *Electronic Beowulf*, edited by Kevin Kiernan, a pioneering digital facsimile (London: British Library, 1999). He was also one of the editors (with Carpenter and Shaw) of *Towards the Digital Library: the British Library's Initiatives for Access Programme* (London: British Library, 1998). He was from 2000 to 2007 the founding director of the Centre for Research into Freemasonry in the Humanities Research Institute at the University of Sheffield. He is currently Librarian at the University of Wales at Lampeter. His publications include *English Historical Documents* (London: British Museum, 1988) and, with Elizabeth Hallam, *The British Inheritance* (London: British Library and Public Records Office, 1999). He has also written articles on the Peasants' Revolt of 1381 and the history of the British Library.

Jane Stevenson gained her M.A. in Archive Administration at the University of Liverpool. Shortly after qualifying she was appointed Curator of Archives and Manuscripts at the Royal Institute of British Architects, and then moved on to gain more technical experience at the University of Leeds working on their Research Publications Information System and Virtual Science Park. She now works for the MIMAS National Data Centre at the University of Manchester, which hosts online services for the UK higher education, further education and research community. For the last five years Jane has worked for the Archives Hub service, a gateway to descriptions of archives held in UK higher and further education. For the past three years, Jane has been Training Officer for the UK Society of Archivists Data Standards Group. She is a tutor for the University of Dundee M.Litt. in Archives and Records Management.

Caroline Williams has been Head of Research and Collections Development at The National Archives in London since 2007. Prior to that she was Director of Liverpool University Centre for Archive Studies (LUCAS) and its postgraduate education programme in Archives and Records Management. Her early career was spent in a series of local authority archive services. She is a former chair of FARMER (the Forum for Archives and Records Management Education and Research) in the UK and is a member of the International Council on Archives Section on Education and Training. Current areas of research interest and publication include the history and diplomatic analysis of the record, and the interface between theory and practice.

Acknowledgements

The chapters in this book began life as presentations to the Society of Archivists Conference at Lancaster in September 2006. A day session entitled 'What are archives?' gave each of us the opportunity to air issues which we felt were of great significance to the archival profession in the UK but which, for one reason or another, had been given little coverage either by the profession or in the professional press. I would like to take the opportunity on behalf of my colleagues to thank the Society for providing a forum for discussion and also to thank our varied professional organizations for the support which enabled us to attend the Society's annual conference that year.

Since the conference, many people have contributed to the emergence of this book: authors of the chapters which follow; colleagues and students with whom we have had vigorous debates and fruitful discussions; and Ashgate Publishing Ltd, whose editorial staff helped us create a readable and coherent text from a set of loosely defined ideas: to all then, my thanks.

List of Abbreviations

AHRC	Arts and Humanities Research Council
ARC	The professional journal for archives, records management and conservation
ARMReN	Archives Records Management Research Network
ASIS&T	American Society for Information Science and Technology
AX-SNET	Archival eXcellence in Information Seeking Studies Network
CASBAH	Caribbean Studies for Black and Asian History
FARMER	Forum for Archives and Records Management Education and Research
HATII	Humanities Advanced Technology and Information Institute, University of Glasgow
MIMAS	Manchester Information and Associated Services
SLAIS	School of Library, Archives and Information Studies, University College London
TNA	The National Archives UK

Preface

Sometime in 2006, a significant moment occurred. It was one which brought a number of people – archivists and academics – together to exchange ideas not so much about archives, but rather about the impact of the world out there upon archives, archivists and users of archives. Traditional archive tenets do not really allow consideration of such a Hegelian position – indeed, traditional archival theory does not normally have much to do with philosophical notions of any kind. At the outset of the 21st century, however, we all felt that a new perspective was needed. Archivists by and large look backward: despite pressures of the modern world – search rooms to be staffed, educational programmes to be arranged, funding bids to be written, targets to be met – the stuff of their world is historical and their approach to life is, in many cases, both introspective and harmonious with this view. By contrast we were trying to look forward and to adopt a wider perspective: looking at archives from the outside, rather than from the inside. Since 2006, others have begun similar work; this confirms in us the conviction that the time is right for debate and discussion, and the realization that a new set of answers to the question 'What are archives?' is beginning to emerge.

Louise Craven
March 2008

Introduction

Louise Craven

In the first decade of the 21st century, archives and the archival profession in the UK face challenges and changes unmatched in any other period. In recent years, new ways of thinking and writing about archives have emerged. These have coincided, on the one hand, with huge technological developments which have brought profound social, political and epistemological changes in their wake and, on the other, with a significant shift in the role of archives in cultural and heritage contexts. At the same time, the social and political role of the archive and the text have become prominent discourses in academic disciplines concerned with cultural studies, with politics, sociology, philosophy, linguistics, history and literary criticism. Some indication of the intellectual activities which focus upon archives can be gauged by the number and nature of transdisciplinary conferences concerned with the philosophy of the archive, the ontology of the archive and with the nature and relevance of the archival narrative, taking place in 2008.[1] Even a year or two ago this simply would not have happened.

At the centre of all this, the archivist stands at something of a crossroads: the familiar world of paper documents is fast giving way to electronic born-digital records. These records pose considerable challenges in terms of storage and preservation and generate questions which strike at the very foundation of the archivist's profession: questions about authenticity, original order, the unique record, custody and meaning. To a profession which has long focused on the 'how', rather than the 'why' of archival work, these collective developments – technological, social, political, academic and professional – present hugely significant issues.

Through the themes of 'Continuity and Change in the Archival Paradigm', 'The Impact of Technology', 'The Impact of Community Archives' and 'Archival Use and Users', this book seeks to contribute to those new ways of thinking and writing about archives. It considers relevant theoretical developments in the field, looks at those immense changes brought by the Internet, considers their impact on the role of archives in society, and seeks to set archives in a cultural, political and social context.

---

1 *The Philosophy of the Archive*, Dundee, 10–11 April; *The Ontology of the Archive* is the first seminar in a research network series on the reuse of archival material across the disciplines, hosted by the University of Manchester, 28 April; *Archives Fervour: Archives Fever*, conference presented by the Department of English at the University of Wales at Aberystwyth, 28 July 2008.

Theme I: Continuity and Change in the Archival Paradigm

This theme highlights changes in the world of the archivist and indicates areas of change and continuity in the archival paradigm. The first chapter, 'From the Archivist's Cardigan to the Very Dead Sheep', gives an overview of the shifting landscape and highlights some of its significant trends. The title indicates changes which the archivist may have experienced: moving from a traditional role – often portrayed (and parodied on the archivists' own professional UK list-serv) as the passive, cardigan-wearing dusty bureaucrat – into a dynamic proactive professional facing and managing all the challenges of the present and the future and actively contributing to those new ways of thinking and writing about archives, as typified in Uriel Orlow and Ruth MacLennan's groundbreaking study of 2004, *Re: the Archive, the Image and the Very Dead Sheep.*

In Chapter 2, Andrew Prescott ponders the textuality of the archive and asks if archival documents, like all texts, are subject to interpretation. Is the language in which historical documents are written subject to similar analysis and, if so, which theorists might help us understand archives in this new way?

In Chapter 3, Caroline Williams discusses traditional attitudes toward personal papers and organizational archives and asks if, in the digital age, these attitudes have any continuing relevance.

Theme II: The Impact of Technology

In the second theme, Michael Moss and Jane Stevenson consider the impact which digitization has made upon archives and archivists from two very different standpoints. Moss asks whether we need a new definition of the archive in the digital context. En route to his conclusion he considers the epistemological and ontological essences of the archive, the fundamental responsibilities of the archivist in paper and digital environments, and questions the archivist's understanding of context, authority, purpose, authenticity, evidence and truth. By contrast, Stevenson looks at all these developments from the purely practical angle: if you want to be a digital archivist, this is what you need to do.

Theme III: The Impact of Community Archives

The third theme looks at the use of cyberspace by different communities and groups. Andrew Flinn focuses on the pressure groups posing questions to those archival conventions which govern acquisition and deposit when the items to be acquired and deposited are transitory, topical and changing. Aside from problems of process and technique in preservation, Flinn asks what we should collect and preserve and, as saliently, who should have the responsibility for this part of our national political heritage, in the UK today.

In Chapter 7, Andrew Prescott, continuing themes and debates developed in earlier chapters, looks at the exile and at exiled archives: he asks 'Where is the exile?', 'How do archives treat the exile?' and 'Can theoretical debates reshape our understanding of familiar collections and archives?'.

Theme IV: Archival Use and Users

The final theme takes the topic of archive users and from very different standpoints asks who they are and what we know about them. Andrea Johnson's approach is from the computer science environment informed by empirical study, by observation and by the evaluation of archive users. She looks at the systems which users must confront in that elusive search for the digital document.

Gerard Collis's essay, Permitted Use and Users, asks why some people are permitted to see archives whilst others are not, and he ponders the questions: what are archives for? who are archives for? are archives elitist? and what is really the difference between archives and museums? To explore these questions Collis takes us to archives and museums in Britain and Ireland and to museums in Germany and Australia; and we travel 17,000 years into the past to the caves at Lascaux, and 10,000 years into the future to the nuclear waste repository in Nevada.

Theme I
Continuity and Change in the Archival Paradigm

Chapter 1

From the Archivist's Cardigan to the Very Dead Sheep: What are Archives? What are Archivists? What do They Do?

Louise Craven

Introduction[1]

> The first chapter in this collection of essays introduces the reader to notions of change and continuity in the world of the archivist. It looks at five specific areas which have experienced transformation or significant development in the past ten or so years. It explores the nature and impact of these developments and asks what, if anything, the archival profession might do in response.

Walk into a record office today and what do you notice? How busy it is! Computer terminals, microfilm readers, racks of popular historical journals, posters and notices for all kinds of societies and activities, 'email here', signs to the café, the local history room and the shop; but most of all, it's the sheer number of visitors and the buzz of activity which surrounds them which is striking.

In Britain today, the general functions of a record office might be said to be those of custodianship and storage of records which have been selected for permanent preservation, together with the provision of a public service. These general functions of course incorporate all those specialized ones of helping the public find what they want, cataloguing and the creation of finding aids, preservation and conservation, and the wider outreach roles of developing education, supporting local history and reaching new audiences. Like the theory which governs our profession, these functions are very much rooted in the second half of the twentieth century.

Compare the professional certainties of those decades with the developments of recent years which have affected archivists, archives and record offices in profound ways: technological advances and the popular use of the Internet; developments in the cultural and heritage sectors; a media profile which has made 'archives' a household

---

1 In this chapter, 'archives' refers to archives, record offices and manuscript libraries of the public sector, open to all; 'record' is used in its widest sense to incorporate documents, manuscripts, films, digitized documents and records of all kinds; and 'archivists' and 'record managers' refer to all those individuals working in archives, record offices and manuscript libraries.

word; electronic records whose usage is assured by a *Modernising Government* (Cm 4310 1999) agenda; and just becoming visible and audible are some debates in the academic world of an multidisciplinary nature which perceive archives in a wholly different way.

Technological Change

Firstly then, technological changes have brought new archives and led to a new way of thinking about archives. Whilst it is not quite true to say that everything has changed because of the Internet and Google, almost everything has: the Internet has changed what we do, what we talk about, how we go about finding things; it has changed our way of thinking and it has changed everyone's expectations. In a wider context, we now look on a world in which theories of knowledge and ownership of knowledge have irrevocably shifted. The individual and the community, not the organization or the government, are the significant units now: our world and our place in it changed beyond all expectation since the coming of the World Wide Web.

Other contributions to this book address specific aspects of the changes which new technology, community software and social software have brought, and some of the challenges of electronic records are discussed later in this chapter. Here, then, I want to look in a general way at the changes which those technological advances have made to the record office itself and to the demands upon the archivist.

For the archivist, in a purely practical sense, all these developments in cyberspace mean that an online catalogue and a website are now standard requirements of every record office, and an Internet connection is expected. It means that the archivist now needs to be skilled in old and new techniques, familiar on the one hand with medieval diplomatic documents and on the other with the requirements of searching for genealogical and historical information on the Web. What we noted above about the ambience of the record office brings its own pressures on record office staff: sheer numbers of visitors with huge expectations. Shifts in post-war demographic patterns and the huge growth in pension provision in the last three decades of the twentieth century mean that the majority of visitors to record offices in Britain (actual or virtual) are over 60, with leisure time to pursue meaningful activities. These meaningful activities are mainly educational, probably family history or local history, and overwhelmingly of a wider heritage and cultural nature.

Changes in the Context of Heritage and Culture

The notion that archives are about identity, heritage and culture is certainly a prominent one: it is shared by government, by policy makers, by funding bodies and by umbrella archival organizations in the UK. The report of the Archives Task Force (ATF) *Listening to the Past, Speaking to the Future* (2004) and the report of the Mayor's Commission on African and Asian Heritage (MCAAH) *Delivering Shared Heritage* (2005) both made specific recommendations to help archivists develop and present their collections in ways synonymous with a diverse, vibrant and thriving multicultural Britain.

Underpinning the re-thinking of archive collections in this context is CASBAH[2] (Caribbean Studies for Black and Asian History) which identified sources for black and Asian history in archives, libraries and media collections in the UK (Fig. 1.1). The CASBAH Project was funded by the Research Sector for Libraries Programme (RSLP) and was active in the years 2000–2002.

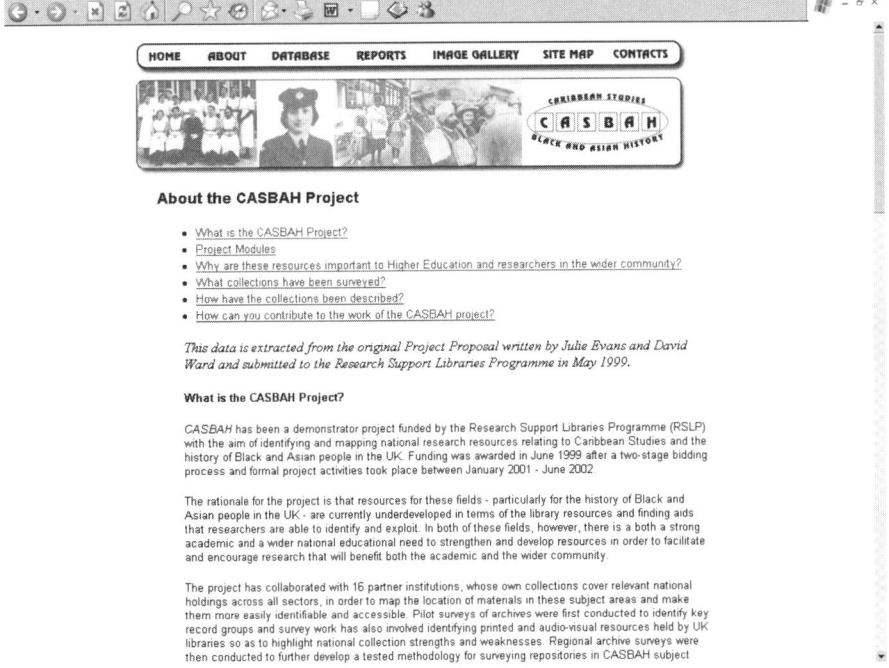

Figure 1.1   Homepage for the CASBAH website (by courtesy of the Institute of Commonwealth Studies)

A major outcome of the CASBAH project was its *Survey Tool* which advocated the *revisiting* of collections already catalogued to find sources of relevance to black and Asian studies (CASBAH 2002, Aims 2). Research underlying the *Survey Tool* led to the conclusion that there were indeed a great many sources for black and Asian history in the archives and libraries surveyed for the project, sources which might not at first glance appear to be relevant. Family and estate collections, for example, were found in many cases to reveal a great deal about landholding in the West Indies, about the ownership of slaves and about trade. These findings have been taken forward recently by the Museums Libraries and Archives Council (MLA) in a pilot project called *Revisiting Archive Collections* which is aimed at developing a methodology for capturing and incorporating new and hidden information into archive catalogues (Newman and Reilly 2007). This in itself signals a significant

2 <http://www.casbah.ac.uk/> accessed February 2008.

departure in archival theory and practice: though the *Revisiting Archive Collections* project is in its early stages, its very existence indicates a recognition that the role of the archivist is changing. The study of archives, like the study of history, is coming to be recognized as a dialogue between the present and the past. In the same way, then, as the historian undertakes revisionist research of topics previously investigated, the archivist will uncover and present new views of archival collections in response to critical issues which shape today's cultural landscape.

Outside the confines of this specific project, and as part and parcel of the developing awareness of archives as a resource for diverse cultures and heritage, archivists have been urged by funding bodies, by government and by their own parent organizations to develop audiences in the light of the identity, heritage and culture of potential user communities.[3] However, it is not altogether clear what this means. Take the concept of identity, for example: it is not at all evident that archivists have a shared understanding of what the concept means in relation to archives. In 2006, research carried out at the School for Library, Archive and Information Studies (SLAIS) at the University of London showed that there had been little work done on archives and identity overall (Flinn et al. 2006); and two research seminars held in 2007 have not yet changed these circumstances.[4] Moreover, the education of archivists in Britain today does not really equip them with a knowledge or understanding of identity in any detailed or specific sense. Indeed, different definitions of identity are to be found in the chapters below. It might help here if we try to define terms: what after all is *identity* about and what does it really mean? Though the ATF report and that of the Mayor's Commission are both very helpful in defining heritage and culture for archivists, identity remains a difficult concept: topical, contentious, problematic. It seems that we may need to look to other disciplines for guidance.

For the sociologist Steven Miles, identity is about consumption (1996). For Anthony Easthope in *Englishness and National Culture* (1999), identity is about language (see his preface); for J.E. Toews in *Cultural Reference and Public Memory* identity is about memory and the built environment (2004). For some, of course, identity is perceived to be a political tool (Anderson 1983; Mann 2005; Arel and Ruble 2006). For the historian Jacques Le Goff, identity is about memory and the past (1992) whilst Stuart Hall, writing about the meaning of identity to members of the West Indian community, talks about a process of negotiation with dialogues of post-colonialism (Hall 1990, 225). By contrast, for the archivist Jeannette Allis Bastian, identity is about collective memory and history (Bastian 2003, 3). Others feel that identity is about place; a sense of place being fundamental to personal identity and health, bestowing psychological well-being (Young 1992, 15; Etherton 2006, 227).

---

3 See for example, Cm 4516 (1999); Heritage Lottery Fund (HLF) (2000), *Audience Development Plans; Helping your Application*; HLF's project (2005), *Remembering Slavery in 2007*.

4 ARMReN's *Archives and Access* incorporated presentations on identity by Andy Flinn and the author, September 2007; *Witness Seminar on Identity* was hosted by the National Trust Scotland, October 2007.

Clearly, no general consensus as to the meaning of identity emerges. Perhaps colleagues in other sectors of the heritage and culture domain can help. Andrew Newman, lecturer in Museum Studies at the International Centre for Cultural and Heritage Studies at the University of Newcastle upon Tyne, found in his recent research on identity that an individual's identity is constructed and multifaceted, and that it changes in response to information, experience and circumstance (Newman 2006). He examined the use of museums in addressing problems of social exclusion and found that museums contribute to social inclusion through their key role in facilitating identity construction. And he found that the way in which exhibitions are themselves constructed can exclude or include individuals.[5] In his research Newman used a standard circuit of culture model based on representation, production, consumption, regulation and identity, developed by Paul Du Gay (Du Gay et al. 1997, 3).

Du Gay's work is central to any understanding of the significance of culture and the cultural, and explains to us why the study of culture has come to occupy a much enhanced role, not only in the social sciences but in the economy and in society in the UK in general. No longer seen as an inferior to, and merely reflective of, economic and political processes, cultural processes are recognized to be constitutive of the social world in general and, most significantly, to be the producer of social meanings. These social meanings regulate the functioning of all social practices we see around us; an understanding of the cultural conditions of all social practices is recognized to be essential to inform any understanding of how culture and society work. The study of culture is thus crucial for understanding all forms of production and consumption, as well as of the media, of film, of narratives of every kind, of all cultural and heritage institutions, of museums and of archives.

Newman's research and Du Gay's methodology are not generally known in the archives sector but their application to archives is immediately useful in generating questions like: do archive exhibitions and events facilitate or inhibit identity construction in the same way? If so, what might we do about this? Does this mean that an exhibition of, let's say, any kind of archival document, *excludes* as well as *includes* visitors? and so on.

Decades of research into critical aspects of the role of museums in society and the perception and use of museums by members of the public have established the museums sector in the UK at the forefront of knowledge and understanding of the country's heritage and culture. As a result, museum professionals have a great deal to tell the archival profession in the UK and archivists have a great deal to learn.

The Report from the Mayor's Commission on African and Asian Heritage (MCAAH) made only too clear the crucial role which archives play in lending understanding and intelligibility to the UK's shared heritage. In this context, the archival profession needs to think about how it can collaborate with other heritage professionals, how it can gain an understanding of those crucially important cultural concepts, and how that understanding might shape practice enabling it to deliver audience development in the light of identity, heritage and culture.

---

5 See also Shimamura-Wilcocks 2007.

Archives and the Academic Context

> The acid test of any theoretical innovation is the question 'What new fields and types of action does the theory open up to us that we did not or could not see before?' (Bennet 1987, 64)

In recent decades, the UK's archives sector has not been noted for its academic research. The historian-archivist of the mid-twentieth century has disappeared: chased away by Jenkinsonian notions that passive archivists are good archivists on the one hand, and by increasing practical demands from access, use, collection development and management on the other. By contrast, the discussion of, and discourses about, archives in other academic disciplines have attained a new profile in recent years.

Recommendations of the MCAAH Archives Diversification Subcommittee concerning academic research in the archives sector, together with the established research centre at the School of Humanities Advanced Technology and Information Institute (HATII) at the University of Glasgow, the recently developed Archives and Records Management Research Network (ARMReN) at SLAIS and that taking shape at the Centre for Archive and Information Studies at the University of Dundee, indicate that change is on the way, but it might be useful here to consider briefly the debates around archives within other academic disciplines.

Archives and Archaeologists

Record-keeping has long been recognized as an indicator of the development of civilization by archaeologists and anthropologists. David Keightley has shown us in astonishing detail the use of oracle bones as records in Bronze Age China (Keightley 1978). At the end of the nineteenth century J.P. Mahaffy explained to us the archive activities of the ancient Greeks (Mahaffy 1877, 391, 395). More recently, new techniques of epigraphical analysis have brought greater understanding of archive functions of late Roman and Byzantine inscriptions (Roueche 1989).

Archives and Historians

Historians have of course discussed documents, sources and archives from the foundation of their discipline. Recent *Unleashing the Archives* conferences have given new ideas about archives a prominence amongst some historians: we see how archives may be presented as evidence, as myth, as personal statement, as construction and manipulation.[6] Many historians, though, prefer to discuss

---

6 *Unleashing the Archives Conferences* held by the School of Advanced Studies in collaboration with the National Archives and the Institute of Historical Research in November 2004 and 2005 incorporated the following areas. *Archives as epic*: Alan Thacker, 'Bede and the Creation of an English Epic'; Louise Craven, 'Epic, Group Identity and the Archive in the Modern World. *Archives as evidence: 'The Bloody Sunday Enquiry'*: Paul Bew, 'The Historian's View'; Richard Norton Taylor, 'The Journalist's View'; Cathryn McGahey, 'The Lawyer's View'. *Archives as personal exploration*: Katrina Dean, 'Biographical Actors'; and Andrea Levy, 'Archives, Fiction and Autobiography'. *Archives as constructions and*

archives in a routine sources-and-methods sort of way, which has been standard down the decades. A theoretical analysis of 'what is history' accompanied by 'how to do historical research' for undergraduate and post-graduate students has been a recognized historiographical contribution from the great historians of very different persuasions since Sir Herbert Butterfield's *Whig Interpretation of History* in 1931. R.G. Collingwood's *The Idea of History* (1946), E.H. Carr's *What is History?* (1961), Sir Geoffrey Elton's *The Practice of History* (1967) and Richard Evans's *In Defence of History* (1997, 2004) are noted landmarks in this long historiographical tradition.

Ian Anderson's work on academic users of archives (Anderson 2004) is of a different order, engaging with archivists to better provide historians and other academics with what they need: this dialogue is unusual, for historians' discussion of sources has traditionally been detached from archivists.

Recently, the archive has also been at the centre of a lively discussion between social historians and cultural historians in debate about theories, methods and perceptions. It is to this discussion that the cultural historian Carolyn Steedman refers when she talks about the new politics of the archive (2002, 2–3), of which more below.

Archives and Literature

Records and archives are intertwined through the narratives of modern English and European literature like a golden thread. Records are found in Chaucer's 'Prologue' to *The Canterbury Tales* and in Shakespeare's *Henry VI Part 2*; archivists are described in Cervantes' *Don Quixote* and archives by Sterne in *Tristram Shandy*. Patents generate Swift's *Drapier's Letters*; wills and deeds determine fate in Dickens's *Bleak House* and Wilkie Collins's *Woman in White*, while muster rolls appear in Kipling's *Kim*. A demon archivist and librarian emerges in Mervyn Peake's *Gormenghast*, one with ulterior motives in Martha Cooley's eponymous novel, and perhaps the first to realize the power of the archivist in Jose Saramago's *All the Names*. The archivist is insane in Sebastian Faulks's *Human Traces* and the archivist in Travis Holland's *The Archivist's Story* in 2007 is a man tortured by both conscience and the Soviet regime.[7] There are of course many more such examples.

This whole area, the presentation and representation of the archivist in literature through the ages, would seem an excellent context for research: it informs our understanding of the central place which archives have held historically and continue to hold in our culture today.

---

manipulations: Charlotte Rouche, 'The Ancient World: the Concept of the Archive Wall'; and Richard Cox, 'The Modern World'. See also Albie Sachs (2005), <http://www.ahrc.ac.uk/news/events/previousevents/unleashing_the_archive.a> accessed February 2008.

7 Chaucer (2003) 11; Henry VI Pt 2 (2000) IV vii, 16–17; Cervantes (2000) 475 ; Sterne (2003) 35; Swift (1935) 4, lines 20–24; Fielding (1966) 25; Dickens (2000) 4, 11, 126, 546–60; Collins (1868) 74; Kipling (1995) 175; Peake (1992) 375; Cooley (1998); Saramago (1997) 3; Faulks (2006) 184, 254; Holland (2007).

Archives and Other Disciplines in the Humanities

In philosophy, politics, psychology, sociology and language, a more critical theoretical view of archives as a whole has developed, reflecting a concern with the importance of archives to society, rather than with archives as simply holders of historical sources. This interpretation, given currency by the French philosopher Michel Foucault in the 1960s, was developed by the semiotician and post-structuralist Jacques Derrida in the later decades of the twentieth century. Derrida is perhaps most well known in this context for *Archive Fever: a Freudian Impression*, published in 1996. Derrida's writing has stimulated new ways of thinking about archives amongst archival theorists in the UK, the Netherlands, North America, Australia and South Africa (see, for example, Ketellar 1999; Harris 2002; McKemmish 1994; Nesmith 2002; Moss 2006; Tyacke 2002; van Zyl 2002).

For both Foucault and Derrida, interest in archives stemmed from an interest in language, texts and meaning. For Foucault, 'the archive is the first law of what can be said; the system that governs the appearance of statements as unique events' (1966, 79–131); for Derrida, the archive was the beginning of modes of thought and events (1996, 1). From both, a new perception of archives is presented, one which understands archives to be the source of power and control, the shaper of language, the determinant of a new way of seeing society.

One of Derrida's major contributions to the philosophy of archives is, of course, about meaning. It was in this context that Derrida described what it is that the archivist actually *does*: the archivist's defining role lies in the relationship to context and the creation of meaning. 'Context gives the archivist credibility.' The archivist also gives title and order: '… there could be no archive without titles … and without the criteria of classification … of hierarchization … of order' (1996, 4).

The strand of philosophical enquiry concerning archives and texts, language and meaning has been continued in France and the UK by post-structuralists and postmodernists, by literary and film critics and by those involved in cultural theory and cultural studies. Deconstruction of the text – mainly literary and philosophical texts – is significant to all strands, not simply to understand the bourgeois nature of the text (as deconstruction was initially intended) but rather as it has become more popularly known, to uncover the *other* meanings of the text. In the postmodernist world, one text can have many meanings and many readings.

As new philosophical schools have developed, archives have been treated by some academics in the same way as other disciplines: as architecture, history, literature and so on have been dealt with by the linguistic turn, so have archives. The 'linguistic turn' is understood as being the notion or realization (depending on which view you take) that written and spoken language can only relate to itself, not to any higher truth; so there is no *correct* interpretation of anything, only lots of interpretations.

The cultural historian Carolyn Steedman develops some of these philosophical strands in *Dust* (2002). Her book is about historical perceptions of the nineteenth century, it is about narrative structures in the text, and it is a response to Derrida. Steedman's work is relevant to the archival profession today because her approach is so different from that of other writers about archives, her interpretation and comments are illuminating, and some of her assertions invite a response from archivists.

At the outset we are presented with a very different Archive Fever: not the abstruse Derridean psychoanalytical searching for a moment of inception to be recovered, but a pressured almost frantic feeling brought on by too many records in the archive and not enough time (2002, 27–19). Steedman's continuing dialogue with Derrida goes on to shape the early part of the book. The view that the founding of national archives in various countries in Europe in the early nineteenth century was part of the development of the nation state is not new, nor is the understanding that different legal systems enable the writing of certain kinds of histories because they require different types of records to be kept, but both are placed in a new Derridean context (2002, 38–67).

Steedman's developing central theme, the close examination of the texts of nineteenth-century novels, demonstrates that the use which authors made of documents as background to their writings had crucial implications for the novels themselves, for the novels' critical interpretation, and for today's popular understanding of nineteenth-century social history (2002, 89–111). It also suggests a new area in archive studies: archives as source and resource, not just for history, but for literature and cultural studies.

Dust also brings to light the work of other cultural historians whose findings are more than relevant to archives today. Writing about the emerging bourgeois society in the West Midlands in the mid-nineteenth century, Donald Lowe comments that 'Bourgeois society tried to consume the past in order to attenuate somewhat for its estrangement to the ... present' (Lowe 1982, 40–41). Is that what we are seeing around us on the Internet and in record offices across the country today?

Leading on from this then, we might ask if the archive profession has anything to learn from these new perspectives. The impact of Derrida has already been noted. Heather MacNeil has demonstrated elsewhere the value which techniques of literary criticism can bring to the understanding of a finding aid (MacNeil 2007) and Terry Cook and Tom Nesmith, amongst others, have considered postmodernism in the specific contexts of archival theory and the education of archivists (Cook 2001, 14–25; Nesmith 2002). These examples suggest that ideas from different disciplines can be very valuable in the archival context.

In record offices today we are experiencing a vast surge in popularity led by family historians. Media coverage boosts this hugely, but the growth in genealogy and interest in personal history had begun long before the TV series *Who Do You Think You Are?*. Archivists, however, still know little about the users of archives and record offices: little about why records *fascinate*. Following these examples then, let us see if any new perspectives on use and users can be elicited from these wider philosophical trends. Would a postmodernist view of the archival text, with understanding drawn from literary criticism, cast any new light on our perception of users?

Readings and Meanings

Let us take a death certificate,[8] a nineteenth-century attestation form for enlistment into the militia[9] and a twentieth-century Cabinet minute[10] as representative of archival documents, and see if these have many readings and many meanings; and, if so, whether findings here anticipate any explanation of the recent huge surge in demand.

The family historian looking for her great-great-grandfather, the statistician looking for deaths from pneumonia, and the local historian interested in mortality and urbanization, all find different things in a death certificate. The political historian looking for the shaping of policy over Northern Ireland, the postgraduate student interested in environmental issues and the economist looking for evidence of the first oil crisis, all find different things in the Cabinet minute. The social historian looking for the physical details of men joining the militia in the 1830s, the family historian seeking to piece together a picture of his or her ancestor, and the military historian looking for the statistics of enlistment from the Home Counties, all find different things in the attestation papers. Clearly then there can be many readings and many meanings of an archival text.

In a way, archivists always known this – in this much they are, like Laurence Sterne, among the first post-modernists – but they have not stated this, nor have they employed any kind of multidisciplinary theoretical framework or language in which these interpretations can be examined, and within which further questions might be generated.

The notion of the text having an identity of its own is in a sense axiomatic with certain kinds of archival documents. We have seen above that different individuals all take different things from an archival document, but many archival documents also have an administrative and legal meaning of their own: a will, a contract, a deed. Letters perhaps do not fall into this category: in the 1980s, the literary critic Terry Eagleton noted that the letter was at once the most intimate and the most treacherous of all archival documents because it is open to so many interpretations (1982, 54–5). Literary critics would call this administrative or legal meaning the 'authorial meaning' of the text. Debates around the 'authorial meaning of the text' and indeed whether a text can have an authorial meaning at all have engaged literary critics for some years (Culler 1986, 3, 4) though this is not something which has previously concerned archivists.

Let us just think for a moment about what it is that actually happens when an individual experiences an archival document. We have said above that because different people are looking for different things, that the archival text then *means* different things to different people. But we do not know what 'meaning' is in this context. Some years ago, the literary critic S. Pradhan (Pradhan 1986, 67) developed

---

8 Certificate: <http://www.gro.gov.uk/gro/content/deaths/obtainingdeathcertificates/index.asp> accessed 10 October 2007.

9 TNA WO 96: War Office: Militia Attestation papers 1806–1914.

10 <http://www.nationalarchives.gov.uk/documentsonline/download.asp?T=1111480&S=I/07/01081019H&E=PRO%5F1111480> accessed 10 October 2007.

the notion that a reader's understanding of the meaning of a text could be equated with its use; that is, the use a reader makes of the information. This notion of the meaning in the text has been taken much further recently by the cultural psychologist Urs Fuhrer in *Cultivating Minds: Identity as Meaning Making Practice* (2004).

Cultural psychologists are concerned with processes not entities, with the mediational processes through which subject and world mutually create each other, and with the analysis of those processes. Fuhrer sees identity and culture as processes through which individuals can experience themselves as agents of their own meaning making activities. Fuhrer then equates meaning with identity and defines identity as a process through which the self continually constructs or reconstructs meaning and identity through social and or cultural mediation (Fuhrer 2004, preface, 171–255). In the archive then, an individual finds meaning in an archival document because the document means something to him and, at the same time, because of that individual's cultural or community identity the individual finds other meaning, other things to identify with. Over time then, identity as meaning making is perpetually constructed and reconstructed through the experience of archival documents.

This certainly has resonance with Andrew Newman's findings about identity in museums which we discussed above. More importantly for archivists, it provides new insights into the experience of users of archival documents, and enables archivists to hypothesize that, for example, the demand for archival documents will simply continue over the years to come as documents are continually becoming different things to different people. Based on these insights, archivists might also choose to make assumptions about further use; these assumptions might then inform policies about users and audiences.

We asked earlier if archivists had anything to learn from advances in other disciplines: the answer is an overwhelming yes.

Archives in a Media Context

Running parallel with these developments are those in the media context – that colossal surge of interest in genealogy and family history referred to above which is boosted by television programmes like *Who Do You Think You Are?*.[11] Archives are now a household word. The series has invested genealogy with celebrity status, enabled topics which once were rarely discussed in society and never in the family (such as incest and illegitimacy) to be aired, encouraged a re-thinking of poverty and hardship and given new meaning to the phrase 'an accident of birth'.

Alongside *Who Do You Think You Are?*, the History Channel and historical documentaries all add to a general raising of the profile of history and of archives, as do the popular serial publications – *Family History*, *Local Historian*, *Ancestors* – which despite fierce competition from other sources have maintained their circulation in recent years.[12]

---

11 <http://www.bbcwhodoyouthinkyouare.com/> accessed 10 October 2007.

12 Figures from *Ancestors* 2006 and 2007 indicate a monthly purchase and subscription rate of about 5,000 and 1,000 respectively. I am grateful to Simon Fowler, editor of *Ancestors*, for this information.

What has this huge popularity done to archives? Firstly, it has made genealogical research seem easy, which sadly it is not. Secondly, it has boosted the demand for access to archives both onsite and online. At the National Archives (TNA) this demand was the main reason for the launching of the DocumentsOnline site which enables people to view actual documents and, if they so wish, to purchase a copy (digitized image) of the document (Fig. 1.2).[13]

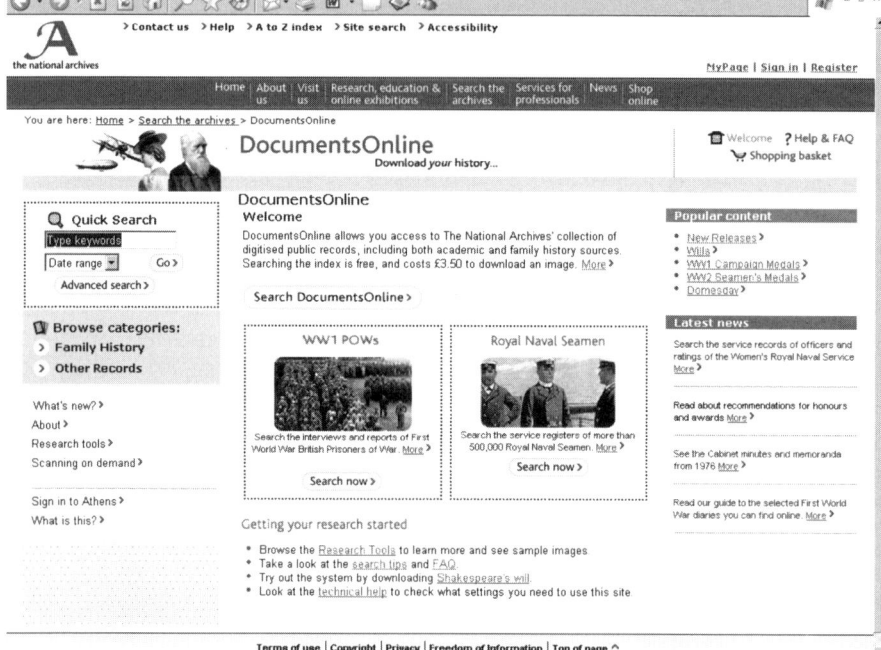

Figure 1.2   Homepage for DocumentsOnline, on the website of The National Archives (by courtesy of The National Archives)

DocumentsOnline is hugely popular and, not surprisingly, it is the documents which tell about people which are the most sought after. Wills, medal rolls from the First World War, seamens' medal rolls from the Second World War and Victorian prisoners' photographs are the documents most frequently ordered in the years since online documents were first made available.[14]

Currently there is little empirical evidence as to the impact of archival images available on the Internet, but the figures alone are staggering: since digitized

---

13 Digitized images of some very popular/iconic docs (like Shakespeare's will) are available free and the service is free on site.

14 Wills can be found in PROB 11; campaign medals (First World War) and seamen's medals (Second World War) can be found in a number of War Office series (WO); Victorian prisoners' photographs are from PCOM 2.

images of documents were first made available in 2004, there have been 66 million downloads from online sources of TNA documents.[15] Consider for a moment what this availability might mean for an individual: what is it that happens when a person experiences an archival document on the Internet?

At the record office or archive there's a ritual to be followed: a procedure of finding out how to find, of getting the reference, then ordering and waiting; then the thrill of the document arriving bound up in a bundle and having to search for it, the excitement of touching the paper and seeing the handwriting, then discovery: 'there it is! ... there is what I was looking for!' – the meaning and identification we talked of above.

The experience online is quite different. The relationship between an individual and the digitized image here seems to be more like that experienced by a person watching a film: visual and intimate, as described by Thomas Elsaesser (1981, 271): 'pressured by time ... marked off very clearly by lights down and lights up ... giving a sense of enclosure ... more radical than television, play or music', and in which the online text, as we understand from our earlier discussion, is like Colin McCabe's classic realistic text, in which a hierarchy of discourses compose the text (McCabe 1981, 217).

Both in the record office and online, there is the excitement of finding what you have been searching for; or not finding it but finding something else of relevance, of meaning to you. In *The Long Revolution* (1961), one of the founding texts of cultural studies in Britain, Raymond Williams described what happens when a reader reads a book: 'a structure of feeling' develops between the reader and the text (Williams 1961, 64–88). That 'structure of feeling' depended with each individual on his or her own experience and culture; that is, what he/she brought to the text and the meaning in the text. This seems to have much relevance to the archival context: the 'structure of feeling' surrounds the reader with understanding, identification, almost with enlightenment. This certainly has a resonance with the experiences of volunteers at TNA who have been working on the Southwell Workhouse Project (Fig. 1.3). One volunteer said, 'It has given a remarkable insight into the activities ... lives and minds of those associated with the workhouse ...' and another, '... a buzz knowing that you ... are finding some new aspects of history not always understood before'.[16] 'A structure of feeling' between record and reader does seem an appropriate description of these experiences.

To return then to our viewer of online documents: having found a meaningful document, he or she has purchased and downloaded a copy, in the process of which the document may itself have acquired a new quality, one which might affect both provenance and context. It is clear that some users of archival documents are quite fascinated by archival context: they want to understand the archival context and provenance because it gives historical accuracy and authenticity to the document they have found. But many are *not* fascinated by archival context at all: they are concerned only with the document *itself*, with the information it provides about their

---

15 TNA Chief Executive's Office, September 2007.

16 'Living in the Shadow of the Workhouse': Comments from Southwell Workhouse Research Group, TNA 2007: <http://www.nationalarchives.gov.uk/partnerprojects/workhouse/default.htm> accessed 10 October 2007.

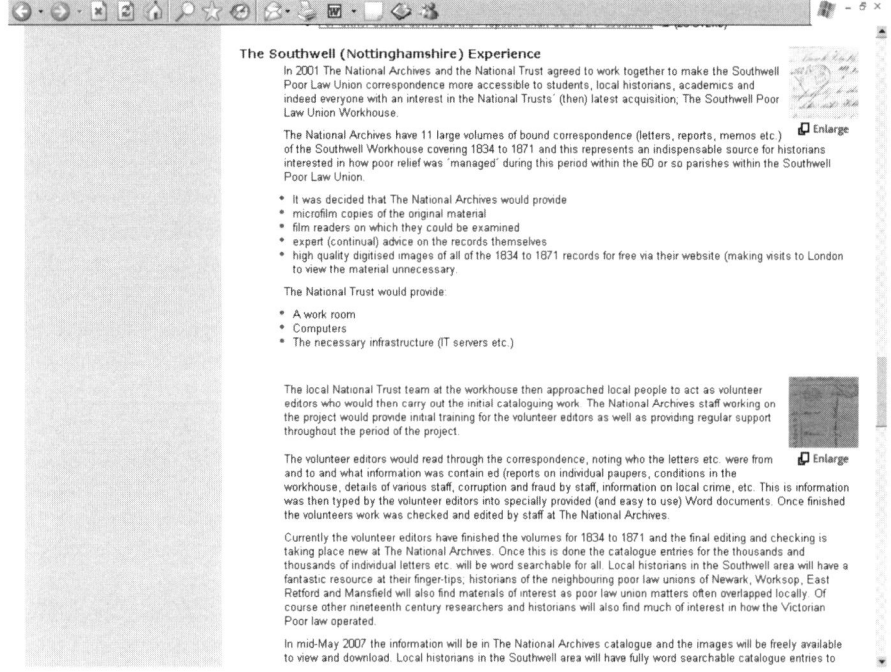

Figure 1.3   Homepage for The Southwell (Nottinghamshire) Experience, on the website of The National Archives (by courtesy of The National Archives)

own family and with the *meaning* it gives to their own lives. In purchasing a copy of a will, say, the reader may feel that it has been removed from its archival context and that it is being placed and owned in its family context, where it really belongs: here then, *the content has become the context*. And this shift of context, from the archive to the individual, is of course re-emphasized and reinforced by programmes like *Who Do You Think You Are?*.

This shift also has echoes of ideas in archive theory concerning provenance and users put forward most recently by Tom Nesmith. Nesmith endorses the more flexible view of provenance endorsed by Sue McKemmish which presents a re-conceived view of the 'logical, virtual and multiple relationships between records and their contexts of creation' (McKemmish 1994, 193). It is this view of provenance which Nesmith has taken further in a post-modernist interpretation, stating that 'multiple creators become but the beginning of [a record's] history, as the actions taken by an archives, and those *who use* records therein, are also part of the creation process'. In Nesmith's view, records 'become active agents in creating what we perceive and are not passive carriers of objective facts …' and 'those who make, transmit, keep, classify, destroy, archive and *use records* … are co-creators of the records and thus of the knowledge they shape' (Nesmith, 2007, 3–4). This shift, which incorporates the context of the user, marks a real development in the meaning of provenance and generates new questions about the popular context of the archival text and about the political and social legacy of archives.

The Challenge of Electronic Records

'The trouble with archivists is that they have electronic records but paper minds …'. (Overheard at a conference, 2006)

Of all the challenges which the archival profession is experiencing today, that from electronic records is perhaps the most enduring. The fundamental distinction to be drawn between paper records and electronic records is this: with paper records, the *paper* (or parchment or vellum) must be preserved, for this is the authentic record; with electronic records, it is the *information* which must be preserved, for that is the authentic record.

It follows from this that almost everything from the functions of a record office to the foundations of archival practice are significantly changed by electronic records. Immediately, though, it is the sheer scale of electronic document creation and of the resources required for digital preservation which astound: the Digital Preservation Coalition, the body which is taking forward digital preservation, is international in membership and global in outlook.[17] Work on this scale is necessary because it is recognized that the challenges of digital preservation are too large and diverse to be resolved by any single organization or country.

Many of the major issues arising from electronic records have already been discussed elsewhere: custodianship and storage (Cook 1992, 38; Tough 2006, 20–22); the appraisal of electronic records (for example Hosker and Richmond 2006); risks posed to future information and knowledge (Duranti and MacNeil 1996; Ross 2000, 3); the challenges to traditional archival principles of arrangement and original order (Duff 2006, 109–10, and quoting Bearman 1993, Headstrom 1993 and Wallace 1995); and privacy, security and ethics in the digitized world (MacNeil 2002; Currall 2006; Lemeiux 2007). In what follows, those issues of archival practice and archival theory which have not been discussed so fully are touched on.

Archival Practice in the Electronic World

As the electronic environment has completely transformed the material with which the archivist works, it seems reasonable to ask whether cataloguing and the production of finding aids are any longer really necessary, given powerful search engines, digitized records and automatic indexing. This question is particularly relevant because elsewhere in the digital world, online catalogues have been identified as barriers to the constructive use of digital resources (Lynch 2003, 210), and traditional archival finding aids have been seen to *inhibit* users' access (Menne-Haritz 2001).

Catalogue descriptions, or metadata, are defined in the paper world by the *International Standard for Archival Description (ISAD (G))* (2000)[18] and this

---

17　<http://www.dpconline.org/graphics/index.html> accessed 8 October 2007.
18　<http://www.ica.org/en/node/30000> accessed 8 October 2007.

will continue to be needed to provide authority and context, to give information about related materials and to help the user navigate the vast amount of archival material now available online. It is likely, however, that the cataloguing metadata accompanying electronic records will change to incorporate technical metadata and additional metadata added at instances of migration, and that the standard will undergo continual revision over the coming years. During this period it will also become clear whether automatic means of gathering and presenting metadata, like the collection of website titles from HTTP headers now being developed by Heritrix and by the International Internet Preservation Consortium (IIPC), prove worthwhile (Brown 2006, 78).

In some ways, electronic records need cataloguing metadata for survival and use. This is firstly because paper records have a set of 'signs' which we absorb automatically: just as typefaces tell us things about the meaning of the words they convey, the outward form of paper records tells us about the significance and authority of the content within. A book bound in red leather says 'I'm important!', the way documents are folded in a bundle, the format of a pipe roll, the use of treasury tags, ties and legal pink tape: these are all ways of telling us about the documents before we look at them. Secondly, the archivist's intervention here – putting the documents in order, describing them and producing finding aids – simply reinforces this notion of importance, and gives the user an indication of what to look at and where to start. Signs of conservation are similarly significant: 'ooh, this has been repaired: it must be valuable!'. Electronic records have no such signs, no way of saying 'I'm important!'. Moreover, in the digital context, characterized by the automatic transfer from an electronic records management system (ERMS) to an archive's digital storage and online presentation system, rearrangement and description by an archivist is unlikely. Without metadata and good titles then which identify records as valuable to administrative, business, research and historical contexts, and which enable a search engine to grab both title and reference, they might sink without trace, simply unnoticed by the user.

New Forms and Formats

New forms of records in the digital world – websites, blogs, wikis – pose interesting new challenges to archival theory. Adrian Brown points out that a fundamental challenge arises from the structural, temporal and informational qualities of the Web, which render it 'almost impossible, in terms of interconnectedness … to define any given website in terms of absolute boundaries'. As a result, it 'may be more helpful to regard a website as a conceptual grouping of information experienced by a user, rather than as an artefact with any coherent physical existence'. Moreover, the similarity of websites to any paper archive collection breaks down when 'the paper paradigm of discrete, enumerable and physically locatable information objects is rapidly rendered obsolete' and 'the nature of much of the informational content of the Web defines traditional categorisation: "publication", "record", "artefact" become meaningless' (Brown 2006, 26).

Websites may be created by a number of people and updated by still more: the archival principles of 'creator' and 'provenance' are not altogether easily defined in this context. Websites may be dynamic rather than static – or be a mixture of both. This has brought new kinds of archiving possibilities: 'snapshots' over time and a variety of new techniques based on the differing selection methods (that is, unselective, thematic or transactional) based on what has actually been used. For the archivist, however, describing an object which is still *dynamic* is an unprecedented departure from traditional archival practice and theory.

The organic nature of websites is a feature shared with other new record formats: blogs and wikis are also typified by collaborative authorship and by regular updating which mean they exhibit the lack of boundaries characteristic of websites. All share the problem that when these new formats are archived, links to other sites no longer function: a quality which at best irritates, and which at worst – and much more significantly – can erode the original function of the record.

Records of new forms and formats do then present new issues to both digital preservation and presentation; they also posit fundamental questions and challenges to traditional archival theory and archival practice.

Professional Status

As the foundations of traditional archival theory are being challenged by the digital context, the archivist's role in that context has also generated debate amongst archivists. Some see it as essential that archivists have a more active role in the creation of records than ever before. The need for this is simple and urgent: electronic records just cannot be managed without highly visible archiving from the outset (Bearman 1994; Duff 1996; Duranti and MacNeil 1996; Nesmith 2002). An alternative view is put forward below by Michael Moss, who identifies involvement with the creation of digital records as undermining the fiduciary responsibility of the archivist.[19] At the same time another change in the archivist's professional activities and status can be identified. In 2006, Helen Tibbo and Wendy Duff emphasized the merits of collaboration with technical specialists (Tibbo 2006, 28–30; Duff 2006, 110) – a collaboration which they saw working fruitfully and equitably. Whilst the archivist works with IT specialists, IT specialists for their part seek the archival perspective to their work. In practice this works, and in reality this collaboration has been growing since the first archival website was developed. Perhaps less expectedly, other changes brought by the needs of digital preservation have generated a different balance between archivists and other technical specialists. Whilst appraisal and selection remain functions of the records manager or archivist, the transfer of electronic records to the archives, the process of ingest, and the handling of those records for preservation and presentation do not. These activities, nationally and internationally, are carried out by experts in digital preservation (Ross 2006, 115–153). Whilst this is proper and essential, it does mean that what was once the preserve of the archivist is no longer so.

Whilst the archivist's role in records creation is still a matter of much healthy debate, ownership and control over the processes through which records pass to the archives has, by contrast almost silently, already shifted to technical colleagues.

---

19 See Chapter 4 in this volume.

Overall, it may be too early to say what the full impact of the development of electronic records will be on the archive profession both nationally and internationally. It can be said with certainty, however, that the change from paper and parchment to born-digital has not been one of degree but of kind: a paradigm shift which has brought profound changes and challenges to every aspect of the theory and practice in the profession in the UK.

Concluding Thoughts

The first chapter in this collection has looked at the impact upon archives and archivists of technological advances, at developments in the heritage and cultural context, at new discourses about archives in academic disciplines, at archives in the popular context and at the specific phenomenon of electronic records. Other chapters will address in detail certain of the issues already raised. Here then, at the outset, what can we conclude about the implications of these changes and emergent new perspectives for the archival profession in the UK?

There seems to be the need for re-thinking archival policy and practice in four areas: in relation to other heritage and cultural professions; in response to academic debate; in terms of archival theory; and in education and training.

Other Heritage Professions

The archival profession in the UK needs to know more about both the knowledge and practice of other heritage professionals. Archivists need to develop and establish both a long-term dialogue and collaborative work with colleagues from the wider heritage sector. The archival profession needs to be proactive in this area and needs to do this now.

The Academic Context

Recent developments in a number of academic disciplines based on human society – politics, sociology, philosophy, archaeology, history, linguistics – demonstrate an understanding of the importance of archives to all societies. As significantly, perceptions, perspectives and ideas in those disciplines give valuable insights into questions raised in the archival profession today. Archivists need to develop a forum for the discussion of these ideas with colleagues from different disciplines; and archivists need to initiate as well as contribute to these discussions through transdisciplinary conferences and interdisciplinary publications.

Archival Theory

We have seen that the MLA's pilot project, *Revisiting Archive Collections*, is changing some aspects of archival theory and practice. Electronic records meanwhile are posing a number of challenges to other fundamental principles underlying traditional theory. In a quite different context, Derridean ideas, postmodernist interpretations and the insights provided by literary criticism are presenting new concepts and new discourses about archives. Within the professional archive community itself, some theorists are turning the notion of provenance on its head. These philosophical concerns, challenges to theory and emerging discourses about archives together indicate that some reconsideration of archival principles is already under way and suggest that a review of archival theory as a whole would be timely.

Education and Training

Over ten years ago Terry Eastwood, Tom Nesmith and Carol Couture called for a reformed archival curriculum to meet contemporary needs and asked 'What will the archivist need to know in the twenty-first century?' (see their respective contributions to *Archivaria*, 1996). In the intervening decade, when archivists everywhere have witnessed a colossal shift in almost every aspect of their profession and of the world around them, have we in the UK done enough to prepare the archivist for the challenges of the twenty-first century?

Postgraduate archive courses in the UK have indeed made changes to incorporate the demands of access and management and to accommodate some of the technical requirements of digitization. But critical analysis of what archives actually are and what an archivist actually does, in a philosophical sense, remains patchy: enthusiastically embraced by some courses, completely passed over by others. At the same time, there is little recognition within the wider profession that any post-diploma development would be beneficial – little opportunity then during an archivist's career to develop any detailed understanding of the why, rather than the how, of being an archivist.

The profession in the UK is focused on practice and process: it is pragmatic and long has been. But now we need to think about how we might change this. We need to think about the establishment of a discipline which will incorporate archives and the activity of archiving as a whole, and the study of how archives have been understood throughout history, of how views and understanding of archives have changed and are changing – an archive-ography if you like (that we have no word for this – unlike our colleagues in museums – speaks volumes), a body of knowledge and activity which will allow us to contribute to and to initiate new thinking about archives. We need to think about how we can incorporate this into archival courses and into continuing professional education in the UK.

At present we are asking and expecting archivists to become skilled in old and new technologies and to make decisions on cultural and heritage grounds without giving them the knowledge and skills they need to do so. Most crucially, we are not enabling would-be archivists to gain the knowledge, understanding and skills necessary to develop as culturally informed, technically able archivists, with historical understanding, which is what is needed in the early years of the twenty-first century.

In the record office, where we began, we noted the pressures and demands on today's archivists: we need now to address both the requirements of the present and the challenges of the future.

References

Anderson, B.R. (1983), *Imagined Communities: Reflections on the Origin and Spread of Nationalism* (London: Verso).

Anderson, I. (2004), 'Are you being served? Historians and the search for primary sources', *Archivaria*, 58, 81–130.

Archives Task Force (ATF) (2004), *Listening to the Past, Speaking to the Future: Report of the Archives Task Force* (London: Museums Libraries and Archives Council).

Arel, D. and Ruble, B.A. (eds) (2006), *Rebounding Identities: the Politics of Identity in Russia and Ukraine* (Baltimore MD: Johns Hopkins University Press).

Attridge, D. et al. (eds) (1987), *Post-Structuralism and the Question of History* (Cambridge: Cambridge University Press).

Bastian, J.A. (2003), *Owning Memory: How a Caribbean Community Lost its Archives and Found its History* (London: CARIBA on behalf of UNESCO).

Bearman, D. (1994), *Electronic Evidence: Strategies for Managing Records in Contemporary Organisations* (Pittsburg PA: Archives and Museum Informatics).

––––––– (1993), 'Archival Principles and the Electronic Office', in Menne-Harritz, A. (ed.), *Information Handling in Offices and Archives* (New York: Saur), pp. 177–93.

Bennet, T. (1987), 'Texts in History', in Attridge, D. et al. (eds).

Bennet, T. et al. (eds) (1981a), *Culture, Ideology and Social Process. A Reader* (Milton Keynes: Open University Press).

––––––– (eds) (1981b), *Popular Television and Film* (London: British Film Institute).

Beyea, M. et al. (eds) (2004), *The Power and the Passion of Archives. A Festschrift in honour of Kent Haworth* (Ottawa: Association of Canadian Archivists).

Bishop A. et al. (eds) (2003), *Digital Library Use: Social Practice in Design and Evaluation* (Cambridge MA: MIT).

Brothman, B. (1999), 'Declining Derrida', *Archivaria*, 48, 64–88.

Brown, A. (2006), *Archiving Websites. A Practical Guide for Information Management Professionals* (London: Facet).

Butikofer, N. et al. (eds) (2006), *Managing and Archiving Records in the Digital Era* (Baden: Hier + Jetzt).

Caribbean Studies for Black and Asian History (CASBAH) (2002), *Archives Survey Tool. A Guide for Archivists, Record Managers and Researchers to assist with the Survey of Archive Collections relating to the History of the Caribbean and of Black and Asian People in the UK.*

––––––– (2000–2002), *The CASBAH Project: Identifying and Mapping National Research Resources for Caribbean Studies and the History of Black and Asian People in Britain.* Supported by the Research Support Libraries Programme (RSLP).

Carr, E.H. (1961), *What is History?* (London: Macmillan).

Cervantes, M.G. [1605–13], *The Ingenious Hidalgo Don Quixote*, trans. J. Rutherford (London: Penguin, 2000).

Chaucer, G. [?1386–87], *The Canterbury Tales*, trans. N. Coghill (1951) (London: Penguin, 2003).

Cm 4310 (1999), *Modernising Government*, White Paper (Norwich: TSO).

Cm 4516 (1999), *Government Policy on Archives* (Norwich: TSO).

Collingwood, R.G. (1946), *The Idea of History* (Oxford: Clarendon).

Collins, W. (1868), *The Woman in White* (London: Wordsworth).

Cook, T. (2001), 'Fashionable nonsense or professional rebirth: postmodernism and the practice of archives', *Archivaria*, 51, Spring, 14–35.

———— (1992), 'The Concept of the Archival Fonds: Theory, Description and Provenance in the Post-Custodial Era', in Eastwood, T. (ed.).

Cooley, M. (1998), *The Archivist: a Novel* (London: Abacus).

Couture, C. (1996), 'Today's students: tomorrow's archivists', *Archivaria*, 42, 95–104.

Craven, L. (2007), 'Epic, group identity and the archive in the modern world', *Archives*, 32 (117), 144–58.

Culler, J. (1986), 'Introduction', in Valdes, M.J. and Millar, O. (eds), *The Identity of the Literary Text* (Toronto: University of Toronto Press).

Currall, J. (2006), 'Security and the Digital Domain', in Tough, A. and Moss, M. (eds).

Derrida, J. (1996), *Archive Fever: a Freudian Impression*, trans. E. Prenowitz (Chicago IL: University of Chicago Press).

———— (1976), *Of Grammatology*, trans. G.C. Spivak (Baltimore MD: Johns Hopkins University Press).

Dickens, C. [1852–53], *Bleak House*, with introd. by Peter Ackroyd (London: Folio Society, 2000).

Du Gay, P. et al. (eds) (1997), *Doing Cultural Studies: the Story of the Sony Walkman* (Milton Keynes: Sage in association with the OU).

Duff, W. (2006), 'A New Order Meets an Old World: the Impact of Digital Objects on the Archival and Records Management Professions', in Butikofer et al. (eds), pp. 105–114.

———— (1996), 'Ensuring the preservation of reliable evidence: a research project funded by NHPRC', *Archivaria*, 42, 28–45.

Duranti, L. and MacNeil, H. (1996), 'The protection of the integrity of electronic records', *Archivaria*, 42, 46–66.

Eagleton, T. (1982), *The Rape of Clarissa: Writing Sexuality and Class in Samuel Richardson* (Oxford: Blackwell).

Easthope, A. (1999), *Englishness and National Culture* (London: Routledge).

Eastwood, T. (1996) 'Reforming the archival curriculum to meet contemporary needs', *Archivaria*, 42, 80–8

———— (ed.) (1992), *The Archival Fonds: from Theory to Practice* (Ottawa: Association of Canadian Archivists).

Ellis, M. and Greening, A. (2002), 'Archival training in 2002: between a rock and a hard place', *Journal of the Society of Archivists*, 23 (2), 197–208.

Elsaesser, T. (1981), 'Narrative Cinema and Audience-Oriented Aesthetics', in Bennet, T. et al. (eds) (1981b).

Elton, Geoffrey (1967), *The Practice of History* (London: Fontana).

Etherton, J. (2006) 'The role of the archives in the perception of self', *Journal of the Society of Archivists*, 27 (2), 227–46.

Evans, J. and Hall, S. (eds) (1999), *Visual Culture: the Reader* (London: Sage).

Evans, R. (1997, 2nd edn 2004), *In Defence of History* (London: Granta).

Faulks, S. (2006), *Human Traces* (London: Vintage).

Fielding, H. [1749], *Tom Jones*, with introd. by R.P.C. Mutter (London: Penguin, 1966).

Flinn, A. et al. (2006), Unpub. paper on identity (School of Library Archive and Information Studies: University College London).

Foucault, M. (1972), *The Archaeology of Knowledge* (London: Routledge).

———— (1966), *The Order of Things: an Archaeology of the Human Sciences* (New York: Harper).

Fuhrer, U. (2004), *Cultivating Minds: Identity as Meaning Making Practice* (London: Routledge).

Greene, M.A. (2002), 'The power of meaning: the archival mission in the postmodern age', *Archivaria*, 65, 42–55.

Hall, S. (1990), 'Cultural Identity and Diaspora', in Rutherford, J. (ed.), *Identity, Community, Culture, Difference* (London: Lawrence & Wishart).

———— (1981), 'Cultural Studies: Two Paradigms', in Bennet, T. et al. (eds) (1981a).

Hamilton, C. et al. (eds) (2002), *Refiguring the Archive* (London: Kluwer).

Harris, V. (2006), 'The Archive is Politics', in Beyea, M. et al. (eds).

———— (2002), 'A Shaft of Darkness: Derrida in the Archive', in Hamilton, C. et al. (eds).

Headstrom, M. (1993), 'Descriptive practices for electronic records: deciding what is essential and imagining what is possible', *Archivaria*, 36, Autumn, 37–63.

Holland, T. (2007), *The Archivist's Story* (London: Bloomsbury).

Hosker, R. and Richmond, L. (2006), 'Seek and Destroy – an Archival Appraisal Theory and Strategy', in Tough, A. and Moss, M. (eds).

Jenkinson, H. (1922), *A Manual of Archival Administration* (London: Edward Arnold).

Johnson, C. and Rankin, M. (2006), 'Records Professionals in a Multimedia Age', in Tough, A. and Moss, M. (eds).

Keightley, D.N (1978), *Sources of Shang History: the Oracle Bone Inscriptions of Bronze Age China* (Berkeley CA: University of California Press).

Ketellar, E. (1999), 'Archivalisation and archiving', *Archives and Manuscripts*, 27, 54–61.

———— (1996), 'Archival theory and the Dutch manual', *Archivaria*, 41, 31–40.

Kipling, R. [1901], *Kim*, with introd. by J. Baylen (London: Everyman, 1995).

Le Goff, J. (1992), *History and Memory*, trans. S. Rendall and E. Claman (New York: Columbia University Press).

Lemieux, V. (2007), 'Balancing access and privacy: using risk management to walk the tightrope', unpub. paper, ARMReN Conference, September 2007.

Lowe, D. (1982), *The History of Bourgeois Perception* (London: Harvester).

Lynch, C. (2003), 'Colliding with the Real World: Heresies and Unexplored Questions about Audience, Economics and Control of Digital Libraries', in Bishop, A. et al. (eds).

McCabe, C. (1981), 'Realism and the Cinema: Notes on some Brechtian Theses', in Bennet, T. et al. (eds) (1981b).

McKemmish, S. (1994), 'Are Archives Ever Actual?', in McKemmish, S. and Piggott, M. (eds).

McKemmish, S. and Piggott, M. (eds) (1994), *The Records Continuum. Ian Maclean and Australian Archives First Fifty Years* (Ancora: Society of Australian Archivists).

MacNeil, H. (2005), 'Research Uses of Personal Information: some Ethical Considerations', in Beyea, M. et al. (eds).

——— (2002), 'Providing grounds for trust: the findings of the Authority Task Force of InterPARES', *Archivaria*, 54, 24–58.

Mahaffy, J.P. (1877), *Social Life in Greece. From Homer to Menander* (Oxford: Oxford University Press).

Mann, M. (2005), *The Dark Side of Democracy* (Cambridge: Cambridge University Press).

Mayor's Commission on African and Asian Heritage (MCAAH) (2005), *Delivering Shared Heritage* (London: Greater London Authority).

Menne-Haritz, A. (2001), 'Access – the reformulation of an archival paradigm', *Archival Science*, 1 (1), 57–82.

Miles, S. (1996), 'Cultural capital and consumption: understanding postmodernist identities in a cultural context', *Culture and Psychology*, 2 (2), 139–58.

Moss, M. (2007), 'Choreographed encounter – the archive and public history', *Archives*, 31 (116), 41–57.

——— (2006), 'The Function of the Archive', in Tough, A. and Moss, M. (eds).

Neale, S. (1981), 'Genre and Cinema', in Bennet, T. et al. (eds) (1981b).

Nesmith, T. (2007), 'What is an archival education?', *Journal of the Society of Archivists*, 28 (1), 5–25.

——— (2002), 'Seeing archives: postmodernism and the changing intellectual place of archives', *American Archivist*, 65 (1), 24–41.

——— (1996), '"Professional education in the most expansive sense": what will the archivist need to know in the twenty-first century?', *Archivaria*, 42 (2), 89–94.

Newman, A. (2006), 'Countering social exclusion through identity construction', AHRC Conference on *Material Culture, Identities and Inclusion*, Dept of Museum Studies, University of Leicester.

Newman, J. and Reilly, L. (2007), 'Revisiting archive collections', unpub. paper, ARMReN conference, June 2007.

Peake, M. [1950], *The Gormenghast Trilogy* (London: Mandarin, 1992).

Peters, V. and Richmond, L. (2006), 'Divided No More: a Descriptive Approach to the Record-Keeping Continuum', in Tough, A. and Moss, M. (eds).

Pradhan, S. (1986), 'Minimalist semantics: Davidson and Derrida on meaning, use and convention', *Diacritics: a Review of Contemporary Criticism*, 16 (1), 66–77.

Ross, S. (2006), 'Approaching Digital Preservation Holistically', in Tough, A. and Moss, M. (eds).

———— (2000), *Changing Trains at Wigan: Digital Preservation and the Future of Scholarship* (London: NPO Preservation Guidance. Occasional papers).

Roueche, C. (1989), *Aphrodisias in Late Antiquity: The Late Roman and Byzantine Inscriptions* (London: Society for the Promotion of Roman Studies).

Rutherford, J. (1990), *Identity: Community, Culture, Difference* (London: Lawrence & Wishart).

Saramago, J. (1997), *All the Names*, trans. M.J. Costa (London: Harvill Press).

Shakespeare, W. [?1592], *Henry VI Part 2* (London: Arden, 2000).

Shimamura-Wilcocks, Y. (2007), 'Social inclusion and museums: celebration of "difference", understanding "self" and "other"', *Museological Review*, 12, 81–7.

Steedman, C. (2002), *Dust* (Manchester: Manchester University Press).

———— (1998), 'The space of memory: in an archive', *History of the Human Sciences*, 11 (4), 65–84.

Sterne, L. [1759–67], *The Life and Opinions of Tristram Shandy, Gentleman* (London: Penguin 2003).

Swift, J. [?1735], *The Drapier's Letters to the People of Ireland*, ed. H. Davies (Oxford: Clarendon Press, 1935).

Tibbo, H.R. (2006), 'Creating, Managing, and Archiving Records: Changing Roles and Realities in the Digital Era', in Butikofer, N. et al. (eds).

Toews, J.E. (2004), *Becoming Historical: Cultural Reformation and Public Memory in Early Nineteenth-Century Berlin* (Cambridge: Cambridge University Press).

Tough, A. (2006), 'Records and the Transition to the Digital', in Tough, A. and Moss, M. (eds).

Tough, A. and Moss, M. (eds) (2006), *Record Keeping in a Hybrid Environment* (Oxford: Chandos).

Tyacke, S. (2002), 'Archives and the wider world, *Archivaria*, 52, 1–25.

Wallace, D. (2005), 'Freedom of Information in the Digital Age: a Crisis of Diminished Accountability and Access', in Beyea, M. et al. (eds).

———— (1995), 'Managing the present: metadata and archival description', *Archivaria*, 39, Spring, 11–21.

Williams, R. (1961), *The Long Revolution* (London: Chatto & Windus).

Young, K. (1992), *People, Places and Power: Local Democracy and Community* (London: Local Government Management Board).

van Zyl, S. (2002), 'Psychoanalysis and the Archive: Derrida's *Archive Fever*', in Hamilton, C. et al. (eds).

Chapter 2

The Textuality of the Archive

Andrew Prescott

All texts are selective, diversionary, and amnesia-prone, forgetting or repressing crucial things about their own origins and those of the events with which they deal (Strohm 1998, xii).

In his introduction to *Postmodernism for Historians*, Callum Brown asserts that 'Postmodernism has changed the way in which History as an academic subject is conducted' (Brown 2005, 180). He concedes that 'These changes are not uniformly felt across every topic, every university, every individual historian nor every published book and article.' Nevertheless, in Brown's view the new theoretical and critical insights developed by such figures as Roland Barthes, Michel Foucault, Jacques Derrida and Jean-François Lyotard have changed the agenda of history, prompting the study of new subjects and the exploration of different types of source materials: 'postmodernism has tremendously stimulated the History profession. It has caused excitement, thoughtfulness, the search for works of theory to engage with or refute new ideas'.

Many other historians, however, have been less enthusiastic about the new body of theory. In 1991, Geoffrey Elton published his historical testament, *Return to Essentials* (a title which prefigured the 'Back to Basics' campaign launched shortly afterwards by the Tory government). Elton denounced postmodern theories as 'the intellectual equivalent of crack', warning against the 'cancerous radiation that comes from the foreheads of Derrida and Foucault' (Elton 1991, 41). Elton urged that the professional study of history should be purged of such distractions as cultural history and return to its purest form, the study of political and constitutional history grounded in rigorous criticism of documentary sources: '*Ad fontes* remains the necessary war cry' (Elton 1991, 52).

Although Elton's hard-line views have not found widespread support, many professional historians, particularly in the UK, remain deeply suspicious of theoretical developments, with postmodernism frequently portrayed as a threat to the integrity and viability of history as an academic discipline. Richard Evans's *Defence of History*, first published in 1997, is perhaps the most widely accepted statement of the consensus view of the UK's historical profession on the nature of its discipline. Although Evans rejects the extremes of Elton's back to basics campaign, he affirms the continuing validity of traditional historical technique: 'Through the sources we use, and the methods with which we handle them, we can, if we are very careful and thorough, approach a reconstruction of past reality that may be partial and provisional, and will certainly not be objective, but is nevertheless true' (Evans 1997, 149).

Archivists naturally see themselves as closely (although not exclusively) connected to the study of history and the debate about the 'postmodern threat' to history should be of more than passing interest to archivists, particularly when it bears on the way in which historians make use of original textual materials. However, archivists may wonder whether these debates have any direct relevance to their daily working life. Notwithstanding their ideological differences, Callum Brown and Richard Evans both make extensive use of archival materials in their own historical research. Their theoretical differences apparently have little impact on their respective approach to archives; the archivists who welcome Brown and Evans to their search rooms will not notice any major differences between them.

Many archivists will feel that such debates about critical theory are of little value in confronting the day-to-day issues affecting the operation of record offices, which every day become more pressing. The list of such practical preoccupations is a familiar one. More and more institutional records are generated as every year goes by. The growth of both electronic and paper records creates new problems of selection, access and storage. Archivists have to grapple with new freedom of information and data protection requirements. Listing backlogs show no signs of dwindling. Conservation issues become more complex, extensive and expensive. As staff become scarcer, it becomes more difficult to keep search rooms open. Archivists struggle to compete with other cognate professions, such as librarians and museum curators, in securing a reasonable slice of the limited funding and resources available for 'heritage' activities. In this context, the archivist may feel justified in dismissing debates about such impenetrable matters as postmodernism, semiotics and structuralism as an irrelevance. Certainly, many archivists reading Richard Evans's defence of a form of history based on the familiar rules of documentary criticism will feel a sense of relief and reassurance that historians will continue to study documentary sources in archive search rooms. Nothing to worry about there, the archivist might think, and thank goodness, because there are more pressing bread-and-butter problems.

The archivist's peace of mind may however be disturbed by glancing at the development of museum studies in recent years. In a lecture given in 1967 and published by the French journal *Architecture/Mouvement/Continuité* in 1984, Foucault suggested that every society created special spaces, which he called (as a counterpart to imaginary utopias) heterotopias. According to Foucault, these heterotopias are highly stylized expressions of the society's power and social structures. Among the types of heterotopias discussed by Foucault were cemeteries, prisons, theatres, gardens and brothels. Museums and libraries, suggested Foucault, were particularly striking examples of heterotopias:

> … there are heterotopias of indefinitely accumulating time, for example museums and libraries. Museums and libraries have become heterotopias in which time never stops building up and topping its own summit, whereas in the seventeenth century, even at the end of the century, museums and libraries were the expression of an individual choice. By contrast, the idea of accumulating everything, of establishing a sort of general archive, the will to enclose in one place all times, all epochs, all forms, all tastes, the idea of constituting a place of all times that is itself outside of time and inaccessible to its ravages, the project of organizing in this way a sort of perpetual and indefinite accumulation of

time in an immobile place, this whole idea belongs to our modernity. The museum and the library are heterotopias that are proper to western culture of the nineteenth century (Foucault 1984).[1]

Foucault's insistence that the character of a museum reflects the social and cultural structure of the society which creates it has encouraged a greater sense of self-awareness among museum curators. There is now a much greater consciousness of the way in which a visit to a museum involves a complex interplay of social and cultural identities, drawing in curators (both past and present), visitors, administrators and objects. In choosing themes for display, selecting objects and deciding on appropriate forms of interpretative commentary, the curator makes many cultural assumptions about the importance of the theme of the exhibition, the significance and character of the museum and its collections, and the nature of the museum's visitors. The visitor in turn brings a further set of different cultural assumptions to bear. Funders, administrators and trustees also have their own equally distinctive preoccupations. In this web of interlocking cultural identities, the meaning of the objects themselves is far from fixed, shifting according to the context of the display, the reason for the selection and the nature of the person viewing it. In the words of Susan Crane, museums are 'flexible mirrors' with a 'convex potential for multiple interpretations and participation (that is, by those who have either kind of personal historical consciousness: as veterans or survivors, or as historians)' (Crane 2003, 332).

The new theoretical insights offered by the academic discussion of museums have had a direct impact on curatorial practice in museums, affecting all aspects of curatorial activity from conservation to display. This 'new museology' demands a shift of emphasis in the activities of curators away from day-to-day practical issues towards a greater awareness of the cultural contexts of all aspects of museum activities. As Peter Vergo has put it:

> Beyond the captions, the information panels, the accompanying catalogue, the press handout, there is a subtext comprising innumerable diverse, often contradictory strands, woven from the wishes and ambitions, the intellectual or political or social or educational aspirations and preconceptions of the museum director, the scholar, the designer, the sponsor – to say nothing of the society, the political or social or educational system which nurtured all these people and in so doing left their stamp on them (Vergo 1989, 2–3).

To date, there has been no similar engagement by UK archivists with the implications of new theoretical and critical tools for the practice of their profession. This is surprising, since the new theories show a strong engagement with text. A central theme of new theoretical discussions is the limitations and deceptions of text as a medium in which to encapsulate human experience. Text is always biased, always limited and always deceptive. Even if the creator of the text were capable of transcending such aspects of his or her own humanity as gender, social status, religion and education to produce a wholly objective account of reality, each reader draws on a completely different set of experiences in interacting with the text. Moreover, the very limitations of human language itself prevent it from adequately conveying

---

1 Cited from: <http://foucault.info/documents/heteroTopia/foucault.heteroTopia.en.html>.

a historical experience; it is quite simply impossible to convey a battle, a revolt or a famine through the restricted set of symbols we use for communication. Above all, text does not exist in a vacuum. Every text carries with it memories and references (both by its creator and in the reader's mind) to countless other texts – just think of the way in which Western texts of all periods are shot through with cross-references to the Bible. Even pictorial images and material objects function effectively as texts. We understand and interpret pictures in textual terms, reducing pictorial imagery to representations of sounds. Our understanding of reality is trapped in a textual paradigm. Hence Derrida's comment that 'there is nothing outside of the text' (Derrida 1976, 158). The limitations and deceptions of text make it impossible for us ever to achieve Ranke's aim of showing history 'how it actually was'. We cannot use documentary criticism to create a time machine; text is not a sufficiently perfect tool for these purposes.

It is not surprising that many historians have consequently seen postmodernism as the negation of the historical enterprise, but this is far from the case. Elton loudly insisted that there was an actual historical reality which could be recovered – events do happen and their existence cannot be denied. However, Elton was too good a historian to think that history was simply the recovery of events. He defined history as 'not the study of the past but the study of present traces of the past' (Elton 1969, 20). Insofar as those traces are overwhelmingly textual, our relationship with the past is constantly mediated by the limitations and uncertainties of the texts which survive. Our investigation of the past is an exploration of those very uncertainties and ambiguities.

As soon as we accept the limitations of our understanding of the past, a far richer intellectual and emotional engagement with the past is possible. Instead of treating 'historical sources' as mere quarries of historical fact, we begin to understand the richness of the cultural universe inhabited by these texts and develop a fuller appreciation of the cultural intersection between past and present. Roland Barthes, the most subtle and sensitive decoder of texts, provided a striking illustration of the way in which the pithiest of texts can convey the richest of messages. He described a walk in a quiet village of south-western France:

> I had occasion to read, within a few hundred yards, on the doors of three villas, three different signs: *Vicious Dog*, *Dangerous Dog*, *Watchdog*. This region, evidently, has a very lively sense of property. But that is not of such interest as this: these three expressions constitute one and the same message: *Do Not Enter* (or you will be bitten). In other words, linguistics, which is concerned only with messages, could say nothing about them but what is very simple, very banal; it would by no means exhaust the meaning of these expressions, for this *meaning is in their difference*: *Vicious Dog* is aggressive; *Dangerous Dog* is philanthropic; *Watchdog* is apparently objective. In still other words, through one and the same message, we read three choices, three commitments, three mentalities, or again, three image-repositories, three alibis of ownership ... (Barthes 1986, 106).

The modern UK countryside is equally rich in such canine signifiers. A sign in the form of a Roman mosaic with the inscription 'Cave Canem' speaks volumes as to the cultural and social outlook of the house's owner. By contrast, a cheap printed sticker with a picture of a ferocious dog and the simple statement 'I Live Here' may be taken as indicating an owner at the other end of the social spectrum. I live in a village in mid-Wales and the question of whether or not such signs should be bilingual (or indeed only in Welsh) adds a whole further level to the analysis. It is said that when ordnance survey maps of North Wales were prepared in the late nineteenth century, the English mapmakers were embarrassed to discover that the common house name they had recorded, *Gwyliwch rhag y ci*, meant 'Beware of the Dog'.

Examples of the way in which the simplest of texts can convey a wealth of cultural and social meanings can readily be multiplied. The social pretensions of the seaside resort of Frinton-on-Sea are eloquently expressed by its signs asking visitors not to picnic on the greensward. The invention or borrowing of place-names by estate agents and developers to suggest that particular localities contain upmarket residences is another example of textual manipulation. At the other end of the social scale, Alison Barnes has mapped the distribution of graffiti in New Basford in Nottingham and points out how 'teenagers leave graffiti as a territorial marker and symbolic gesture of their distancing from the world of adults'. Mapping of this archive of graffiti reveals an enormous amount about the social and spatial relationship of young people to the city in which they live (Barnes 2005).

Richard Evans objects that critical analysis of this kind has long been stock-in-trade of the orthodox historian and represents nothing new. In this context, one might think of the Victorian legal historian Frederic William Maitland's insistence that the development of phrases regarded as mere 'common form' frequently reflects fundamental issues in legal and constitutional history (Maitland 1911, 2: 110–173). Similarly, Elton insisted that the 'stifling formality' of legal records could conceal deeper issues which can only be revealed by a precise understanding of the legal and administrative machinery (Holmes 1997, 267). However, the application of new linguistic tools makes the study of semiotics a much richer field of study than that used in conventional historical criticism. Moreover, while the idea that gnomic texts can conceal rich layers of meaning is a familiar one for historians, they rarely put it into practice. Historical works are all too often judged by the quantity of new sources consulted rather than the extent to which the semiotics and layers of interpretation have been investigated. Exegesis is often more fruitful than the triangulation of large quantities of data.

New critical approaches like those espoused by Roland Barthes in his celebrated series of essays *Mythologies* have allowed scholars to use unpromising texts to develop profound cultural and historical insights. Although Robert Darnton would reject the label postmodernist, his enormously influential essay, 'The Great Cat Massacre', is a characteristic example of this methodology because of the way in which it uses a single short document to recapture the social and cultural milieu of Parisian artisans in the eighteenth century (Darnton 1984). Likewise, the study of the Peasants' Revolt of 1381 in England, a well-worn historical subject, has recently been revivified by literary scholars such as Susan Crane (1992) and Steven Justice (1994), who have made a careful analysis of the language, audience, imagery and textual interconnections of the well-known letters in Middle English said to have been composed by the rebel leaders. Using such methods, Crane and Justice have provided vivid insight into the ideological programme and mentality of the rebels and elucidated the wider social impact of the rising.

Crane and Justice confine their attention to 'literary' texts found in chronicles, but their work helps break down the boundaries between 'literary' and 'administrative' texts. Paul Strohm takes such methods to their logical conclusion by applying techniques more commonly associated with the analysis of literary texts to 'administrative' documents from formal archives, such as an appeal relating to the controversial mayoral election in London in 1384 (Strohm 1992) or the records of the process in King's Bench by which the Lollard insurgent Sir John Oldcastle was condemned in 1417 (Strohm 1998). Strohm argues that for the scholar there is no distinction between 'literary' and 'administrative' texts; they are all historical texts. In the index to his collection of essays *Hochon's Arrow*, he includes under the technical literary term 'genres' not only such literary forms as 'dream vision' and 'fabliau' but also such archival forms as 'approver's appeal' and 'petition'. The logical conclusion of such a view is that archival texts must be read as closely as poems by Chaucer or Langland, and Strohm argues strongly the case for a more leisured and interpretative reading of archival materials:

> My conviction is that, rather than retarding the historical enterprise, a direct address to issues attending the construction of historical meaning is central to its excitement and its integrity. My objective is thus at once modest and presumptuous: not so much to announce new information, as to offer alternative ways of viewing and entertaining information already considered to be possessed (Strohm 1998, xii).

The potential deceptiveness and uncertainty of historical texts is something of which archivists are often more conscious than historians. All archivists will be familiar with categories of documents whose meaning is entirely false and fictitious. One of the most well-known types of deed is the common recovery which was used to break restrictions on the sale of land and was in origin a record of a fraudulent lawsuit in the Court of Common Pleas. One of the parties in this action was a fictitious character called Hugh Hunt and the land itself was vaguely described. The recovery proceeded by summoning various parties to vouch for the title to the land. A key part was played by the crier of the court who acted as 'common vouchee' and appeared in the court simply to request that the matter be put to a jury. When the crier failed to appear once more in court, the land was awarded to another party notwithstanding any previous restrictions on its transfer. The crier of the court thus appears in a formal court document in a deceptive and fictitious guise, often using false names such as John Doe and Richard Rowe. The common recovery is a completely misleading text, but nonetheless of critical importance in the history of land and the propertied classes.

Fictions such as these multiply throughout the archive. The bill of Middlesex was another example of a fictitious lawsuit which was used very successfully to transfer unrelated cases to the Court of King's Bench. The stewardship of the Chiltern Hundreds is another such well-known fiction but one which has occasionally turned into a reality – in 1842 Viscount Chelsea, who sought to apply for the office in the course of a controversy over election bribery, was refused the office, and Gladstone fretted over whether members of parliament who had committed misdemeanours and wished to apply for the office should be granted what might be seen as an honour. These are very obvious fictions; others are more subtle. Roy Hunnisett has pointed out how during the sixteenth century coroners' inquests began regularly to report that the 'opprobrious words' used during mortal struggles were 'thou art a knave' (Hunnisett 1971, 206). He suggests that this phrase had become a piece of 'common form' – the actual words were probably not so unimaginative or so mild. Hunnisett also notes that many medieval 'proofs of age' were evidently highly artificial documents.

Occasionally, the archive can leave us completely perplexed. In October 1390, a commission was issued to investigate the robbery of Geoffrey Chaucer, at that time Clerk of the King's Works, at Hatcham in Surrey (Crow and Olson 1966, 477–89). A writ discharging Chaucer of liability in the Exchequer states that the poet was robbed of twenty pounds of the king's money, his horse and other property at 'Le Fowle Oak' in Deptford. In April 1391, a group of robbers were tried in the Court of King's Bench. One of the gang became an approver while Middlesex juries also brought indictments against them. These state that Chaucer was robbed of nine pounds and forty four (or forty three) pence at Hatcham near Deptford on 6 September 1390 but also declare that Chaucer was robbed of ten pounds at Westminster on the same day.

Read literally, these records suggest that Chaucer was robbed three times in three separate places within the space of three days. This seems unlikely, although as the editors of the *Chaucer Life-Records* point out, 'Scholarly opinion ranges from a belief that there was only one robbery to the feeling that there were probably three' (Crow and Olson 1966, 488). The proximity of 'Le Fowle Oak' and Hatcham suggest that these two references are probably to a single incident, although whether it took place on 3 or 6 September remains unclear. But how did Westminster come into the account? Perhaps it was added simply to strengthen the claim of the King's Bench, which acted as a court of first instance in Middlesex, to hear the case. We will probably never know.

The process by which such confusions and fictions might occur has been elucidated by Roy Hunnisett in a meticulous comparison of file and roll entries for six inquests taken by the Warwickshire coroner Robert Waver between 1365 and 1372 (Hunnisett 1971). The differences between the information in the file record of the inquest and its final enrolled version are very striking. In one case the file states that the victim was stabbed through the heart with a knife called a 'broche' and died immediately, whereas the roll declares that the wound was inflicted with a baselard and that the victim died three days later. In another case, the file states that the victim was stabbed through the heart with a knife worth one penny by unknown malefactors, whereas the roll merely says that the victim had divers wounds and that the perpetrators were strangers who immediately fled.

The variations between the file and roll versions of Waver's inquests are very reminiscent of the apparent contradictions in the records of the robbery of Chaucer. In some cases, the discrepancies in Waver's records are due to simple scribal error. In others, they appear to be deliberate manipulations intended to protect particular individuals from possible fines and liabilities. The roll entries also apparently draw on further additional information not now available, perhaps records of further interrogations of the inquest jury. Hunnisett points out that the survival of both file and roll is unusual; normally only an enrolment or fair copy survives. He observes that 'It is seldom possible to discover how much of it [the enrolment] can be trusted: which jurors and sureties or even more essential people are ghosts, which dates and valuations are genuine, what exactly happened' (Hunnisett 1971, 227). Noting that it has long been recognized that literary texts, like medieval chronicles, should be used with caution, Hunnisett draws the melancholy conclusion that 'The reliability of many official records seems to be no greater, and from their haphazard mixture of fact, fiction, and error the complete truth can rarely be distilled' (Hunnisett 1971, 227).

L.C. Hector has pointed out how even the most solemn of records, the plea rolls of the royal courts at Westminster, are by no means comprehensive accounts of the proceedings of the court (Hector 1978). The very formality of these records mean that they omit a great deal of legal discussion and manoeuvring, compressing the most complex of debates into a rigid straightjacket of formulaic textuality:

> The rolls entirely ignore everything in the proceedings they record that can be regarded as abortive or irrelevant. Thus the plea abandoned by its proponent or declared inadmissible by the court, the disallowed claim to jurisdiction by the bailiffs of a franchise, the waived or the overruled objection, and the unsuccessful aid-prayer are all passed over in silence as complete as if they had never been advanced. The defendant whose right to appear by attorney is not recognised by the court, or whose letters of protection are revoked by a patent produced by his opponent, is recorded, in an entry indistinguishable in form from hundreds of others on the roll, simply as having defaulted … There is even good reason to think a writ could be quashed, abandoned or replaced by another, without provoking any mention of the fact in the roll (Hector 1978, 268).

However, as Hector points out, while these debates, which were not merely of legal significance but also full of social and cultural interest, were suppressed from the 'official' record, they are recorded in another 'unofficial' text, namely the year books. Hector experimented with the use of file records to identify records of cases reported in the year books, but his fundamental conclusion is a compelling one, namely that an 'unofficial' text can be a more authoritative record of a proceeding in a royal court than the 'official' roll entry.

A record of a legal hearing is a record of an event, and different types of texts respond to that event in different ways. We can only recover the event through its textual traces, and these fluctuate, mutate and shift. The text of the record forms a barrier between us and the event which cannot be penetrated. This is not a phenomenon restricted to medieval records; it is an inherent characteristic of all texts. The same sort of distortions described by Hector can be seen in the records of a much later case, namely the appearance before the Privy Council in 1794 of John Thelwell, one of the leaders of the London Corresponding Society who had been arrested on suspicion of treason (Thompson 1968, 20–21). Two main accounts of Thelwell's appearance before Privy Council survive, one by Thelwell and another in the papers of the Treasury solicitor in the National Archives (TS 963/11). Thelwell refused to answer the questions of the Privy Council and his dramatic account of his interrogation afterwards formed a great set-piece in his public lectures. But Thelwell's description differs fundamentally from that in the Treasury solicitor's papers.

In Thelwell's own account of his appearance before the Privy Council, he seeks to give the impression that the proceedings were highly improvised and thus unconstitutional. He presents the Privy Council as in a state of confusion on his appearance. Thelwell describes how he was called in 'and beheld the whole Dramatis Personae intrenched chin deep in Lectures and manuscripts ... all scattered about in the utmost confusion'. Thelwell adopts a strategy of presenting the whole proceeding as a play (which, since a play is carefully prepared perhaps contradicts his suggestion that the proceedings against him were improvised). In the published version, this comparison with a play is emphasized by the use of elaborate stage directions, printed in italics. In the lecture, Thelwell presumably used his own powers as a mimic to convey a similar effect. Thelwell achieves a comic effect by making William Pitt his main opponent, urging the legal officers on in their interrogation. Pitt is thunderstruck by Thelwell's defiance, repeating himself in his annoyance. The Attorney General and Lord Chancellor act as good cops to Pitt's hard man:

ATTORNEY GENERAL [*piano*]. Mr Thelwell, what is your Christian name?

T. [*somewhat suffering*] John.

ATT. GEN. [*piano still*] ... With two l's at the end or with one?

T. With two – but it does not signify. [*Carelessly, but rather sullen, or so*] You need not give yourself any trouble. I do not intend to answer any questions.

PITT. What does he say? [*darting round, very fiercely, from the other side of the room, and seating himself by the side of the* CHANCELLOR].

LORD CHANCELLOR [*with silver softness, almost melting to a whisper*]. He does not mean to answer any questions.

PITT. What is it? – What is it? – What? [*fiercely*]. (Thompson 1968, 20–21)

In the Treasury solicitor's papers, all this is reduced to a simple exchange: 'Being asked by the Clerk of the Council how he spelt his Name – Answered: He might spell it according to his own discretion for that he should answer no Questions of any kind'. Thelwell thus becomes a truculent artisan rather than a quick-witted adversary reducing the council to confusion. Pitt is not shown as present and is not listed as a member of the board of interrogation at the beginning of the record. Instead, the Treasury solicitor's record claims that Pitt had merely been summoned to appear before the board before Thelwell was brought in order to testify that treasonable documents had been found in Thelwell's possession. This means that the distinctive impression given in Thelwell's account of Pitt acting as the motive force behind the prosecution is completely absent from the official record. Indeed, the textual strategy of the official record is every bit as self-serving as Thelwell's own account. It goes out of its way to suggest that every propriety was observed in the treatment of Thelwell. In Thelwell's account, a key phrase is his declaration that 'I am bold in the consciousness of innocence'. In the 'official' account, the stress is rather the way in which the court sought to help the misguided radical: 'It is no trouble – It is their duty to put questions to you, that it may appear what questions you refuse to answer'.

Both these records are accurate accounts of the event according to their own lights, but they give completely different impressions of what happened. This shows the power of textuality in shaping and filtering our engagement with the past. In an age of dodgy dossiers, the Guildford Four and the Birmingham Six, it is not surprising that we do not share the confidence of our Victorian forebears in the inherent superiority of the official record, but we perhaps still do not give enough weight to the way in which even honest and conscientious descriptions reflect myriad cultural forces. Records are shaped by countless textual precedents. A multitude of practical and historical considerations determine the physical form of the record and the layout of the text. Above all, records are shaped by such characteristics of their creators as their social background, education, religion and gender. A text is a cultural construct of the most complex kind. Much of the fascination of archives and historic texts lies in the way in which their meaning constantly slips through our fingers like quicksilver.

Yet while archivists such as Hunnisett and Hector were supremely aware of the inherent elusiveness and shortcomings of archival texts, in their working lives they were daily confronted with the inescapable physical reality of the archive. Archivists who have worked with the English national archives constantly stress their sheer size and quantity. Roger Ellis, for example, described how, when he began work as an Assistant Keeper at the Public Record Office, 'the majesty of the records themselves fired my imagination from the start. There they lay in their silent caves, great stalactites of history, some left complete, some truncated, as the imperceptible currents of life had turned to run elsewhere, some year by year still growing' (Ellis 1971). On his first day at the Record Office, Ellis was told by his training officer, 'the first thing to remember about this place, gentlemen, is this: that there is any amount of work to be done, and no hurry whatever about doing it'. Similarly, the historical outlook of the historian V.H. Galbraith was famously shaped as a young man by his experiences in seeing the rolls of the medieval Chancery and Exchequer stored in the huge purpose-built racks at Chancery Lane. Galbraith was equally struck by the continuity of office practice at Chancery Lane; as an assistant keeper he prepared transcripts from Domesday Book according to the same procedure as that used by Thomas Powell in the seventeenth century.

Modern theory stresses not only the complex character of individual texts but also the way in which texts interact with one another in a great web of meaning, a phenomenon known as intertextuality. The image of the public records as great geological deposits is in itself a compelling textual construct. This is not to deny the reality of the physical existence of the records; no one who has seen the great banks of chancery enrolments in the National Archives or the mass of enrolled statues in the parliamentary archives will ever forget the sight. But the idea that these records are the result of the continuous organic growth of the English administration is an expression of the nineteenth-century view of the development of the UK's constitution. For hundreds of years, these records had been scattered all over London in a state of chaos and they had only survived as result of administrative inertia. The present arrangement into classes is the result of the herculean efforts by curators like

Harley Rodney, who in the early part of the twentieth century was responsible for developing many of the details of the class arrangement of the public records.

The continuity of the public records was emphasized in the nineteenth and twentieth centuries because they provided a potent emblem of the UK's self-image of a country whose constitution and society had organically evolved over many centuries without major turmoil or cataclysm. The first Deputy Keeper of Public Records, Sir Francis Palgrave, gave the game away when he claimed the primacy of the English public records over the French, alleging that the English public records began at the Norman Conquest whereas the French records only began in the late twelfth century (Cantwell 1991, 163). But of course these earlier years are only represented by the two singular survivals of Domesday Book and the 1130 pipe roll – strip these away, and the English public records do not look much older than the French ones. While historians were fashioning a history which focused on the myth of the seamlessly evolving UK constitution, archivists and historians were rearranging records into a form which gave visible expression to this myth. If the prevailing history of the late nineteenth century had had a different perspective on the UK constitution, the public records would today be radically different in their appearance.

Domesday Book has long been honoured as the *fons et origo* of this great heritage of public records. In recently reporting the availability of an online searchable version of Domesday, *The Daily Telegraph* succinctly described it as 'the oldest and most famous public record in Britain'. In his *Studies in the Public Records*, Galbraith gives pride of place to Domesday, 'the greatest and oldest of our public records' (Galbraith 1948, 121). Domesday is, declared Galbraith, 'a true "public record" for it was made by the clerks of the King's *curia*, and has never been out of official custody' (Galbraith 1948, 89). Yet, in illustrating the administrative importance of Domesday, Galbraith refers to a large number of manuscripts which are not in public custody. Indeed, in describing how the information in Domesday was compiled, Galbraith refers to two manuscripts which embody earlier versions of the information in Domesday, namely the *Inquisitio Comitatus Cantibrigiensis*, now part of a manuscript in the Cotton collection in the British Library, and Exon Domesday, kept in Exeter Cathedral. If these represent earlier and fuller versions of the information collated in Domesday, should they not also be recorded as public records, and indeed as public records of greater authority than Domesday? The only objection to such a view appears to be that they are no longer in 'public custody' (although the *Inquisitio Comitatus Cantibrigiensis* is in the custody of a government-funded library).

Galbraith goes on to discuss two twelfth-century digests of Domesday, the Herefordshire Domesday, which is preserved in an Oxford college (Balliol MS. 350), and the *Abbrevatio* preserved in the records of the Exchequer (The National Archives, E 36/284). The Herefordshire Domesday was, suggests Galbraith, 'an undoubted product of the royal curia from the earlier part of the reign of Henry II'. He argues that it was prepared to assist the Sicilian Thomas Brown in his work in checking matters relating to the king in the Exchequer. The Herefordshire Domesday shows evidence of being used for administrative purposes in the late twelfth century. However, since it is now in the hands of an Oxford college, it is not regarded as a public record. By contrast, the Domesday *Abbrevatio* seems to have had a less practical function. It may simply have been a luxury presentation version of the information in Domesday, evidence of Domesday's continuing prestige but not a product of its use by the royal administration. Yet the *Abbrevatio* is regarded as a public record because it is among the Exchequer records in the National Archives (although it is not clear how it got there), while the Herefordshire Domesday is not considered a public record.

Domesday Book is the oldest public record because it is the oldest thing in the National Archives. It is far from being the oldest UK government record. Many charters, writs and other document issued by pre-conquest kings survive. The tenth-century King Athelstan probably had a writing office which could be reasonably described as a royal chancery (Keynes 1980, 39–83, 134–53). Yet documents produced by this chancery are not considered public records. The oldest authentic instrument produced by an English king is a charter of King Hlothere dated 679, over four hundred years before Domesday Book was compiled. Yet this charter is not considered, as perhaps it should be, 'the oldest public record in Britain', because it is now in the British Library, where it is Cotton MS. Augustus ii.2.

In his discussion of 'What are Archives?', Hilary Jenkinson constantly emphasizes the importance of 'official character'(Jenkinson 1966, 2–14). The first point in his definition of an archive was that 'Archives are documents which formed part of an official transaction'(which the charter of Hlothere did) and 'were preserved for official reference' (which the charter of Hlothere was not, since it was probably preserved in an 'unofficial' monastic archive). Yet Jenkinson's insistence on the primacy of continued official custody as a means of defining an archive leads to some very curious distortions, as immediately becomes evident in his second rule which states that archives include 'both documents specially made for, and documents included in, an official transaction'. Thus, according to Jenkinson, a copy of *The Times* as part of a comprehensive sequence which has been in continuous official custody in the Newspaper Library at Colindale is not part of an archive, but a stray copy of *The Times* in a Foreign Office file is part of an archive. However, this copy of *The Times* could again be considered part of an archive if it forms part of the records of the company publishing the newspaper. This last consideration prompts Jenkinson to admit that the term 'archives' can also be extended to 'collections made by private or semi-private bodies or persons, acting in their official or business capacities'.

It is at this point that Jenkinson's definition breaks down completely. He insists on custody as the fundamental test of the archive: 'The closest definition, therefore, that we can use in this matter is to say that the documents are set aside for preservation in official custody'(Jenkinson 1966, 9). Jenkinson realized that it was impossible to insist that only records which had been continuously in the custody of the administration which produced them should be regarded as archives. He therefore applied the test of continuous custody in the hands of a 'responsible person' (Jenkinson 1966, 37–8). A responsible person was fundamentally a representative of a suitably corporate body who respected the integrity of the archive and took it over *en bloc*: 'there must be no selecting of pretty specimens' (Jenkinson 1966, 41).

It was on these grounds that Jenkinson was unwilling to recognize the collections of Anglo-Saxon and other charters in the British Library as archives, since he regarded them as representing selections. Jenkinson was in fact wrong in his understanding of the structure of the charter collections in the British Library, which (for acquisitions since 1826 at least) often represent complete archives whose identity is to some extent concealed by the methods used for registering and cataloguing individual documents. Nevertheless he was fierce in his insistence that

> No Archivist, even in cases where these documents have been taken over direct from original owners and custody has consequently been preserved unbroken, could possibly allow full Archive value to documents which have been violently torn from the connexion in which they were originally preserved … (Jenkinson 1966, 42).

It is difficult to escape the impression that Jenkinson's rules were to a large extent fashioned to ensure that the British Museum could play no part in influencing the emerging archives profession in the UK. He wanted to ensure the primacy of the practice of the Public Record Office. Jenkinson was already uncertain about the status of many collections in local record offices which modern archivists would certainly claim as archives; he half suggests that parish registers transferred to a record office are not, strictly speaking, archives. He conceals many embarrassing facts that would seem to undermine his arguments, such as the fact that the chancellors' rolls of the Exchequer were from 1833 to 1864 deposited in the British Museum (Stenton 1981, 281; Cantwell 1991, 222), which might seem to compromise their status as archives. Jenkinson makes the British Museum sound irredeemably committed to arbitrary and destructive selection of documents, yet it was only as a result of a complaint in 1838 by the British Museum to the Treasury that the scandal of the sale of ancient documents to a fishmonger by Exchequer officials was brought to light (Cantwell 1991, 49). Above all, Jenkinson did not point out that the British Museum collections include many collections which even by his own definition must be considered archives, such as the archives of the South Sea Company (Additional MSS. 25,494–25,584 and Additional Charters 16281–16293) and the Society of the Free British Fishery (Additional MSS. 15154–15165).

Jenkinson's arguments are remarkably circular: archives are archives because they seem like archives and are looked after by archivists. Moreover, another reason for Jenkinson's insistence on the importance of custody was his assumption that archives should be like the UK's constitutional history: a gradual organic accretion of material conserved by a body of officials of unimpeachable respectability and trustworthiness. The idea that information about, say, the sinking of the *Belgrano* or the events in Londonderry on 'Bloody Sunday' should be inherently less trustworthy because it had been in official custody would have profoundly shocked Jenkinson. It has already been noted how the public records were, during the late nineteenth and early twentieth centuries, moulded into a form which corresponded with prevailing conceptions of UK history. Jenkinson's definition of archive reduced this vision of the country's history to half a dozen rules and thereby locked the archives profession into historical constructs which were already becoming outmoded at the time Jenkinson was writing. The textuality of Jenkinson is rooted in the intertextuality imposed on the public records by Harley Rodney and others. V.H. Galbraith dreamed of an archivist's history in which the past appeared as a vast collection of 'original documents', falling into types, classes and series. The progress of history would appear as a 'slow pageant of slowly changing records, marked from time to time by the occasional disappearance of one class and the gradual emergence of another' (Galbraith 1948, 7–8). It was this kind of archival Darwinian fantasy that Jenkinson sought to impose.

At Sotheby's sale on 20 July 1981, the British Library acquired lot nine, which was a teller's view of account from the Exchequer of Receipt for the half year beginning Michaelmas 1587. This item is now Additional Manuscript 61947. Jenkinson would certainly have denied such a single item, wrenched from an archival class and purchased in a London saleroom, any archival status whatsoever. If such a stray had been acquired by the National Archives it would not have been allowed to sully the purity of the main archival class by being inserted in its appropriate place in the sequence. It would instead have been sent to the sanitized limbo of PRO 30, the class of 'Original records acquired as gifts or on deposit'.

Tellers' views of accounts were half-yearly declarations of receipts and payments in the Exchequer of Receipt, prepared by the Auditor of the Receipt and submitted to the Undertreasurer. Since as a result of the reforms of the revenue courts in 1554, the Exchequer of Receipt handled the bulk of the crown's receipts and payments, the tellers' views were in effect a kind of early form of national balance sheet. They facilitated a closer check on the tellers and gave an impression of the overall pattern of royal income and expenditure. The first tellers' view covered the year from Michaelmas 1559 to Michaelmas 1560 and was apparently introduced at the behest of Walter Mildmay who was appointed Chancellor of the Exchequer in February 1559. The introduction of the tellers' views probably formed an integral part of the attempts during the early years of Elizabeth to get a clearer idea of the state of the royal finances. The existing records of the activities of the tellers, such as the tellers' rolls, were helpful in checking their activities but were so detailed that it was impossible to derive any financial overview from them. The tellers' views did not grow organically from these existing records but represented a radical break with them. For this reason it is unhelpful that the tellers' rolls and tellers' views together with other series such as the jornalia rolls and certificate books are all part of the same class (E 405) in the National Archives, another example of the artificiality and inconsistencies found in the reconstruction of record classes.

Each yearly view comprised two separate half-yearly views. Under Mildmay, these half-yearly views were divided into two parts. The first part summarized the transactions of each teller separately, while the second contained a general statement of income and expenditure in the Exchequer of Receipt. In both sections, receipts were broken down into such broad categories of income as crown revenues, vacancies of bishoprics, first fruits and so on. Payments were summarized as amounts given to individual officers. The balances held by the teller at the beginning and end of each half year were noted and assigned revenues were not recorded, suggesting that the function of the view under Mildmay was primarily as a check on the tellers. After the appointment of Lord Burghley as Lord Treasurer in 1572, the structure of the tellers' views changed, with receipts being more carefully analysed and assigned revenues being added to the income. However, no such analysis of payments was provided, suggesting that Burghley was chiefly concerned with increasing income. This was the format used in the tellers' view for the half year beginning Michaelmas 1587 acquired by the British Library in 1981.

The two half-yearly tellers' views for each year were usually bound together, but this did not happen for the year beginning Michaelmas 1587. The companion view to the one in the British Library, which covers the half year beginning Easter 1588, is in the National Archives where it has the reference E 405/434. However, E 405/434 came into the National Archives under circumstances which would certainly have met with Jenkinson's disapproval. It was sent to William Black in the Public Record Office by Stephen Martin Leake, formerly a principal assistant clerk at the Treasury, on 19 February 1853. In a letter to Black on 1 March, Leake wrote:

> In explanation of the Book & Papers which I left last week and yesterday at the Record Office, I beg leave to inform you that they were found by me in the Loft under the Roof of the Treasury together with many other documents of various dates, in the year 1828 or 1829, when I was directed to ascertain what Depots of Papers then existed in the Treasury Building. They have since remained in my possession, & I found them among my Papers when I retired from the Treasury last year (National Archives, PRO 1/17).

Leake's letter provides vivid testimony as to the chaotic state of the government archives in the first part of the nineteenth century which hardly seems to fall into Jenkinson's definition of 'responsible custodianship'. Moreover, Leake's description of the treatment of this record emphasizes once again the extent to which record classes, far from being geological seams organically laid down over long periods of time, were rather artificial constructs of the late nineteenth century – virtuoso exercises in reconstituting textuality. Presumably the companion Michaelmas 1587 view was also lost for years in a Treasury loft, which explains its eventual appearance in Sotheby's. But why is it that these two half-yearly views were never bound together so that they were separated in this way?

The answer appears to be that the system of compiling the views was altered halfway through the year. The view for the Michaelmas term was compiled in the format adopted in 1572. In the view of the Easter term, a summary analysis of payments was inserted. This appears to have an emergency measure, linked to Burghley's attempts to cope with rising war costs. Presumably the sudden change meant that it was felt unhelpful to bind together the half-yearly views for 1587–88. Thus, the 'stray' acquired by the British Library, far from being likely to distort our understanding of the development of the record class because it has been removed from its original context, in fact adds appreciably to our understanding of the development of this form of record at a momentous time. The format of the tellers' views was to change frequently again in the years after 1588 as the government struggled with its finances. By the time of James I, the general statements of income and expenditure were to become the dominant element in the tellers' views, eventually leading by a long path to the emergence of the auditors' declaration books.

The impression given by the National Archives classification is that the tellers' views were a single series. However, from 1572 duplicate tellers' views survive outside the National Archives. Indeed, for Easter 1576, two tellers' views survive outside the National Archives (British Library, Egerton MS. 806, ff. 5–14v; Additional MS. 34215, ff. 1–13). Clearly, the nature of this record series is different from that suggested by the class arrangement in the National Archives. Indeed, it is not entirely certain that the sequence in the National Archives is drawn from a single class – given the evident chaos of the Treasury records at the time of their transfer to the Public Record Office, it is entirely possible that the National Archives holdings were pieced together from different series. A continuous series of duplicate tellers' views from 1603 to 1608 form Lansdowne MS. 663A in the British Library. Since this is precisely the period leading up to the emergence of the new class of declaration of accounts, the development of the new record class can only be understood by reference to the documents in the British Library – firmly non-archival by Jenkinson's definition.

The absurdity of a definition of archives which privileges the concept of official custody is vividly illustrated by the story of the tellers' views of account. The British Library's Lansdowne MS. 663 formed part of the papers of Sir Julius Caesar, an official who was directly involved in the discussions of royal finance leading to the creation of the new record class. The manuscript has been in far more responsible custody since that time than was the case with the Treasury records, many of which had to be retrieved with police assistance from 'Workshops and Cellars, Public Houses and other places' (Cantwell 1991, 49). By contrast, the line of provenance of Lansdowne MS. 663 can be firmly traced. Yet the National Archives series should, according to Jenkinson, be given priority. One of Jenkinson's concerns was that, by transfer to a library collection, evidence of the working of the administration could be destroyed. Yet in the case of the tellers' views, the arrangement of the records in the National Archives, by giving the impression that a record class consisted of a single sequence, conveys a misleading view of the administrative use of the document.

If custody is not the test of an archive, is content? It would be difficult to imagine a more gnomic or forbidding administrative document than a tellers' view. If a type of text could be seen as characteristic of an archive, it would be the tellers' view. Are archives simply administrative documents in technical language? However, as has been seen, the tellers' views fluctuate in their layout, structure and function. Although these records consist primarily of numbers, the constantly changing presentation of these figures reflects as eloquently as any literary text the impact of political crises and events. These tellers' texts, as they shift and change in their format, are as deceptive and elusive as one of the spy's reports which Burghley also anxiously scrutinized.

In short, the tellers' views are texts like any other. It is difficult to develop a schema which would draw a clear and consistent textual distinction between an account of the payment of a pension to Christopher Marlowe, the coroner's inquest on his death or one of his plays. One of the central themes of modern literary theory has been the attack on the idea of the canon, the assumption that certain works are privileged because they have been the subject of intensive critical scrutiny. Jenkinson's insistence on the primacy of records which have been in continuous official custody can be seen as a similar attempt to create a canon. The result of the attack on the literary canon has been to open up new types of texts to scholarly discussion and analysis. The literary scholar is now seen less as an arbiter of taste and good critical judgement and more as someone who can reveal the different cultural and social layers and significations in any type of text, whether it is a *Carry On* film, a play by Shakespeare, a Victorian penny dreadful, a 'Beware of the Dog' sign or indeed a tellers' view of account.

In this context, do archives have a distinctive textuality which marks them apart? The conclusion, as Hunnisett indicated in his discussion of the difference between file and roll versions of Warwickshire coroners' inquests, has to be 'no'. Archives are texts (with all the complications, significations and difficulties implied by that term) like any other texts. As the work of Paul Strohm indicates, texts such as coroners' inquests or pipe rolls have to be examined in just the same way as a poem by Chaucer or a monastic chronicle. Yet this is far from being the negation of the archival enterprise; Strohm's own work illustrates abundantly how the use of techniques more generally associated with literary criticism can result in a far richer engagement with the cultural world of the historic text.

Such a conclusion might indeed be seen as an affirmation of a distinctive aspect of the intellectual traditions associated with UK archives. While great archivists such as Hunnisett or Hector might demonstrate by their work the shortcomings of archival materials in an attempt to produce a Ranke-style reconstruction of the past, they nevertheless demonstrated throughout their professional service and their published writings a constant fascination and engagement with archives. Those huge stalactites and stalagmites of the public records are one of the most imposing survivals of past ages. Since we are doomed constantly to engage with the past, we are also doomed always to be fascinated by these huge textual survivals. This was a point appreciated by Galbraith. While Galbraith's idea of an archivist's history may at one level be seen as a statement of the Whiggish constructs which pervade that nineteenth-century reconstruction we call the National Archives, at another level Galbraith's insistence than the past should be seen as a pageant of records is a more evocative and truer statement of the nature of our historical engagement than the conviction of a Richard Evans or a Geoffrey Elton that a historian sitting in a Cambridge college room can recreate the past.

These are issues which were developed very effectively by Galbraith in his *Introduction to the Study of History*, published in 1964. Galbraith gently qualifies some of the more rigidly empirical claims made for the study of history. Noting that a description of history as a science suggests an alignment with the school of Ranke and J.B. Bury, he adds that 'we are doing no more than stating an ideal, however unattainable in practice' (Galbraith 1964, 3). He also takes a genial side-swipe at ideas of historical objectivity: 'its only completely impartial exponent is the Recording Angel … "bias" is all right so long as you come clean about it' (Galbraith 1964, 4). Records had been seen by Acton as the basis for a new scientific history which would attain to ultimate truth. This vision had faded as the records were more closely studied and better understood. In fact, they had turned out much like literary sources – as deceptive as all texts.

Records, no less than the literary sources, are generally compiled from other documents, often unknown to us and … they rarely tell the whole truth. Records, in fact can no more be taken at their face value than chronicles … it will be found that most records – from Acts of Parliament to balance sheets of public companies and diplomatic notes – have some sort of bias of their own, and seek to conceal the truth or part of it (Galbraith 1964, 13).

In consigning the ideals of Ranke and Acton to the dustbin, Galbraith nevertheless urges new generations of scholars to continue their engagement with the archives, simply as great textual monuments of the past which form part of a common human heritage and deserve to be preserved: 'they are an inexhaustible and an invaluable inheritance' (Galbraith 1964, 80). Towards the end of his life, it was this process of textual engagement that Galbraith remembered and cherished, rather than any great discoveries which emerged. In a final declaration which verged on the relativistic, Galbraith stated that:

> The past itself is dead, and the books we write tombs of learning, except insofar as they live in the consciousness of their readers. So conceived, we travel pleasantly, but by the nature of things we never arrive. The main job of the academic historian … is to convey this sense of kaleidoscopic change to his audiences; if so, his own views will never reach finality (Galbraith 1970, 7).

So, to return to the question posed at the beginning of this essay, and one which loomed large in the discussion of the session at the conference of the Society of Archivists which led to the present publication, what does this mean for the common or garden working archivist? Does it matter? Galbraith's insistence on the value of studying the archives for their own sake is very poetically expressed, but it is not really the sort of language which would convince the chairman of a local authority committee. If archives in their textuality are 'selective, diversionary, and amnesia-prone', what is the point of keeping them – and of having archivists?

The first answer to these questions lies in the very limitations of the archives. They may be deceptive, elusive and often plain wrong, but this in itself tells us a great deal about our engagement with the past. If we understand the limitations of the archive, we get a clearer and sharper perception of the superficiality of our own engagement with the past. These lessons, if rightly understood, have significance for all areas of human endeavour, from politics to philosophy. In fact, the challenge of theory and its refusal to accept views of the world which simply reflect prevailing power structures has encouraged scholars to look at forgotten and neglected people and social phenomena. This interest in 'uncanonical' aspects of history has prompted scholars to look at different types of records and to explore neglected archives. The emphasis on a 'bottom-up' view of history has led to the use of new and different types of records. At a purely practical level, then, theory means that scholars want to use new types of records. This has immediate implications for the selecting and listing of records. Types of record which would have been selected for destruction thirty or forty years now attract great scholarly interest, with major implications for the treatment of, for example, personal instance papers.

However, such shifts in scholarly interest are bound to occur and must be regarded as part of the normal operational environment of the working archivist. A more profound challenge is the argument that breaks down the distinction between the 'official' archive and other types of text, such as private papers, printed ephemera and books. In a scholarly environment which sees all these materials simply as historical texts (and indeed treats material culture as a kind of further textuality), it is difficult to sustain the view that archives should remain a profession distinct from librarianship and museum curatorship. Such boundaries are in any case increasingly being blurred by the impact of new information technologies. As a first step, the challenge of theory demands (as Caroline Williams has argued elsewhere in this volume) that archivists should revisit their view of private papers and collections of manuscripts. Beyond that, links may increasingly develop with specialists in other disciplines concerned with historic texts. The collection of seventeenth-century printed pamphlets and ephemera in the British Library's Thomason Tracts is textually much like an archive, only failing Jenkinson's tests insofar as they do not emanate from a corporate body. The Newspaper Library at Colindale is clearly an archive; the issues confronting librarians dealing with collections of official publications are much like those confronting archivists. Indeed, archives and collections of early printed material, newspapers, 'grey literature' and bindings all look very much like textual 'heterotopias' and Foucault's designation may be useful in redefining the archive.

The other impact of theory is on the audience for the archive. Modern political demands to widen access and reflect the diverse nature of UK society derive from a postmodern ethos which emphasizes heterogeneity and seeks to undermine monolithic power structures. The anxieties about archives and archive keepers in Derrida's essay *Archive Fever* reflect a common preoccupation of theorists with the nature and character of the power structures which control and shape of knowledge. The archivist is seen as a power figure, the *bête noire* of theorists. The challenge to become more accessible, to attract new audiences, to explore diversity and identity and to seek out the alienated and forgotten is a challenge which has sprung directly from the new body of theory, and cannot be fully understood without reference to it.

The idea that the archivist should not wholly control a catalogue, that users should be invited to comment and contribute on it and should not be locked out of the dialogue which surrounds the record, is a concept which springs directly from the discussion by figures like Barthes, Foucault and Derrida of the relationship between text, author and reader. The recent launch of by the National Archives of 'Your Archives' with its invitation to 'Add further information to this Catalogue entry on Your Archives or see what other users may have written' is a direct result of the impact of such theoretical discussion.

It can be anticipated that the launch of 'Your Archives' will very quickly reshape our idea of the structure of an archive catalogue and with it our view of the archive itself. Barthes, in contemplating why many people do not read books, suggested that one reason was the 'facticity' of the library. The very scale of the library and its rigid organization is overwhelming and intimidating, discouraging readers. The other problem, declared Barthes is that:

> The Library is a space one visits, but not that one inhabits. We should have in our language, versatile as it is said to be, two different words: one for the Library book, the other for the book-at-home (let us use hyphens, producing an autonomous syntagm whose referent is a specific object); one for the book 'borrowed' – usually through a bureaucratic or magisterial mediation – the other for the book grasped, held, taken up as if it were already

a fetish; one for the book-as-object of a debt (it must be returned), the other for the book-as-object of a desire or an immediate (without mediation) demand (Barthes 1986, 38).

Much the same could be said about archives. Archivists need to become less preoccupied with a 'bureaucratic or magisterial mediation' – with the defence of the archives – and should instead seek to promote that lust for the archive grasped, for the record held and taken up as a fetish.

References

Barnes, A. (2005), 'Graffiti: Overground Archaeology or Environmental Crime', *Temporary Type: 4th Annual Friends of St Brides Library Conference*, at <http://stbride.org/friends/conference/temporarytype> accessed July 2007.

Barthes, R. (1986), *The Rustle of Language* (Oxford: Blackwell).

Brown, C.G. (2005), *Postmodernism for Historians* (Edinburgh: Pearson).

Bullough, D. and Storey, R.L. (eds) (1971), *The Study of Medieval Records: Essays in Honour of Kathleen Major* (Oxford: Clarendon Press).

Cantwell, J. (1991), *The Public Record Office 1838–1958* (London: HMSO).

Carbonell, B.M. (ed.) (2003), *Museum Studies: an Anthology of Contexts* (Oxford: Blackwell).

Crane, S. (2003), 'Memory, Distortion and History in the Museum', in Carbonell, B.M. (ed.).

——— (1992), 'The Writing Lesson of 1381', in Hanawalt, B. (ed.).

Crow, M. and Olson, C. (1966), *Chaucer Life-Records* (Oxford: Clarendon Press).

Curtis, L. (ed.) (1970), *The Historian's Workshop: Original Essays by Sixteen Historians* (New York: Knopf).

Darnton, R. (1984), *The Great Cat Massacre and Other Episodes in French Cultural History* (London: Allen Lane).

Derrida, J. (1976), *Of Grammatology* (Baltimore MD: Johns Hopkins University Press).

Ellis, R (1971), 'Recollections of Sir Hilary Jenkinson', *Journal of the Society of Archivists*, 4, 261–75.

Elton, G.R. (1991), *Return to Essentials: Some Reflections on the Present State of Historical Study* (Cambridge: Cambridge University Press).

——— (1969), *The Practice of History* (London: Fontana).

Evans, R. (1997), *In Defence of History* (London: Granta).

Foucault, M. (1984), 'Of Other Spaces (1967)', *Michel Foucault, Info at* <http://foucault.info/documents/heteroTopia/foucault.heteroTopia.en.html> accessed July 2007.

Galbraith, V.H. (1970), 'Afterthoughts', in Curtis, L. (ed.).

——— (1964), *An Introduction to the Study of History* (London: C.A. Watts).

——— (1948), *Studies in the Public Records* (London: Thomas Nelson).

Hanawalt, B. (ed.) (1992), *Chaucer's England* (Minneapolis MN: University of Minnesota Press).

Hector, L.C. (1978), 'Reports, Writs and Records in the Common Bench in the Reign of Richard II', in Hunnisett, R. and Post, J.B. (eds).

Holmes, C. (1997), 'Geoffrey Elton as Historian', *Transactions of the Royal Historical Society*, 6th series, 7, 267–79.

Hunnisett, R. (1971), 'The Reliability of Inquisitions as Historical Evidence', in Bullough, D. and Storey, R.L. (eds).

Hunnisett, R. and Post, J.B. (eds) (1978), *Medieval Legal Records Edited in Memory of C.A.F. Meekings* (London: HMSO).

Jenkinson, H. (1966), *A Manual of Archive Administration* (London: Lund Humphries).

Justice, S. (1994), *Writing and Rebellion: England in 1381* (Berkeley CA: University of California Press).

Keynes, S. (1980), *The Diplomas of King Æthelred the Unready, 978–1016* (Cambridge: Cambridge University Press).

Maitland, F. (1911), *Collected Papers* (Cambridge: Cambridge University Press).

Stenton, D.M. (1981), 'The Pipe Rolls and the Historians, 1600–1883', *Cambridge Historical Journal*, 10 (3), 271–92.

Strohm, P. (1998), *England's Empty Throne: Usurpation and the Language of Legitimation 1399–1422* (New Haven CT and London: Yale University Press).

——— (1992), *Hochon's Arrow: the Social Imagination of Fourteenth-Century Texts* (Princeton NJ: Princeton University Press).

Thompson, E.P. (1968), *The Making of the English Working Class* (Harmondsworth: Penguin).

Vergo, P. (ed.) (1989), *The New Museology* (London: Reaktion).

Chapter 3

Personal Papers: Perceptions and Practices

Caroline Williams

'There's gotta be a record of you some place
You gotta be on somebody's books'

Dire Straits, *On Every Street*

Introduction

Different countries have arrived at a range of different models for managing their public and private archives. In some there is a conscious attempt to keep the acquisition, custody and management of public archives distinct from that of private ones. In others, public and private – and personal – archives coexist happily side by side within the same archival institution. Below the national level disparate solutions are to be found at a local and regional level too – but in either case, while public archives institutions might well host archives of private and/or personal origin it is less likely that a private or in-house archive repository will acquire records of public bodies or authorities.

The range of current models is due to a number of factors (political, cultural and historical) that have influenced the development of national and other archival institutions over time. In general, however, models are driven by comparable imperatives. These relate mission and aims, the nature of the source of an archival institution's authority, its legislative environment and its sources of funding. Depending on these the archives will develop a goal or mission that aims to fulfil the requirements and needs of identified stakeholders, capture and acquire records and archives in compliance with a defined acquisitions policy and encourage appropriate access to its resources.

The exploration of perceptions and practices in the management of personal papers will be undertaken within this broad context. This paper explores the nature of personal records and where this overlaps with those of private and official records; the growing tendency to personal self-expression and the impact on personal record keeping; the 'traditional' role of the archivist and historian in relation to both organizational and personal papers and how this might be changing; and the standards and tools available to the archivist to assist in their management. It ends with the suggestion that more attention be paid to the management of personal papers, in particular in a digital environment, and that one place to start is in the education and training of records and information professionals.

Context

At a political level most countries will prioritize the care of their publicly created records, whether as evidence of governance or indispensable to cultural heritage (or both), above their private and personal ones. Decisions about how records of public authorities should be managed in part rest on the nature of regulation within a country, and depend on legislative and administrative arrangements – of which there are many models. Strong central state control and management of public archives has featured in communist countries, for example. Duchein (1992) notes that before 1991, in Bulgaria, Czechoslovakia, Poland, Romania and the USSR all these countries' archives were deemed part of the State Archives Fonds as defined by Lenin in 1918 – *apart* from papers of a strictly personal nature. A different kind of centralized management is a feature of federated constitutions: in Australia and the US, state archives, overseen by a national archive, have responsibility for public federal archives in their regions. An example of a less centralized model can be seen in Switzerland where individual cantons make their own archival arrangements, ungoverned by national regulation, while the UK shows a separatist tradition in relation to the archives of its constituent countries (Mackenzie 1999). No doubt one could cite further examples of such varied administrative arrangements. A similar range of models is discernable in the management of private and personal papers too where less regulated arrangements are likely to be in place. Papers may reside mainly in national libraries or state historical societies as well as in private, commercial, charitable, academic or other archival institutions. Some national archival institutions take in both public and private papers – the National Archives of Scotland, Library and Archives Canada – while UK local authority archives services also provide for public and private deposits. Others, like The National Archives of England and Wales and the National Archives of Australia are the repositories solely for the records of government, although The National Archives has a supervisory role in relation to archives held privately. These arrangements, and the 'public archives tradition' versus the 'historical manuscripts tradition' inherent in the US will be discussed below.

There is a cultural dimension at play here too. The degree of central control that is in place is itself a reflection of different national cultures. Ketelaar (1997) has argued that the variety in archival systems can best be understood by considering cultural differences. He explores European archival approaches in the light of Dutch anthropologist Gert Hofstede's investigation into national cultural differences with respect to power distance (the distance between the citizen and the source of power), individualism (the degree of autonomy citizens are happy to exercise) and uncertainty avoidance (the level of risk they are willing to expose themselves to). He shows that the more relaxed the regime the more flexible are the solutions for archives (and other services too). This hypothesis could be further pursued in relation to the management of personal papers, although it is not within the scope of this paper to do so.

The context of personal papers within the landscape of public and private ones needs to be identified before a consideration of their management and use is undertaken. It is generally perceived that records of public authorities are overwhelmingly those of organizations, of corporate bodies both large and small. As discussed below, although these might also retain series of personal papers, this is not an overwhelming characteristic. Records of private origin are equally likely to include those of organizations, commercial, charitable and so on. They too may well include personal papers, especially where the boundaries between the corporate and personal function and activity are hard to define.

Personal papers are those created by an individual during his or her lifetime. All individuals active in public life will, consciously or not, create a personal archive that documents the different facets of their public activities alongside their private ones. It can be difficult to discern the precise boundary between public, official and personal in some instances. As Cook (1999, 32) notes, politicians and military personnel are likely to have an awareness of the interest of posterity and the public in their activities, and in the records that bear witness to these. There may be a clear case for such papers to be deposited in a public institution because of the public interest they retain and because access is assured. Winston Churchill's papers went to Churchill College Cambridge, those of Field Marshal Viscount Montgomery of Alamein to the Imperial War Museum, for example. Here the purely personal are likely to be accessioned along with the official and semi-official. Others may be retained privately, by families and their descendants, like the papers of the Dukes of Devonshire at Chatsworth House.

There is a wide range of collections of personal papers centred on individual, often occupational, functions. In the UK these are often to be found in national, university and specialist libraries: literary papers at John Rylands University Library, military papers at King's College London, medical papers at the Wellcome Library, papers of botanists at Kew Gardens, and of politicians at London School of Economics, for example. These alone represent a substantial and significant contribution by individuals of personal contributions to national and international affairs – political, economic, social, cultural. Such collections often exhibit similar traits and contain predictable series (correspondence, publications, etc). It can be difficult, because these are often generated in unselfconscious record systems, to demonstrate where distinction between the personal 'official' and the personal 'personal' might lie. And ultimately personal records may come to reside in official archives and *vice versa*.

The survival of the mass of personal papers generated by individuals of lesser public standing, and those that reflect a private as well as a public function, is less likely to be assured and has always been to some degree serendipitous. Small quantities may be deposited in local archives in the geographical area where an individual lived. Others, based on occupation, may be found in archives with collecting remits in the specific area. While the safety of personal papers is today to some degree assured – even if this is sometimes by chance rather than design, their survival in the *future* is less so. These may be becoming increasingly prolific but their sustainability in the longer term will depend on those with an interest in their maintenance overcoming the challenges of preservation in a rapidly changing digital environment.

Personal Records and Personal History

Personal records are everywhere. Records *about* people are generated and maintained *by* organizations– schools, hospitals and the state. As aggregated data such information about people has long been used in the formation of social, demographic and economic policy by central and local government as a basis of long-term planning, and to measure the effectiveness of those policies. Such records are usually defined as 'official' because they are generated by organizations with a specific business function and purpose. Some official personal records are created by official bodies and retained by individuals for evidential purposes: passports, driving licences and examination certificates.

Personal records, as noted above, are also generated *by* people as part of the processes of living, working and leisure, individually and communally. These – letters, working papers, diaries, journals, sketchbooks, photographs such as those held in local history collections and community archives – may be deemed unofficial, for reasons that will be considered below. But we cannot of course insist on clear definitions: as already noted in many cases it may be impossible to distinguish what is personal and what is work-related – semi-official perhaps – in the papers created by individuals – politicians, writers, scientists – and so on.

From the research viewpoint personal records – of both kinds – are of value in all kinds of studies. Social scientists use official data sets in order to understand human conditions and behaviour; while unofficial personal records are more likely to put flesh on the bones, to underpin biographies and genealogical research and to provide the basis for cultural and community history. Both, but perhaps the latter rather more, form an important part of our collective memory.

In addition to the records of individuals engaged in pursuing particular careers there are the collections of the purely personal that display no purposive activity, but are merely 'evidence of me'; in Sue McKemmish's words 'a kind of witnessing' on a personal level, '… a way of evidencing and memorialising our lives – our existence, our activities and experiences, our relationships with others, our identity, our "place" in the world'. We probably do not have many of these in our holdings, probably because they appear ephemeral – but they are increasingly 'out there' and we need to consider whether it is anybody's job to see that any of them become part of the history of our times.

There is perhaps an increasing conscious desire to *create* and *collect* personal history too, based on the aspiration to leave some kind of a footprint or trace behind. Those so inclined have always been able to keep diaries, personal memoirs, correspondence and so on as a record of lives lived. But there is an increasing opportunity today – through technology – to do so more easily (if more ephemerally): after all anyone can start a weblog and web-based software is the medium for many a community archive. Minority and indigenous groups, community archives and individuals are creating new spaces – elbowing into the space traditionally perceived as inhabited by conventional archives, whether organizational or personal. Records created in this way may be more selfconscious, and may be generated in order to actively document current actions and concerns, rather than be simply the unconscious residue of past activities and transactions.

Personal records generated through Web 2.0 enabled social software have found a whole new platform for their creation and dissemination. This raises a new series of questions too, about their values to the future, their ownership, appraisal and preservation. Facebook, Flickr, personal blogs and so on sustain an important representation of the voice of society: archivists need to be ready to consider the challenges they pose.

Engagement with personal histories is certainly creeping up the agenda too. Interest in genealogy has been growing for years and has escalated as a result of the Internet and television programmes such as *Who Do You Think You Are?*. 'This,' says Michael Moss (2007), 'is for many the interface between history and the archive, even though most of our ancestors have left only the shallowest footprints on its surface; a name in a directory, a poor law register, a census or a list of emigrants.'

Individuals and individual testimonies are increasingly being given value and new interpretations found. In terms of social history the research emphasis has moved away from concentration on political, economic and social elites to a consideration of the evidence of individual lives as lived by all and any members of society, including women, workers, immigrants, ethnic, religious and other minorities. Such 'identity' history involves a micro or 'bottom-up' approach that requires not only a re-examination of existing archives but the active collection of personal papers, oral histories and the papers of community and campaigning organizations (Flinn 2006).

There are other drivers too. The social benefits of personal histories, memory boxes and life story books which are now used by doctors, mental health and social workers as therapy in cases of physical and mental pain relief, family loss, separation and adoption are becoming increasingly apparent (Etherington 2006).

Archives, Manuscripts and Personal Papers: 'Definitions'

Given the apparent value accorded to the papers, memories and histories of individuals it would seem on the face of it that the management of such evidences falls squarely within the archivist's remit. However the archival establishment has always paid less attention to the management of personal papers than to those created by organizations – even to the conventional personal papers generated by 'eminent', often 'establishment', individuals in the official or semi-official capacity described above. Such letters, memoirs, diaries, scrapbooks, literary output, antiquarian notes, photos, etc., have often been considered as falling more within the purview of the librarian than the archivist, and identified as 'manuscripts' rather than 'archives'.

This question of definition is vexed. Are personal records 'archives'? To those outside the archive world this might seem to be a non-question. Indeed the 'traditional' idea of archive – or maybe the view that archivists rather than anyone else have traditionally held – is one for the minority. The following quote, from an American textbook (Hunter 2004) gives us a definition of personal papers that appears even to deny their archival attributes:

> Archives are generated by organizations or institutions; manuscripts are generated by individuals or families ... the holdings of an archival repository are called 'records'... [and] the holdings of a manuscript repository are called 'papers' ... the custodian of

organizational records is called an archivist, while the custodian of personal papers is called a manuscript curator.

Not all Americans agree, however. Richard Cox provides a robust rebuttal when he says:

> There is really no room for disagreement. Archivists are archivists. Archives are archives. Archives are composed of records. Historical manuscripts are composed of records, and they constitute archives. Manuscript curators are responsible for records *and* archives (Williams 2006, citing Cox 2001, 24).

Although this reflects practice embedded in the American public archives tradition and historical manuscripts tradition, similar views have been held in the UK, if in a less extreme way. The British Library has always been the traditional repository for the papers of notable individuals, as has the National Library of Scotland.

However, this historical development has led to the perception that those who manage personal papers are a breed apart from those who manage the records of organizations. Attempts have recently made to deny this distinction. Sue McKemmish, in defending her 'Evidence of me …' article of 1996, says:

> It [her article] does not see the archivist who looks after personal archives as a separate species. Such an archivist is not our equivalent of the platypus for early nineteenth-century natural scientists, a species which cast doubt upon their existing taxonomy of knowledge. Archivists looking after personal records can be found in all recordkeeping spaces, and not necessarily in the streams of 'dysfunction' or 'otherness'… Archivists in government institutions or working for businesses are concerned with personal records, regional archivists with the recordkeeping of the individual people in their region. Libraries and museums collect personal records and increasingly are recognising the need to employ an archivist to manage them (Upward and McKemmish 2001).

Organizational Archives

As professional archivists we remain strongly influenced by Hilary Jenkinson (1966), whose definition of archives required that they were generated to support official, business administrative or executive transactions – although those created by private or semi-private bodies were admitted in this, personal transactions were not. However, Jenkinson was positively liberal compared with others. R.L. Poole (1857–1939), Keeper of the Archives at the University of Oxford, defined the archives of an ecclesiastical institution as essentially two kinds: grants of privilege and title deeds of property. Such items as letter books might exist 'but these do not come properly under the definition of archives', quotes Vaisey (Procter and Williams 2003). Today a letter book would certainly fall within the definition as official, transactional and evidence of a particular function or activity. I think even the most traditional archivist would permit a definition of a record to include any thing that provided evidence of some kind of transaction, provided it had content, context and structure – and would include, for example, a contribution to a blog, a note to the milkman, a voice-mail message from the subject's mother-in-law – archives of an entirely personal nature.

Personal Papers

Thus, despite American definitions, personally created papers may certainly exhibit the attributes required of records. They provide recorded evidence of the activities of the creator, whether official (letter to the bank) or personal (text message to son). However, they obviously reflect an individual rather than a corporate records system, which may be idiosyncratic and inconsistent. It is unlikely that there will be a file plan, built-in retention periods, a conscious transition to archives (although vital records might be carefully stored). In addition, as noted earlier, the distinction between official and personal is often unclear: are letters written on the beach in Cannes by Gordon Brown and sent to his permanent secretary in Whitehall 'official'? Is his record of an official meeting held at Chequers but kept amongst his family papers 'official'?

Moreover, while many personal records that reflect personal and official interactions *are* transactional many others will not comply with strict rules of recordness. Literary drafts, research notes, diaries, news cuttings, antiquarian notes, ephemera, might tell you a lot about the creative process that supports the creator's function and output but are not in anyway transactional and lack the essential quality of 'recordness' as defined in the International Standard ISO 15489. And in practical terms no archive is going to refuse to take in an interesting set of data or information sources simply on the grounds that it does not have sufficient 'recordness'. Cunningham (1996) notes the narrow-mindedness and corporate myopia of archival theoreticians whose definition, because it centres on the notion of 'transaction', would therefore exclude such materials despite the obvious evidence contained therein.

A consensus appears to have emerged which defines a record in transactional terms … It skirts the slippery concept of the evidential nature of records and excludes such non-organisational material as personal diaries and literary drafts, the 'recordness' of which to me is defined by their evidential qualities.

However, definitions of 'archive' are many and various and go far beyond the those familiar to the archive professional. Even within the profession we are urged to broaden our notion of the archive: indeed, postmodern writers argue that individual and collective memories – archives – are represented not only in textual material but also through oral and audiovisual records, literature, songs, dance, art and artefacts too (McKemmish et al. 2005, 153). If 'archive' can be taken to mean anything used to store memory we may have to realign our thinking. Even if we do not think it our responsibility to manage such non-textual materials as these I believe we do need to consider at least how we currently manage conventional personal papers now, and how we propose to manage them once they are all produced and deposited electronically.

'Values' in Organizational and Personal Papers

As a result of education, training and accepted theory and practice archivists are naturally drawn to organizational archives that exhibit the evidential and organic qualities readily perceptible in them. We argue that they are more authentic because of the context of their creation and we seek to preserve evidence that is authentic and reliable and that can testify to business process. (We used to seek to preserve them for their objectivity and truth and hence their impartiality, but we now accept that this is not a sufficiently nuanced approach.) In addition we have argued that because organizational archives are generated by 'agents' (semi-detached officials) who have no overt interest in their content the evidence contained in them is all the more reliable. It certainly appears that records produced in organizations have rich contextual layers that appear to support such contentions. Authenticity and reliability can be demonstrated through an analysis of provenance, functions, activities and transactions and their products. They can be cross-checked against other documents, both external and internal, to provide those evidential attributes so valued for corporate accountability. Organizations are created to undertake particular functions and where there are a number of similar institutions (lots of hospitals, crown courts, schools) all doing the same thing, additional credibility results from this critical mass of evidence and tends to provide a more substantiated account of events and trends.

Personal papers on the other hand are valued for their content, the informational aspects described by Schellenberg, rather more than those evidential contextual ones. Evidence of organizations, functions and business process is not what is primarily sought here. It is as much to do with what they are *about* as who created them and why that engages people. The contexts and values of personal records are centred on the individual, and so have a direct relationship with the individual. Their contents are likely to tell you more about 'individual creators, their predilections and prejudices than you can ever expect to learn about a faceless administrator in the organizational record' and reveal information about the individual's cultural and social setting. 'There are here glimpses of the inner soul as well as its outer manifestation in public activities' (Hobbs 2001). Thus, partly because they are often random in content, context and survival, personal papers have been viewed as less 'archival', less 'reliable' than those generated by organizations. They are more likely to yield information at a micro, individual level – from which it is harder to draw broad empirical conclusions.

Use

Archival records of organizations provide a good base for research, and many historians continue to value the traditional empirical approach to writing history that places value on the evidence base of administrative records.

Hitchcock (2006) says:

> Both the methodologies of the social sciences and the evolution of the (historian's) profession have effectively given prominence to specific types of information and relationships that privilege organic archives, interpreted by professionally trained individuals, as the source of legitimate truth. As a result we are unconsciously led to give unwarranted prominence to the *institutions* of past societies, in preference to groups and individuals defined in more inchoate ways, who did not leave well-structured archives.

This is what archivists want to hear: it confirms one of the archivist's earliest *raisons d'être*: we value the evidence produced by organizations because it is deemed to be objective. Yet we have always known that administrative records can be unreliable, even if they are authentic. We recognize that although a document might be produced by an authentic system this does not mean that its content is necessarily reliable or accurate.

Here is an example. What could be more official than a writ of summons (TNA C219/14/3) for the Wiltshire parliamentary boroughs, 1433, from the records of Chancery in the irreproachable custody of The National Archives? And what more flawed? This document provides the names of men elected to parliament, each attested by the sheriff or returning officer as well as two sponsors (Fig. 3.1). A brief check of the list of names of these sponsors, on the right-hand side of the page show these to be: 'Thomas God; John Save; Henry Alle; Richard This; John Faire; Henry Compayne; Laurence Ande; Henry Gyffe; John Theyme; Richard Grace'. It is perhaps too much of a coincidence that these surnames, expressed in modern English, read 'God save all this fair company and give them grace'.

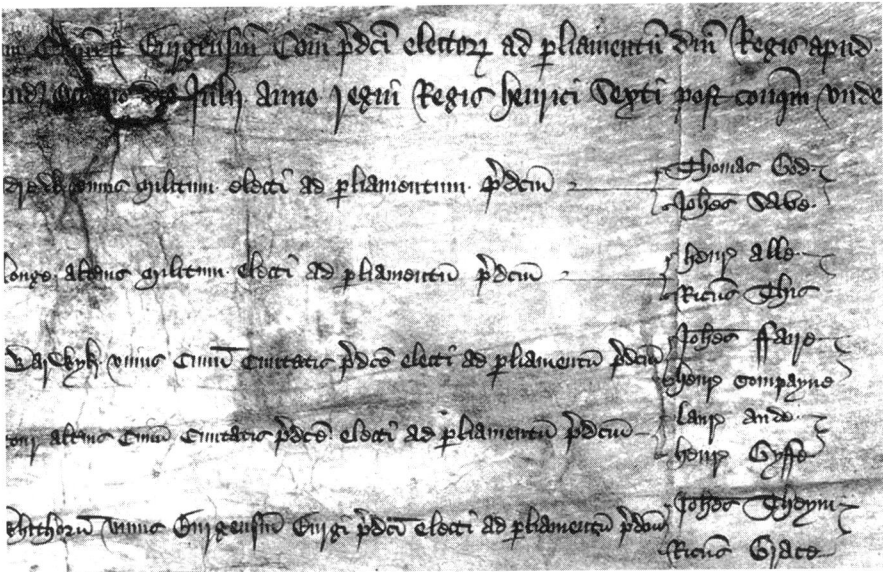

Figure 3.1 Writ of Summons, 1433. C219/14/3 (by courtesy of The National Archives)

So administrative, evidential records can be just as unreliable as the less systematically generated personal papers. And as Galbraith (1964, 13) reminds us, 'records, no less than the literary sources, are generally compiled from other documents, often unknown to us and ... they rarely tell us the whole truth. Records, in fact can no more be taken at their face value than chronicles' – that other intensely personal form of remembering.

Personal records are perhaps more likely to be valued by literary and cultural historians and biographers than by constitutional and administrative historians. Medieval historian Andrew Prescott (2006) recognizes the value of the personal perspective when he discusses the merit of the chronicler: 'the 19th-century view that legal and administrative records are superior (to chronicles) as historical evidence because their official provenance gave them an objective character has now been thoroughly discredited'.

Did we know this? Clearly Hitchcock and Prescott seem slightly at odds, and there is a debate to be continued here.

Personal papers may of course be used to satisfy administrative/evidential approaches too, where research is less concerned with an individual *per se* than as an office-holder or contributor to public events. Many of the personal collections noted above include material about holders of public office. These have characteristics of both private personal papers and the records of public institutions – clearly it is not useful to attempt to impose rigid distinctions here.

Clearly whatever evidence survives, of whatever kind, is grist to the researcher's mill, and making distinctions between their respective values can be taken too far. Michael Moss (2006, 232) reminds us that, however trustworthy or not archives might be, researchers do not depend on them alone. 'A single archive is rarely the panopticon of a user's knowledge. Argument is based on evidence drawn from a variety of archives, some held in recognised repositories, some in private hands and some drawn from printed sources' – and from non-textual ones too.

Archival Standards and Methodologies

Archival theory, systems and processes have primarily been developed to support organizational and administrative records rather than personal papers. They are clearly more directed to support the 'corporate and collective, as opposed to the individual and idiosyncratic' (Hobbs 2001). Cunningham (1996) says (in Australia) that as an archivist in a library he felt he was among 'members of a sub-tribe' who for 60 years have scratched their heads and 'pondered exactly how to apply the lofty principles of Sir Hilary Jenkinson to the personal papers of individuals'.

Few professional methodologies and standards for acquisition, appraisal, arrangement and description have been explicitly developed to support the requirements of personal papers, although these are not specifically excluded.

Appraisal methodologies have been built around the needs to manage organizational or government records – macro appraisal, functional analysis, file classification schemes and so on assume hierarchical aggregations of material. Documentation strategies and acquisitions policies are top-level appraisal methodologies of value to collecting archives, but these operate at the collection level rather than within collections themselves. Appraisal of personal papers is likely to rely on an analysis of content rather than of function.

In terms of appraisal, archivists of personal papers need to recognize the outcomes of the methods they choose. Will their appraisal approaches be the same whether they are dealing with private manuscripts or a collection of official records?

Are they aiming to document the personal life, prioritizing items that illustrate the early years, family and personal relationships, and so on (that is, through the eyes of a potential biographer)? Or will s/he highlight those that prioritize the career and public life? Dalgleish (1996) notes that the result of concentrating on the latter in relation to members of US Congress been much duplicated material about the office (because of the similarity of processes) but very little biographical data. Selection will inevitably reflect organizational acquisition goals and perspectives.

Arrangement and description methodologies too tend to assume that all archives are composed as aggregates that can be manipulated in hierarchical structures – fonds, sub-fonds, etc. Standards such as the General International Standard Archival Description (ISAD(G)) (International Council on Archives, 2000) and the *Manual of Archival Description* (MAD) (Procter and Cook 2000) encourage the exhibition of evidential qualities and organizational structures, but although they permit the arrangement and description of personal records they do not offer much guidance. Indeed, MAD has references on only six pages to the management of personal papers. Where ISAD(G) terminology is not adopted, for example in the US, hierarchical methods of arrangement are still very apparent.

It is not always possible or desirable to arrange personal papers in this way. Solutions are as often based on arrangement by theme, subject or chronology as on hierarchy. An example of the difficulties that can arise in the arrangement of personal papers highlights this problem. Patrick Cadell, former Keeper of the Records of Scotland, has been working with the papers of Jimmy Logan, the Scottish actor and comedian. How, he wonders, do you accommodate in your arrangement constant use and reuse (and therefore change and adaptation) of the same material, whether scenes, pantomime scripts or music? And how do you arrange gags (jokes) – many hundreds of them – some of which are in numerical sequence, others arranged by author, others by subject (mother-in-law, bus, shop, tradesman)? What do you do with treasured gagboxes passed down from older comics?

In 1996 Sue McKemmish asked for functional requirements for personal recordkeeping and for socio-historical evidence. She attempted 'to define a way in which archivists might look at personal papers', asserting that 'archivists can analyse what is happening in personal recordkeeping in much the same way as they analyse corporate recordkeeping'. 'Just as they can identify significant business functions and activities', she states, 'so they can analyse socially assigned roles and related activities and draw conclusions about what records individuals in their personal capacity capture as evidence of these roles and activities' (Pollard 2001, 156).

In response to challenges from South African archivist Verne Harris, Pollard (2001, 146) argued that the records continuum model is just as appropriate for managing personal records, believing that one can use the continuum 'to structure … exploration of issues relating to personal recordkeeping, identity and memory, and the role of archivists in transforming records as a form of "evidence of me" into part of the "evidence of us", an aspect of collective identity and memory'. There is clearly the potential for more focused work to be undertaken in this area – and those managing personal papers must be the best equipped to contribute to taking forward the development of standards and methodologies.

We all appreciate the benefits that the application of standards brings – not least in offering strategic solutions and raising the professional profile. Standards-based database management eases the work of the archivist, and interoperable searching that of the user. Preservation standards help to ensure the sustainability of data in the long term. Metadata standards support description and retrieval of any digital object. Archival description and authority standards facilitate the intellectual control of holdings and access to them. Guidelines for appraisal are sufficiently flexible to allow their application to personal records as well as organizational ones. Even if the 'fit' is not always exact as far as personal papers are concerned, all these have proved to be useful. Checking online catalogues of personal papers shows that the arrangement of personal papers of those with public duties can fairly easily be dovetailed into hierarchies that are amenable to ISAD(G) requirements, often chronological or by correspondent, rather than by the provenance or function-based solutions usually provided for organizational archives.

However, it seems that some new methods of generating personal records are less likely to involve adherence to standards, whether descriptive or indeed preservation-based. Individual and community (micro) responses to recordkeeping are now competing with the institutional (macro) ones for whom standards and methodologies provide useful tools. For example, the increasing development of community archives needs make no reference to established services and practices, potentially challenging the monopoly of traditional archival institutions. The development of user-generated finding aids using Web 2.0 social software and wikis means that a whole new generation of personal records is being created well beyond the traditional means of managing them.

The Technological Imperative

The overarching concern, both in the case of emerging social software and new ways of generating personal records, is a technological one. In terms of their assured preservation, personal papers are in any case more vulnerable than those generated and maintained by organizations. Nearly all records are now created electronically, whether for personal or corporate purposes. Many organizations are getting to grips with managing corporate records through electronic document and records management systems. Where organizations manage their own archives such systems can allow for the long-term sustainability of records and their transfer to archives – the Seamless Flow process at The National Archives, for example. But where records have been separated from their parent body – or personal records from their creator – finding adequate solutions is more complex. Collecting archives will now be faced with acquisitions and accruals in digital form, on possibly obsolescent formats that they are unable to access. Personal papers will fall into this category, where the contents of computers have been downloaded into a variety of formats that then may cross an archival threshold but with inaccessible content. The Paradigm Project, working on the papers of politicians, has established that for records created by individuals to be preserved and to continue to be accessible it is necessary to take proactive steps. It is necessary to negotiate with depositors *before* material is sent to the archive and ensuring what they are creating is stored on a sustainable format. This has huge resource implications for any organization seeking to acquire and sustain archives after, say, 1990.

Since the overwhelming challenges – and likely solutions – for professionals required to manage records and archives today will be focused on technological aspects of recordkeeping it is axiomatic that those tasked with this management role have the appropriate knowledge and skills to do so. These skills will increasingly require knowledge and expertise in digital systems and processes. Curricula of postgraduate programmes vary. While all place knowledge and understanding of principles, concepts and processes of recordkeeping at the centre of the curriculum, some concentrate their elective modules on areas of interpretation and contextualization of the document (palaeography, diplomatic, administrative history) while others emphasize requirements of current records and information more than of archival documents. Few concentrate heavily on the technical expertise that will be needed to care for the future – entirely digital – archive. It has been noted recently that archivists have often tended to shy away from dealing with the physical attributes of documents, leaving that side of the work to conservation and preservation experts. Steve Bailey (2007) notes that:

> The technicalities of paper preservation, of de-acidification and inert gas encasement are not by and large carried out by archivists and records managers but by specialist conservators … few of us understand the … hard … science … required to preserve physical records … Certainly long before electronic records came into being archivists were already struggling with any form of record not stored in what could be described as a direct visual media: sound recordings, celluloid and video tape being prime examples … Digital records are, perhaps, just the latest and most extreme example of our reluctance to get our professional hands dirty and deal with the material aspects of the items we manage. The difference now of course is the sheer ubiquity of digital information which means we cannot just pass this off to special collections to manage. Every user, every organisation and every archive in the country now creates electronic information as a matter of course. It is very definitely our problem.

A useful piece of work would be to identify what technical knowledge and expertise should be taught, both on the postgraduate programmes and in continuing professional development, that would better fit archivists and records managers to operate successfully. Programmes responsible for turning out professional archivists and records managers will need to place at the centre of students' studies guidance – conceptual and practical – on the creation, maintenance and management of digital materials, whether born-digital or generated in surrogate digital formats. This includes an understanding of the nature of digital objects in all their forms and involves managing the creation, curation and sustainability of, and access to, digital surrogates; managing the born-digital record in relation to capture, workflow, appraisal and retention and so on. Moreover, recruits need to be encouraged from untraditional disciplines – social and physical sciences and IT that include elements relating to technology – as well as the usual arts-based history and languages ones, where technology is not an issue that is confronted in any detail in undergraduate programmes. The perception of what it is to be an archivist or records manager must change too so that those attracted to the profession are in no doubt about the nature of their work in the 21st century.

Conclusion

Personal papers comprise an important archival genre. While the records of public bodies and organizations contribute primarily to knowledge about infrastructures, contexts and frameworks of business, society and politics, papers of individuals enable biographical, prosopographical, occupational and genealogical study at a personal and collective level. Their successful management and exploitation by a range of archival bodies has demonstrated their value in terms of the content they hold and their indispensable use and value to research. That it might become more challenging to acquire and manage the digital personal papers of the future should merely serve to encourage archivists and librarians to ensure that they have the requisite skills to do so professionally and sustainably.

References

Bailey, S. (2007), 'Taking the road less travelled by: the future of the archive and records management profession in the digital age', *Journal of the Society of Archivists*, 28 (2), 117–124.

Cook, M. (1999), *The Management of Information from Archives*, 2nd edn (Aldershot: Gower).

Cox, R. (2001), *Managing Records as Evidence and Information* (Westport CT: Quorum).

Cunningham, A. (1996), 'Beyond the pale', *Archives and Manuscripts*, 24 (1), 20–26.

Dalgleish, P. (1996), 'Personal records of Members of Parliament', *Archives and Manuscripts*, 24 (1), 86–101.

Duchein, M. (1992), 'History of European archives and the development of the archival profession in Europe', *American Archivist*, 55 (Winter), 14–24.

Etherington, J. (2006), 'The role of archives in the perception of self', *Journal of the Society of Archivists*, 27 (2), 227–48.

Flinn, A. (2006), Seminar: *Archives and Identity: Whose Stories? Whose Archives?*, University College, London, <http://www.ucl.ac.uk/mellon-program/ seminars/2006-2007/abstracts/flinn.shtml> accessed 2 February 2008.

Galbraith, V.H. (1964), *An Introduction to the Study of History* (Cambridge: Cambridge University Press).

Hitchcock, T. (2006), 'Digital searching and the problem of the ventriloquist's dummy', paper presented at *AHRC Experts Virtual History and Archaeology Seminar*, Sheffield.

Hobbs, C. (2001), 'The character of personal archives: reflections on the value of records of individuals', *Archivaria*, 52 (Fall), 126–35.

Hunter, G. (2004), *Developing and Maintaining Practical Archives* (New York: Neil-Schumann).

International Council on Archives (2000), *General International Standard Archival Description* (ISAD(G)) (Paris: ICA).

Jenkinson, H. (1966), *A Manual of Archive Administration*, 2nd edn (London: Lund Humphries).

Ketelaar, E. (1997), 'The difference best postponed? Cultures and comparative archival science', *Archivaria*, 44 (Fall), 142–8.

McKemmish, S. (1996), 'Evidence of me …', *Archives and Manuscripts*, 24 (1), 28–45.

McKemmish, S., Gilliland-Swetland, A. and Ketelaar, E. (2005), 'Communities of memory', *Archives and Manuscripts*, 33 (1), 146–175.

Mackenzie, G. (1999), 'Archives – the global picture', *Archives*, 101, 2–15.

Moss, M. (2007), 'Choreographed encounter – the archive and public history', *Archives*, 32 (116), 41–57.

———— (2006), 'The Function of the Archive', in Moss, M. and Tough, A. (eds), *Record Keeping in a Hybrid Environment: Managing the Creation, Use and Disposal of Unpublished Information Objects in Context* (Oxford: Chandos).

Pollard, R. (2001), 'The appraisal of personal papers: a critical literature review', *Archivaria*, 52, 150–163.

Prescott, A. (2006), Untitled paper sent to author, 9 May.

Procter, M. and Cook, M. (2000), *Manual of Archival Description*, 3rd edn (Aldershot: Gower).

Procter, M. and Williams, C. (2003), *Essays in Honour of Michael Cook* (Liverpool: University of Liverpool Press).

Upward, F. and McKemmish, S. (2001), 'In search of the lost tiger, by way of Sainte-Beuve: re-constructing the possibilities in "Evidence of me"', *Archives and Manuscripts*, 29 (1), 22–43.

Vaisey, D. (2003), 'Now and Then: Reflections on Forty Years in Archives', in Procter, M. and Williams, C. (eds).

Williams, C.M. (2006), *Managing Archives: Foundations, Principles and Practice* (Oxford: Chandos).

Theme II
The Impact of Technology

Chapter 4

Opening Pandora's Box: What is an Archive in the Digital Environment?

Michael Moss

In his 1955 presidential address to the Society of Archivists, Hilary Jenkinson speculated on the future of archives in England. Reflecting on a half-century working with records interrupted by two world wars, he was alive to the impact that new technologies were having on the conduct of business, 'equipped with telephones, motor cars and aeroplanes we are getting back to the oral, substituting it for written communication'. He challenged those who argued that such developments made 'it necessary to revise our views about the nature and treatment of Archives'. Perceptively he observed that

> ... the mere manufacture of documents is only one element in the creation of Archives: another and much more potent one is their preservation for reference; that is to say their substitution not merely for the spoken word but for the fallible and destructible memory of the people who took part in whatever the transactions may have been that gave rise to them. *Recordari* still means, as it meant in the twelfth century, to remember. So long as memory is a necessary part of the conduct of affairs so long will it be necessary to put that memory into a material form, and so long as that is necessary so long will you have Archives, whether they take the form of writing on paper or parchment or palm leaves by hand or that of steel tape (shall we say) engraved by mechanical means with microscopic grooves which enable you to reproduce at will the voices of men who forgot or have been themselves forgotten (Jenkinson 1980, 321–2).

Despite all the welter of developments in information and communication technologies that have taken place in the succeeding half-century, this prediction remains a valid defence of the archive against those who might wish either to appropriate its functions or, as in Jenkinson's day, to substitute some other definition. Rooted as his thinking was in medieval history, he had no difficulty in admitting to the archive other forms of recording than paper; for him the act of archiving was in recording or preserving the 'Documents in the Case', whatever the form, and communicating them to the 'student public' (Jenkinson 1980, 323).

Such an emphasis on inscription and preservation was to be echoed by Michel Foucault some years later in *The Archaeology of Knowledge* in rather more convoluted language: 'The archive is not that which, despite its immediate escape, safeguards the event of the statement, and preserves, for future memories, its status as an escapee; it is that which at the very root of the statement event, and in that which embodies it, defines at the outset the system of *enunciability*'. Foucault insisted that the archive does not 'unify everything that has been said in the great confused murmur of a discourse', but 'differentiates discourses in their multiple existence' (Foucault 1989, 146). Derrida, writing forty years after Jenkinson, shared much the same perspective, albeit with at times a radically different gloss: 'there is no archive without consignment in an *external place* which assumes the possibility of memorialisation, of repetition, of reproduction, or of reimpression' (Derrida 1998, 11). At much the same time Brown and Davis-Brown argued that inscription was fundamental to the concept of the archive and the library: 'Only with the advent of writing, and hence the textual embodiment of a shared memory exterior to particular minds and performances, can archives and libraries be thought of as specific spaces for storing important documents' (Brown and Davis-Brown 1998, 18). Eric Ketelaar commented:

> Archives are memory because they are evidence. They are not only evidence of a transaction, but also evidence of some historic fact that is either part of the transaction itself, or that may be traced via the transaction, or that which is otherwise embodied in the record, or in the context of the archiving process (Ketelaar 2006, 188).

The evidential fiduciary function of the 'archive' is fundamental to compliance with international regulation and rule of law or more sinisterly, as in Travis Holland's novel *The Archivist's Story*, to support the actions of a totalitarian regime (Holland 2007). Holland's archivist, Pavel Duborov, was charged with cataloguing the confiscated papers of Russian poets, playwrights and authors during the Stalinist purges and then destroying them after their creators have been killed. Gordano, which claims to be 'the leading email, calendaring and collaboration messaging suite', advises its customers that 'email archiving has particular application for organisations that need to comply with regulatory obligations such as Sarbanes-Oxley' (Gordano 2007). In both these examples the archive is transient, destroyed when its purpose is fulfilled, whereas in most definitions it enjoys a permanence with 'potentialities' that 'awaits a constituency or public whose limits are of necessity unknown' (Osborne 1999, 55).

The evidential view of the archive has been criticized in the intervening half centuries by those, including Ketelaar, who consider it to be rooted in a positivist and constructivist approach to the past which they deftly seek to replace in a digital environment with a postmodern perspective that take ideas from both Foucault and Derrida. In a remarkable flight of rhetorical fancy, Hofman considers 'the archives can be seen as a node in a web of relationships with respect to records, clustering records into larger meaningful whole and embodying them on the one hand, and as a building block in collective memory on the other' (Hofman 2005, 154). Galin and Latchaw argue that the concept of the archive has been destablized by 'the emergence of large-scale, widely accessible digital databases of print documents', and are drawn to Foucault's metaphor of *heterotopia* to describe certain digital archived spaces because of the fruitful ways it *'reflects and subverts current economic and cultural assumptions about academic publishing'* (Galin and Latchaw 2001). This chimes with notions that 'as the backdrop to all scholarly research stands the archive' or a body knowledge, which in itself is open to positivist accusations (Velody 1998, 1). There is long pedigree to such a definition to be found in titles of many journals that begin with '*Archif*' or '*Archiv*' or 'Archive' that date back to the nineteenth century. Ketlaar considers: 'A digital document is not a thing in and of itself. ... [It is] no more than an interpretive moment in a never-ending conversation with the texts' (Ketlaar 2006, 190). Terry Cook interprets this 'new paradigm' as

> ... a shift away from viewing records as static objects and towards understanding them as dynamic virtual concepts: a shift away from looking at records as the passive products of human or administrative activity towards considering records as active agents themselves in the formation of human and organisational memory; a shift equally away from seeing the context of records creation resting within stable hierarchical organizations to situating records within fluid horizontal networks of work-flow functionality (Cook 2001, 4).

The sociologist Mike Featherstone goes further, with 'a powerful counter-image of the archive: the archive as the repository of material which has only been loosely classified, material whose status is as yet indeterminate and stands between rubbish, junk and significance: material that has not yet been read and researched' – Foucault's great confused murmur of discourse (Featherstone 2006, 594).

> In this utopian narrative, an archive is less like the *archivium*, or house, [Derrida's external place] and more like a city that continually expands and grows, that contains numerous pathways. In this dream, new technologies play a central role as the means by which all documents might be put on-line, linked by a vast hypertextual network (Sawchuk and Johnson 2001).

From such vantage points the archive becomes a global contingent collection of unstable 'texts' with questionable 'evidential' value that can be deployed in competing narratives – a 'repository of meanings' (Bradley 1999, 118). The 'text' itself within this digital archive not only becomes fluid, but ceases to be bounded by the written or even spoken word. As a consequence 'the adequacy, propriety, truthfulness of the materials, entities and objects that constitute an archive cannot be judged by their appearance in the archive as such. Only those who work in and around the archive can undertake such claims' (Velody 1998, 12). In some senses this is true of the Internet Archive that acts as a vast safe depository of digital objects – 'We will archive the site you have submitted and you will be able to view it in the wayback machine within 6 months' (Internet Archive). This led Taylor from this perspective to enquire, 'Do we possess the archive or does it possess us?' (Taylor 2002, 246). All users of archives, such as Fergus Roland in A.S. Byatt's novel *Possession*, have experienced such a transition, and even archivists can in a sense become the archive, scrupulously in the words of Sebastian Faulks lunatic archivist trying 'not merely to transcribe, but to redeem' (Byatt 1990, Faulks 2006, 185).

Such a redefinition of an archive represents a return to the cabinet of curiosities or *wunderkammer* of the Enlightenment, before information was differentiated by curatorial practices. In Susan Sontag's novel *Volcano Lover*, largely about Sir William Hamilton's life in Naples, the rocks that he collected patiently and with much physical effort and at times danger from Mount Vesuvius formed an archive, a subset of his extensive cabinet of curiosities of paintings, objects from antiquity, and so on (Sontag 1992). In her description of a visit by the poet Goethe and the artist

Tischbein to Hamilton's collection, their immediate reaction was 'there seemed no method or organization in it'. In a privileged visit to the cellar storerooms, she reported Goethe's amazement at finding an 'entire small chapel', 'two ornate bronze candelabra which he knew had to have come from the excavations at Pompeii. And many objects of no distinction whatsoever' (Sontag 1992, 143). In the *wunderkammer*, just as in the digital environment, the 'text' seems to cease to be bounded by the written or spoken word. It can be pretty much anything, as Jim Blackaby and Beth Sandore observed from their separate perspectives of the US Memorial Holocaust Museum and the Oregon Historical Society: 'Ever wish you could put your fingers on all of the information about a specific topic in a museum, regardless of whether it was drawn from the objects collection, exhibit catalogues, the library's holdings, or the prints and slides collection?' (Blackaby and Sandores 1997). Although such a statement confuses the mechanisms for resource discovery with the location and curation of objects, it draws attention to the fragility of boundaries when objects are reduced to strings of bit stream.

Buckland has observed:

> One can enumerate different types of digital documents and this is necessary because of the need to specify standards in order to achieve efficiency and interoperability. But if one seeks completeness, the process becomes arbitrary and intellectually unsatisfying because it is not clear where the frontiers between documents and non-documents should be (Buckland 1997a; 1998, 1).

In his thought-provoking article 'What is a "digital document"?' and another paper he drew attention to the documentation school of the early twentieth century that had its origins in the library profession, some of whose members argued that three-dimensional objects could be documents, if, as Otlet opined, 'you are informed by observation of them' (Buckland 1997a; 1998, 3, quoting Otlet 1934). For Briet a document was 'evidence in support of a fact' in 'any physical or symbolic sign, preserved or recorded intended to represent, to reconstruct or to demonstrate a physical or conceptual phenomenon' (Buckland 1997a; 1998, 3, quoting Briet 1951, 7). This is a definition that would have contented Sir William Hamilton: the specimens of rock he patiently collected and recorded would be considered documents, while those he left on Vesuvius would not – 'there was moral in these stones, these shards, these dimmed objects of marble and silver and glass: models of perfection and harmony' (Sontag 1992, 26). Although Briet failed to be explicit about when an object could be considered to be a document, Buckland identified four criteria:

1. There is materiality: Only physical objects can be documents,
2. There is intentionality: It is intended that the object be treated as evidence;
3. The objects have to be processed: They have to be made into documents; and, we think,
4. There is a phenomenological position: The object is perceived to be a document (Buckland 1997a; 1998, 4).

This implies 'binding', either internal or external and possibly of different strengths, that allows objects to be recognized as documents and by implication the privileging of content either implicitly or explicitly – the stones left behind on Vesuvius or the documents we intentionally destroy. As Buckland pointed out, later thinkers glossed such a materialistic categorization with a more metaphysical definition. For Barthes the external bindings were stripped away as the objects became 'vehicles of meaning' in themselves; in other words the content became the context (Buckland 1997a; 1998, quoting Barthes 1998, 5). The documentalist perspective speaks to the digital environment and provides helpful guidance in defining what might constitute an 'archive' that is more aligned with our contemporary usage than a definition that restricts contents to the written word.

If we accept (and some do not, as we shall see) that all documents are records of something then it follows that they all have different degrees of bindings to support their authenticity and veracity. A treaty between nations will be bound by a complex and iterative process of drafting and redrafting and by signatures of heads of state and their witnesses and the application of seals. The Scottish Declaration of Arbroath of April 1320 declares its authenticity with a mass of appended seals. The process of binding evidence for use in legal proceedings is intricate, involving careful cross-referencing and an abstraction that may distort the original, which in itself raises interesting questions about authenticity and veracity. As Syme has shown brilliantly in his painstaking analysis of the evidence compiled by Edward Coke to secure the convictions of those charged in the rebellion by Robert Devereux, Earl of Essex, in 1601, 'although the original examination is not literally erased, the words and symbols added to the document modify the prior inscriptions, altering their meaning as well as their physical form' (Syme 2007). Such sophisticated procedures are not required or even desirable for letters between friends, but in the analogue world there are processes of binding associated even with these records, such as headings (address, date and so on), salutations and valedictions, and externally covers with address, sometimes closed with seals and franked postmarks from which the content can easily become detached if the envelope and content are separated. Sir William Hamilton's specimens were in all probability numbered (internal) and registered in a catalogue (external), as was the case with much administrative paper until very recently. Such binding on what could be assumed to be trivial records still supports authenticity and veracity, crucially so in bookkeeping systems that depend on the ability to trace and verify the evidence for every single transaction however small. The foundation of all bookkeeping systems are invoices and receipts for payments for goods or services. These are known as vouchers precisely because they 'vouchsafe' the probity of the transaction recorded. These are often recorded on nothing much more than scraps of papers, but they embody a well-understood process with a description of what the transaction involved and the names of the parties. Although forgery and deception are always possible, only in unusual circumstances such as the century after the Norman Conquest in England may they be the 'rule rather than the exception' (Clanchy 1979, 248). Nevertheless for a forgery to be successful, it must mimic the bindings or processes that endow authenticity. As the diplomatist Duranti explains, establishing the veracity of a document is a reactive not a proactive process:

In both cases, affixing personal seals to the records and preserving them in a secure place would not alone have been sufficient to ensure that the actions and obligations to which the records relate would have been considered valid in the future. Such measures would have guaranteed to posterity the authenticity of the records, but not their reliability (Duranti 1995, 6).

The painter James McNeill Whistler wrote to his mother on 26/27 September 1876:

I come to wish you many happy returns my darling Mother – and to assure you of my fond affection – and my great wish to be with you this day! – Really I have continually promised myself a rest with you at the sea side dearest Mother for I did so enjoy the wee little visit of the while ago – but I have not managed it yet! – Never quite able to get off – Matters at home are [p. 2] getting better – I have managed to pay off many of my debts and am making careful economies – so that soon, with my new works I hope to be in comparitively in smooth water … (Whistler, 2004, 06564).

This perfectly authentic letter is a deceit, for on the very day of his mother's birthday Whistler held a grand dinner party at his home for which the menu survives in his own hand (Whistler 2004, 06854). In the digital environment much of the necessary binding for documents such as these is held externally in the shape of metadata that is often not completed at the time of creation or becomes detached.

Much of the contemporary debate about the ontological status of the 'archive' by archivists fails adequately to explore the criteria and binding attributes that objects must satisfy for inclusion that are assumed in every iteration, even when the archive is taken to be the whole content of the Internet. If they do, it is from a narrow archival perspective that accuses others of appropriating the archivist's vocabulary, which, as we have seen, has been going on for a very long time. The documentalist position may appear to be analogous to that of Hartland, McKemmish and Upward in a chapter on documents in the book *Archives: Recordkeeping in Society* – 'Unless we allow ourselves to become fixated upon paper as the physical storage media for a document, the web of documents in which we live can be seen to encompass many different documentary relationships, both serendipitous and constructed' (in McKemmish et al. 2005, 76). In their subsequent discussion, however, they adopt nine analytical perspectives for documents: form, format, medium, context, authority, content, purpose, technologies and accessibility. By confusing ontological status with taxonomy, as many in the information professions do, they inhibit rather than help our understanding. Form, format, medium and technologies are attributes that assist in classification (taxonomy that some information professionals choose to call ontology), whereas context, authority and purpose are ontological characteristics in the philosophical meaning of the term that help us to decide if an object conforms to the criteria set for the phenomenological properties of a document (ibid. 81). Even when Hartland et al. do consider ontological characteristics, they retreat into taxonomy. Purpose is defined not, as might be expected, as it relates to intention, but described in two analytical examples as 'aide-memoire, evidence of social status, and memorialisation of a family occasion'. This confusion that Buckland addressed directly is obvious in their declaration that: 'We can't exploit or value a document if we don't know what it is and identification of genre, a sub-genre and a form are a starting point' (ibid. 86). Much of the thrust of their argument is to draw a distinction between a document and a record of a transaction. In a subsequent chapter on records, Reed contests that:

> Records are different from other information resources because of this transactional aspect, which makes it important to identify the characteristics that must be present to ensure that records are reliable and authentic. The transactional aspect also makes it necessary to develop techniques for ensuring that records are created and managed in ways that assist in maintaining these characteristics (Reed 2005, 102).

This leads Hartland et al. to the surprising conclusion that storing authoritative transactional records so that they can be accessed are (*sic*) 'the essence of recordkeeping processes, storing them for as long as required is the essence of archiving processes' (ibid. 89). This looks like nothing more than special pleading for 'professional' intervention, predicated on a taxonomical muddle that does not get us as near understanding what an archive might be as the documentalist school.

Brothman, an archivist, in a perceptive essay, suggests the growing interest by archivists in the relationship between records and evidence over the last fifteen years 'exemplifies a complex politics of temporality ... Underlying these efforts to fix these two concepts' semantic value and relationship are manoeuvres to bolster professional identity and to establish the nature of our social commitment' (Brothman 2002, 312). He challenges the archival profession to make its epistemological mind up: 'It remains moot, therefore, whether archivists are in the business of taking measures to preserve records as vessels reliably carrying intended *meaning* or in the business of evoking and then proficiently capturing *incontestable organizational truthfulness* of fact as expressed by injecting "recordness" in "information" systems' (ibid. 326). As I have argued elsewhere, the latter endangers the fiduciary function of the archive (Moss 2005a). Brothman warns: 'Once questions of evidence predominate as primary preoccupations of the archival profession, issues of truth, truthfulness, and proof come to displace concerns about meaning, understanding and interpretation. And so archivists have been crossing several lines, without adequately recognizing that they have done so' (Brothman 2002, 330). Taken together with the outputs of our contemporary audit culture in which, as Strathern puts it, the 'ought' becomes 'is' (Strathern 2000), the danger is that the archive becomes, as Brothman cautions, what the archivist wants it to be (Brothman 2002, 331). This is Derrida's vision of the *archon* (the archivist) – 'The archons are first of all the documents' guardians. They do not only assume the physical security of what is deposited and of the substrata. They are also accorded the hermeneutic right and competence' (Derrida 1998, 2). This is a long way from Jenkinson's timeless *Recordari* – to remember that equates with much modern usage of the term 'archive' where the actions of the recorder (archivists) are both participatory and passive. It would be inconceivable that an archive of scientific data could have an archivist with 'hermeneutic right' as well as 'competence'. I will return to this conundrum.

Archivists' attempts to intervene in the process of creating records are a defensive reaction to the collapse of the curatorial boundaries implicit in the digital environment where traditional library objects elide with what were conventionally thought to be unique documents. When we view a document online, whether it be an image, a text or piece of music, we are looking at an object held uniquely on a server by a provider. The provider may have back-up copies for practical or security purposes, but access is very different from the analogue manuscript and print culture. Before the invention of moveable type users had to travel often long distances to view an 'original' manuscript, or copies had to be laboriously transcribed. With the invention of moveable type many copies could be printed and distributed widely (Burke 2000; Headrick 2000). In the digital environment many users view unique objects, original manuscripts if you like, from anywhere in the world providing they have the connectivity. We can view digital surrogates of Domesday Book held at The National Archives at Kew, or, as I write, images taken on mobile devices of the Saffron Revolution in Burma on blogs from a country where news reporting is severely circumscribed, or broadcasts using similar technology by the most wanted man in the world, Osama bin Laden. Although analogous to an analogue documentary world, digital distribution has the significant differences in its potential to generate multiple copies of documents that, rather than having to be selected for preservation, have to be selected for destruction and, in the way that it privileges content, to generate collections that we might in the analogue call archives. This does not, however, negate the Briet/Buckland criteria for a document apart from its materiality, but as Allison, Currall, Stuart and I have argued the bit stream does have reference (Allison et al. 2005).

If the archive in our digital environment has in effect become a *wunderkammer* of unique objects that can be viewed simultaneously and many times in every part of the world, how does this plurality chime with the analogue equivalent? The content of most paper-based archives is heterogeneous, with perhaps the exception of large homogeneous datasets with strict rules for accession, for example a census – and even here there can be room for doubt (Higgs 1989). In such cases, they rarely constitute the whole archive but form part of a larger whole. They certainly contain plenty of documents that can only be loosely described as transactional records and they contain documents in many formats reflecting available technologies, as Jenkinson implied in 1955. They perform many functions, as Hofman describes in a chapter on archives ranging from the archives of a nation to that of a family or an individual (Hofman, 2005). Their content reflects long chains of intention to preserve evidence, concluding with final selection or appraisal by the archivist that admits them to the archive. From this viewpoint the 'archive' is just another collection, an arbitrary metaphor for a collection of collections sharing common criteria for a document and specific purposes, defined in the analogue by a curatorial imperative that no longer applies in a digital environment. Lagoze and Fielding consider as 'a collection as logically defined in a set of criteria for the selection of resources from the broadest information space' (1998, sec. 3). These may be value-laden, as Derrida would claim or, as Latour is careful to point out in his discussion of collections as 'centres of accumulation', neutral (Latour 1990). They do not have to be one or the other.

The concepts that underpin collections have been explored by Currall, Stuart and myself in two papers (Currall et al. 2004; 2006). In these we argue, drawing on the ideas of Lee and Miksa, that there are, at least two perspectives of what a collection might be (Lee 2000; Miksa 1998). The developer perspective sees the collection in terms of selection and control, whilst the user perspective sees the collection in terms of resource discovery and access. 'In private collecting, these two perspectives are embodied in the one individual, the collector, but where collections are developed and maintained by one party for the benefit of others the role of collector and user may become widely divergent' (Currall et al. 2006, 102). A good example might be the decision of the National Library of Australia only to archive blogs 'when they support the high priority category of academic publications' (Phillips 2003). Another might be the way in which information professions 'allocate individual objects and the collections to which they belong to hierarchies with explicit taxonomies' (Currall et al. 2004, 141). We concluded that from the developer or provider perspective there is a 'pressing need to create taxonomies and associated rules and standards to allocate names to objects for the simple reason that "privileging of the better and, by default, the non-privileging of the rest, remains a significant needed service"' (ibid. 144; Buckland 1997b, supplement to Chapter 6, 6). Mbembe makes much the same point: 'Archives are the product of a process which converts a certain number of documents into items judged to be worthy of preserving and keeping in a public space, where they can be consulted according to well-established procedures and regulations' (2002, 20).

If the term 'archive' is collapsed into 'collections', as would seem to be the case in our contemporary usage, and we agree that complaints by archivists about appropriation will fall largely on deaf ears, the question remains if there is anything about archival collections as a genre within a wider taxonomy that is distinctive. Jenkinson by 1955 was working to a very plural concept of the archive that functions to link memory to the record and to the conduct of affairs in the widest sense, which must subsume as a particular genre the fiduciary juridical function of some archives such as the Public Record Office. The fiduciary juridical function is in some respects about registration and reference that is an attribute common to many collections that lack any particular legal protection. Even what appear to be the most haphazard collections, such as that of Sir William Hamilton or Sir Walter Scott's antiquary Johnathan Oldbuck or the Internet Archive, are not simply contingent (Scott 1816). They embody an intention and logic, albeit temporal and culturally specific. There are many examples of collections that possess a quasi-juridical function that are curated in such a way to hold and manage contents fiduciarily in the discharge of their responsibilities. An herbarium contains specimens of plant life that can be used to identify other specimens. A dictionary, which is a form of collection, contains lists of words and their meanings that can be used to corroborate definitions. Picture galleries and museums not only serve to educate and entertain, but also as reference for other objects. The majority of archives serve as registers and works of reference, whether explicitly juridical or not. Jenkinson himself observed this when he defined archives in 1947 as 'Documents accumulated by a natural process in the course of the Conduct of Affairs of any kind, Public or Private, at any date: and preserved thereafter for reference, in their own Custody, by the persons responsible for the Affairs in question or their successors' (Jenkinson 1980, 237). As O'Neill and Strathern argue, fiduciary action requires more than the observation of auditable criteria – procedures that conform to rules and regulations – it demands responsible behaviour if trust is to be maintained (O'Neill 2002, Strathern 2000). Such collections must not just be securely held, all the surrounding processes must be above reproach so the content can possess a canonical authority. This is a long way from the postmodern position that so problematizes any body of knowledge that truth becomes unknowable.

In these circumstance what might distinguish an archival definition of the archive apart from other collections is not that it holds transactional records, but the fiduciary protection it affords both depositors and users. For depositors it provides back office support to front office actions, providing the records are maintained in such a way that their content can be subsequently validated. The transmission of documents or records to secure storage where access is supervised protects the authors from future misrepresentation as well as allowing them to be held to account. As both Brothman and I have suggested, for the archivist to become involved in the process of creation jeopardises the fiduciary function of the archives (Brothman 2002, 326; Moss 2005b; Moss 2006) and dangerously confuses the front and the back office. It is for the executive to control the process of creation and selection within the framework of risk that will involve back office consultations, but not control. If this is so, archivists have a case for differentiating some archival collections from other collections in substance as well as degree. The curators of herbariums, the editors of dictionaries and the curators of galleries and museums are implicitly involved in collection development as in some of their activities they are archivists. However, when their function is defined as a public archive (*cimiliarchio publico*), their duty, at least in Western democratic cultures, is to preserve records for the benefit of the whole community, which has rights of access, and users can have confidence that when they consult archives they are what they purport to be, at least what they purported to be when they were selected for permanent preservation (Clanchy 1979, 163). In this regard archivists occupy a critical juridical role in establishing or, as Jenkinson put it, record the truth that must be protected by the rule of law. In Evans's words, they record that 'it really happened, and we really can, if we are very scrupulous and careful and self-critical, find out how it happened and reach some tenable though always less than final conclusions about what it all meant' (Evans 1997, 253). Jenkinson, in a lecture at University College London, was emphatic about the duty of the archivist: 'His Creed, the Sanctity of Evidence; his Task, the Conservation of every scrap of Evidence attaching to the Documents committed to his charge; his Aim to provide, without prejudice or afterthought, for all who wish to know the Means of Knowledge (Jenkinson 1980, 258). Without such a creed the archivist is powerless to defend the archive when governments seeks to pervert it, as in Stalinist Russia, or deliberately do not tell the truth, as would seem to be the case in the conduct of the war in Iraq by the US (Chandrasekaran 2006). The neo-conservatives have cynically manipulated postmodern thinking to assert 'truth is not salutary, but dangerous, and even destructive to society – any society', and we could substitute 'archive' for 'truth' (Drury 1997, 1). In other words, if truth is unknowable, there is no need to tell the truth. This is made all the more easy in a digital environment where context is often absent and the processes involved in creating documents in the analogue built up over centuries have been abandoned, making it difficult to assert with any confidence that an object was intended to be treated as evidence (Moss 2005b). As I have argued, the public archive protected by the rule of law must always have the potential to be subversive, to collect the soldier blogs that provide a different perspective on events in Iraq, or even to preserve records in defiance of executive instruction (Moss 2005a; Moss 2006).

Acceptance that the public archive has a duty to capture and care for documents that tell the 'truth' does not in itself resolve a relativist critique of the archive, nor Cook's view that 'there has been a collective shift from a juridical-administrative justification for archives grounded in the concepts of the state, to a socio-cultural justification for archives grounded in wider public policy and public use' that reflects widespread hostility to Federal government in the US, allied to a long-established historical manuscripts tradition (Cook 1997). The tension between the individual life experience and the whole is a necessary characteristic of the archive, exemplified by the popularity of family history that I have explored (Moss 2007). Justice Albie Sachs of South Africa, in an interview with Henry Kreisler of the Institute of International Studies at the University of California at Berkeley, explored poignantly the interplay between the individual intensely subjective experiences and the those of the group. Sachs responded to a question about his recovery from the bomb attack that left him blind in one eye and with only one arm:

> You still have those moments of unconsciousness fading in and out. Communicating with them, hearing a voice. Telling oneself a joke that, as it happened, revived me from fainting again. And that slow, long recovery that's very personal. But then also the knowledge that I'm part of a community, a group, that what got me there wasn't just a purely personal idiosyncratic thing. That I'm in history. There are thousands of others out there crying for me, laughing for me, cheering me on. I'm doing it for them. It's about something. It's about the world out there. It's not about becoming famous or becoming rich or being powerful or enjoying sex. It's about who you are in the world. And that was very, very sustaining (Kreisler 1998).

In Sachs's perception the two narratives are complementary; the one does not in any sense negate the other. Himmelfarb argued that, although historians are prepared to admit a 'relativistic' relativism in the interpretation of sources, few are willing so to problematize them that 'truth' becomes unknowable:

> Where modernism tolerates the obstacles in the way of objectivity as a challenge and make strenuous effort to attain as much objectivity and unbiased truth as possible, postmodernism takes the rejection of absolute truth as a deliverance from all truth and from the obligation to maintain any degree of objectivity (Himmelfarb 1999, 74 and 82).

Ironically she has Republican sympathies and yet this encapsulates for me the approach historians should adopt to the 'archive' of the war in Iraq. I want the truth to be knowable. Far from 'meta-narratives' precluding 'other' narratives, this approach demands their exploration and the archive to sustain them. This is what the philosopher Ricoeur termed the 'historian's spontaneous "realism"', based on the continuum 'of activities of preserving, selecting, assembling, consulting, and finally, reading documents and archives, which mediate and, so to speak, schematize the trace, making it the ultimate presumption of the reinscription of lived time (time with the present)'. This is where, as Duranti argues, verification takes place. For Ricoeur it was the hermeneutic 'use of documents and archives that makes the trace an actual operator of historical time' that enabled 're-enactment', the exploration of the 'pastness of the past', which he describes as 'the telos of the historical imagination, what it intends, and its crowning achievement' (Ricoeur 1985, vol. 3, 183–4). The complex interrelationship of reading text in the present and imagining the past as it actually happened, '*wie es eigentlich gewesen*' as Ranke put it, reaches fulfilment for Ricoeur in the refigured past (Ricouer 1985, 185, quoting Ranke 1824).

Such complimentarity is much more intellectually satisfying than the binary opposition of much postmodern deconstruction. As Ricoeur expresses it, 'The conflict between explanation that connects things together and the horror that isolates ...' (Ricoeur 1985, 188). Although Cook defends postmodern deconstruction against the charge of 'endless relativist critiques', Ricoeur's approach fits better his enthusiasm for its consequences for the 'archive' – it is 'about constructing, about seeing anew and imagining what is possible when the platitudes and ideologies are removed' (Cook 2000, 22). From an archival perspective reinscription is self-evidently a user activity, external to the 'archive' if it is to discharge its fiduciary curatorial responsibilities, but re-enactment and participation in the process of refiguration are not. I am convinced Jenkinson was careful to draw a distinction between the archivist and historian, and is what Eastwood is getting at when he reaffirmed Jenkinson's definition of the archivist as 'a keeper and protector of the integrity of evidence and a mediator of the many interests vested in the positive act of its continuing preservation' (Jenkinson 1980, 258; Eastwood 1993, 237). MacNeil is emphatic:

> Archival custodianship has always been linked inextricably to the protection and safeguarding of evidence. Physical ownership of the records is merely the means by which, historically, archivists have assured that protection. The advent of information technologies does not change the substance of our custodial responsibility; it simply changes the means by which we exercise it (MacNeil 2007).

Of course, archivists possess fictive imaginations with which they explore the 'pastness of the past' when they appraise, catalogue and describe their collections in the present. It would be strange if it were otherwise; it is what after all enables subversion, such as Holland's archivist, Pavel Dubrov's removal of one of Isaac Babel's unpublished stories and hiding it in his basement store:

> Back among the shelves, Pavel wonders: How long would it take to destroy all of this? Every file, every folder, down to the last story, the last poem. He lays a hand against one of the boxes, feels the manuscript in it shift when he pushes against the cardboard, as if someone living lay inside asleep, dreaming. He moves on to another box, then another, letting his hand rest a moment on each of them. *The magnificent grave of the human heart* (Holland 2007, 50).

Such transcendence echoes the re-enactment of Jules Michelet: when wandering 'in those solitary galleries' of the archives, there came to him 'the whispers of the souls who had suffered so long ago and who were smothered now in the past' (Michelet 1974, 11–27, quoted in Steedman 1998, 69). Such re-enactment can be observed amongst those who encounter the 'archive' – a photograph of a grandfather murdered by the Nazis, of whom no other picture survives, in the newly-opened Holocaust archives, or more prosaically the excitement of unravelling from documents the jigsaw pieces of a narrative – the 'enduring passions that researchers develop with the contents of buff folders' (Hamilton et al. 2002, 16). This is perhaps what Derrida had in mind when he described the archive as 'a responsibility for tomorrow' whose meaning will only be known 'in times to come' (Derrida 1998, 36).

We are now nearer an understanding of why the particular archival definition of an 'archive' might be worth defending against its contemporary plural usage that has become synonymous with a collection, a body of knowledge or a bunch of stuff. Pursuing Ricoeur's line of thinking, curators of other collections, as we have seen, are engaged in the process of reinscription. It is what makes their collections what they are and differentiates them from the archivist's definition of an 'archive', which, as I have argued, is as more about the function and activity of preserving the 'Documents in the Case', than the ontological status of the 'documents' themselves that is shared with other collections. There is then no contradiction between the static and dynamic perceptions of the document. They complement one another in a perpetual hermeneutic spiral. An archive in this sense can be and often is a *wunderkammer*, but it is emphatically not a *wunderkammer* 'of material which has only been loosely classified, material whose status is as yet indeterminate and stands between rubbish, junk and significance: material that has not yet been read and researched' (Featherstone 2006, 594). It is a place of 'dreams', of re-enactment for both the user and the archivist (curator), who together always are engaged either passively or actively in the process of refiguration that is never ending.

Acknowledgements

The author is grateful to: James Currall and Susan Stuart for many stimulating interactions; David Jasper for introducing him to Ricoeur; Alistair Tough for his close reading of the text and suggestions; Nigel Thorp, the editor of the Whistler correspondence for the reference to the artist's deceit; and to students on successive classes on the Information Management and Preservation MSc programme at the University of Glasgow, <http://www.hatii.arts.gla.ac.uk/imp/index.htm>.

References

Allison, A., Currall, J., Moss, M. and Stuart, S. (2005), 'Digital identity matters', *Journal of the American Society for Information Science and Technology*, 56 (4), 364–72.

Barthes, R. (1998), *The Semiotic Challenge* (New York: Hall & Wang).

Bell, B. and Alloway, R. (eds) (forthcoming, 2008), *The Reader in History* (Edinburgh: Edinburgh University Press).

Blackaby, J. and Sandore, B. (1997), 'Building integrated museum information systems: practical approaches to data organization and access', at <http://www.archimuse.com/mw97/mw97wed.htm#13> accessed September 2007.

Bradley, H. (1999), 'The seduction of the archive', *History of Human Sciences*, 12 (2), 107–22.

Briet, S. (1951), *Qu'est-ce que la documentation?* (Paris: EDIT). An English translation by R.E. Day (Indiana University) and L. Martinet (Paris), with H. Anghelescu (Wayne State University), is available at <http://ella.slis.indiana. edu/~roday/Briet_preface.pdf> accessed September 2007.

Brothman, B. (2002), 'Afterglow: conceptions of record and evidence in archival discourse', *Archival Science*, 2 (3–4), 311–342.

Brown, R.H. and Davis-Brown, B. (1998), 'The making of memory: the politics of archives, libraries and museums in the construction of national consciousness', *History of the Human Sciences*, 11 (4), 17–32.

Buckland, M.K. (1998), 'What is a "digital document"?', *Document Numérique*, 2 (2), 221–30.

——— (1997a), 'What is a document?', *Journal of the American Society of Information Science*, 48 (9), 804–9.

——— (1997b), 'Redesigning library services: a manifesto', available at <http:// sunsite.berkeley.edu/Literature/Library/Redesigning/supplement.html> accessed July 2008.

Burke, P. (2000), *A Social History of Knowledge from Gutenberg to Diderot* (Cambridge: Polity).

Byatt, A.S. (1990), *Possession: A Romance* (London: Vintage Books).

Chandrasekaran, R. (2006), *Imperial Life in the Emerald City: Inside Iraq's Green Zone* (New York: Knopf).

Clanchy, M.T. (1979), *From Memory to Written Record: England 1066–1307* (London: Edward Arnold).

Cook, T. (2001), 'Archival sciences and postmodernism: new formulations for old concepts', *Archival Science*, 1 (1), 3–24.

——— (2000), 'Fashionable nonsense or professional rebirth: postmodernism and the practice of archives', *Archivaria*, 51, 14–35.

——— (1997), 'What is past is prologue: a history of archival ideas since 1898, and the future paradigm shift', *Archivaria*, 43, 17–63.

Currall, J., Moss, M. and Stuart, S. (2006), 'Privileging information is inevitable', *Archives and Manuscripts – Journal of the Australian Society of Archivists*, 34, 98–122.

——— (2004), 'What is a collection?', *Archivaria*, 58, 131–46.

Derrida, J. (1998), *Archive Fever: A Freudian Impression*, trans. E. Prenowitz (Chicago IL: University of Chicago Press).

Drury, S.B. (1997), *Leo Strauss and the American Right* (New York: Palgrave Macmillan), and for reference see <http://rightweb.irc-online.org/analysis/2004/ 0402nsai.php> accessed September 2007.

Duranti, L. (1995), 'Reliability and authenticity: the concepts and their implications', *Archivaria*, 39, 5–10.

Eastwood, T. (1993), 'Nailing a little jelly to the wall of archival studies', *Archivaria*, 35, 232–52.

Evans, R. (1997), *In Defence of History* (London: Granta).

Faulks, S. (2006), *Human Traces* (London: Vintage Books).

Featherstone, M. (2006), 'Archive', *Theory, Culture & Society: Problematizing Global Knowledge: Special Issue*, 23 (2–3), March–May, 42–4.

Foucault, M. (1989), *The Archaeology of Knowledge*, trans. Sheridan Smith (London Routledge).

Fox-Genovese, E. and Lasch-Quinn, E. (eds) (1999), *Reconstructing History – The Emergence of a New Historical Society* (New York and London: Routledge).

Galin, J.R. and Latchaw, J. (2001) 'What is an archive?', *Hetrotopic Spaces Online: A New Paradigm for Academic Scholarship and Publication*, at <http://kairos. technorhetoric.net/3.1/coverweb/galin/index.htm> accessed September 2007.

Gordano (2007), <http://www.gordano.com/products/Archive.htm> accessed September 2007.

Hamilton, C. et al. (2002), *Refiguring the Archive* (Dordrecht, Boston and London: Kluwer).

Hartland, R., McKemmish, S. and Upward, F. (2005), 'Documents', in McKemmish, S.M. et al., 75–100.

Headrick, D. (2000), *When Information Came of Age: Technologies of Knowledge in the Age of Reason and Revolution 1700–1850* (Oxford: Oxford University Press).

Higgs, E. (1989), *Making Sense of the Census: the Manuscript Returns for England and Wales, 1801–1901* (London: HMSO).

Himmelfarb, G. (1999), 'Postmodernist History', in Fox-Genovese, E. and Lasch-Quinn, E. (eds).

Hofman, H. (2005), 'The Archive', in McKemmish, S.M. et al.

Holland, T. (2007), *The Archivist's Story* (New York: Dial Press).

Internet Archive, <http://www.archive.org/web/web.php> accessed September 2007.

Jenkinson, H. (1980), *Selected Writings of Sir Hilary Jenkinson*, eds R. Ellis and P. Walne (Gloucester: Alan Sutton).

———— (1922), *A Manual of Archive Administration* (London: Lund Humphries).

Ketelaar, E. (2006), 'Writing on Archiving Machines', in Neef, S., van Dijck, J. and Ketelaar, E. (eds), *Sign Here! Handwriting in the Age of New Media* (Amsterdam: Amsterdam University Press).

Kreisler, H. (1998), 'Suffering, survival, and transformation – conversation with Albie Sachs', <http://globetrotter.berkeley.edu/Sachs/sachs-con8.html> accessed September 2007.

Lagoze, C. and Fielding, D. (1998), 'Defining collections in distributed digital libraries', *D-Lib Magazine*, November, at <http://www.dlib.org/dlib/november98/ lagoze/11lagoze.html> accessed September 2007.

Latour, B. (1990), 'Drawing Things Together', in Lynch, M. and Woolgar, S. (eds), *Representation in Scientific Practice* (Cambridge MA: MIT Press), 19–68.

Lee, H-L. (2000), 'What is a collection?', *Journal of the American Society for Information Science*, 51 (12), 1106–13.

McKemmish, S.M., Piggott, M., Reed, B. and Upward, F. (2005), *Archives: Recordkeeping in Society* (Wagga Wagga, Australia: Centre for Information Studies, Charles Sturt University),

MacNeil, H. (2007), 'Archival theory and practice: between two paradigms', *Archives & Social Studies: A Journal of Interdisciplinary Research*, 1 (1) (September), available at <http://socialstudies.cartagena.es/images/PDF/no1/macneil_archival. pdf> accessed September 2007.

Mbembe, A. (2002), 'The Power of the Archive and its Limits', in Hamilton, C. et al.

Michelet, J. (1974), 'Préface de 1869', in *Oeuvres complètes*, vol. 4 (Paris: Flammarion), 11–127. Orig. pub. 1869.

Miksa, F.L. (1998), *The DDC, the Universe of Knowledge, and the Post-Modern Library* (Albany NY: Forest Press).

Moss, M. (2007), 'Choreographed encounter – the archive and public history', *Archives*, 32 (116), 41–57.

———— (2006), 'The Function of the Archive' in Tough, A. and Moss, M. (eds), *Record Keeping in a Hybrid Environment – Managing the Creation, Use and Disposal of Unpublished Information Objects in Context* (Oxford: Chandos Press), 227–43.

———— (2005a), 'Archivist: friend or foe?', *Records Management Journal*, 15 (2), 104–114, also in Aubry, M., Chave, I. and Doom, V. (eds) (2007), *Archives, archivistes et archivistique dans l'Europe du Nord-Ouest de l'Antiquité à nos jours: Entre gouvernance et mémoire* (Lille: Institut de Recherches Historique du Septentrion), 36, 243–53.

———— (2005b), 'The Hutton inquiry, the President of Nigeria and What the Butler Hoped to See?', *English Historical Review*, 120 (487), 577–92.

O'Neill, O. (2002), *A Question of Trust* (London: BBC), available at <http://www. bbc.co.uk/radio4/reith2002/lectures.shtml> accessed September 2007.

Osborne, T. (1999), 'The ordinariness of the archive', *History of the Human Sciences*, 12 (2), 51–64.

Otlet, P. (1934), *Traité de documentation* (Brussels: Editiones Mundaneum – reprinted 1989, Liège: Centre de Lecture Publique de la Communauté Française).

Phillips, M.E. (2003), 'Balanced scorecard initiative 49 collecting Australian online publications', at <http://pandora.nla.gov.au/selectionguidelinesallpartners.html> accessed September 2007.

Ranke, L. von (1957), *Fürsten und Völker: Geschichte der romanischen und germanischen Völker von 1494 bis 1514* (Wiesbaden: Willy Andersen).

Reed, B. (2005), 'Records', in McKemmish, S.M. et al.

Ricoeur, P. (1985), *Temps et récit*, vol. 3 (Paris: Editions du Seuil), trans. K. Blamey and D. Pellauer (1988) as *Time and Narrative*, vol. 3 (Chicago IL: University of Chicago Press).

Sawchuk, K. and Johnson, S. (2001), 'Editorial/introduction', *Canadian Journal of Communication*, 26 (2), available at <http://www.cjc-online.ca/viewarticle. php?id=636&layout=html> accessed September 2007.

Scott, W. (1816), *The Antiquary*, chapter 3, electronic text available at <http://www2. arts.gla.ac.uk/SESLL/STELLA/STARN/prose/WSCOTT/ANTIQUAR/contents. htm> accessed September 2007.

Sontag, S. (1992), *The Volcano Lover – A Romance* (London: Cape).

Steedman, C. (1998), 'Memory: in an archive', *History of Human Sciences*, 11 (4), 65–83.

Strathern, M. (2000), 'Abstraction and decontextualisation: an anthropological commentor: E for ethnography', available at <http://virtualsociety.sbs.ox.ac.uk/GRpapers/strathern.htm> accessed September 2007.

Syme, H.S. (2007), 'Judicial Digest: Edward Coke Reads the Earl of Essex, 1601', in Bell, B. and Alloway, R. (eds).

Taylor, J. (2002), 'Holdings: Refiguring the Archive', in Hamilton, C. et al.

Velody, I. (1998), 'The archive and the human sciences: notes towards a theory of the archive', *History of the Human Sciences*, 11 (4), 1–16.

Whistler, J.M. (2004), *The Correspondence of J.M. Whistler*, online edition (Glasgow: Centre for Whistler Studies, University of Glasgow) at <http://www.whistler.arts.gla.ac.uk/correspondence/index.htm> accessed September 2007.

Chapter 5

The Online Archivist: A Positive Approach to the Digital Information Age

Jane Stevenson

The literature that has been produced in recent years on electronic record keeping and digitization is huge, and the challenges of the digital age and ever-changing world of technology have been well documented. Archivists and records managers face the massive task of dealing with the management of an increasingly diverse range of records, and the selection, cataloguing and preservation of archive material. The focus within our profession tends to be on how technology is impacting on our role in terms of dealing with electronic records and digital preservation. We often consider the challenges of dealing with digital records and archives and the skills needed for this, but aside from this the digital age gives rise to other implications for the role of the information professional. We need to think about the potential of technology within our profession, and how technology will influence the behaviour and expectations of users of archives. We all have a sense that the roles of archivists and records managers are changing, but what does this mean in practice, in terms of the skills set needed in the twenty-first century and the ways that we communicate, disseminate information and build relationships with users and colleagues? It is important to think about where we, as archivists and records managers, place ourselves within this world and how we equip ourselves to be effective within it.

Information professionals are increasingly taking a more user-centred approach to their work. Many of the latest technical innovations encourage individuals to become empowered to create, manipulate and use information in ways not previously envisaged. In this climate, the methods that individuals use to discover and interact with archive materials are going to continue to develop at a fast pace, and we can have little idea what may lie in store in ten or twenty years' time. There is likely to be a move away from the traditional view of the professional as gatekeeper and controller of resources, but what does this mean for the role of the archivist of the future? We cannot predict what is going to happen in the fast-paced world of technology, but what we can do is to ensure that we are aware of technical developments and trends, so that we can take the opportunities that technology provides to enhance and improve what we do and meet users' needs as effectively as we can.

In this chapter, I want to focus on the skills that we will need to develop in order to interact with, and benefit from, the advances taking place in the digital world. I will refer more specifically to archivists than records managers, because in general archivists are more concerned with dissemination of information to a wider audience, although clearly the need for technical awareness applies broadly to all sorts of information professionals. I am not going to discuss our relationship to archives themselves, be they digital or paper-based; rather, I am going to consider our use of technology and the crucial role of the World Wide Web.

I use the word 'technology' in this context to refer to information technology. This is generally considered to refer in the broadest sense to all matters concerned with the design, development, installation and implementation of information systems and applications. I am using it to refer in particular to the processing and dissemination of information. I want to think about the possibilities that technology opens up for us and our attitude to what is out there and available to us in the digital world. It is fundamentally our attitudes to technology and our willingness to understand and use it that will determine how much we take advantage of the opportunities that it presents.

An Evolving Skills Set

Archivists generally have good organizational skills, which are important for ensuring a methodical approach to appraisal, sorting, cataloguing and description. In recent years, archivists have also become more adept at communication, marketing, advocacy, raising the profile of archives and using archives in an educational context. The development and application of a whole range of skills has become essential, as we continue to work to ensure that society appreciates the importance of preserving, using and understanding historical records. However, technological developments are now having a major impact on the role of the archivist in terms of cataloguing, communication, dissemination, collaboration and participation, and in these areas we need to be engaged with technology and use it to our advantage. The majority of archivists have a humanities background, and they may have an interest in palaeography and an appreciation of the value of historical documents, but often they have little interest in the role of technology. It may be that we need to think about attracting people to the profession who have a greater enthusiasm for working with technology, combining this with an interest in the more traditional and core competencies of the archivist.

Increasingly, technology will be integral to the role of the archivist. It is our best means of disseminating information, improving access and promoting our collections. We therefore need to have an awareness of what is potentially available to us, and understand the implications of the solutions that we adopt. The reality is that our profession is having to move in new directions and we have to adapt and change, to develop new skills and new approaches to fit in with the search-orientated information environment. If we want to disseminate information about archives as widely and effectively as possible, we need to have an understanding of how this can be done. We need to know how to share and exchange data, how to structure finding aids to enable sophisticated searching, what the advantages and disadvantages are of using controlled vocabularies, how we can continue to engage new users, how to explain the uses and benefits of archive material for all manner of research and educational purposes and communicate effectively with a global audience. We should be thinking about such issues as exposing data to search engines, promoting effective cross-searching and harnessing user expertise and opinion. The aim is to ensure that archive services take advantage of technology in useful and appropriate ways. The importance of this to employers is reflected in the Workforce Study of the 2004 Archives Task Force, which found that 50 per cent of practitioners saw training in information and communication technology as the most important training need (Museums Libraries and Archives Council 2004). The vision of a 'Knowledge Web', where we provide seamless access to the collections and services of archives, and indeed of archives, libraries and museums, offers something of enormous benefit to users. Realization of this will require leadership, commitment and widespread support, and it will also require archivists with technical awareness to work together with colleagues on the technical challenges that this ambitious aim presents.

A New Mindset

One of the first hurdles that we have to overcome is our general mindset when it comes to technology. We need to develop a more positive perspective, where we are willing to experiment and explore, to share ideas, to be receptive to new ideas and developments that might be beneficial to us. There are so many options available to us that it can be daunting to know where to start. We cannot investigate everything, nor is it the case that all technical innovations are going to be worth embracing. However, as far as possible, we need to have an awareness of what is available to us and what is worth using and, equally importantly, to know what we are rejecting. At the same time, we need to take a realistic approach based on institutional aims and objectives, the resources available to us and the requirements of archive users.

Relationships with Users of Archives

The relationship that we have to our users and the ways that we engage with them are intimately bound up with how we think about and provide access to archives, and this is something that is fast changing. Integral to an effective strategy for dissemination and communication is the need to know about the user community and user behaviour and also the need to appreciate user expectations.

Users of archives are increasingly physically remote, but we still tend to measure success primarily in terms of personal visits to an archive repository. This is not surprising, as our profession is generally focused on the physicality of documents and the secure accommodation that we need to provide for them, and the understanding and interpretation of physical archives is crucial to many areas of research. Perceptions of access are now shifting due to the increasing numbers of electronic resources available online, but it is still the case that personal visits to repositories and physical contact with the archives themselves are seen as the main goal in terms of user statistics, and therefore in terms of the success of the record office. It is vital that we continue in our traditional role, preserving archives and making them accessible within the reading room for those many researchers who wish to use the physical documents and to have the advantages of access to related documents and other materials, as well as the benefits of an archivist on hand to help and advise them. Indeed, part of our advocacy role is the need to put forward persuasive arguments that access to the actual physical artefacts is still of the utmost importance. Effective preservation and arrangements for secure user access are therefore still crucial roles for the archivist. But, at the same time, the demands of users are changing and the relationships that we have with users are broadening out. We now have the opportunity to reach people in different ways and to increase our user-base to include new audiences. A growing proportion of people want remote access with full-text online and easy access to digital objects, and we are making efforts to meet these needs by undertaking digitization projects and by exploring ways of linking to digital content.

One of the great advantages of the Web that is particularly pertinent to archivists is that it can enable people to find information on an obscure subject or a little-known individual. If archives are described effectively and the descriptions are available on the Web, people across the world can locate materials that are of interest to them. This advantage is a practical example of the concept of the 'long tail' (see Anderson 2006), a term originally used in a business scenario to describe the situation where low-demand items become more profitable because they collectively outsell popular items, and now applied more broadly to refer to the importance of minority tastes and niche markets within the online environment. With the removal of geographic boundaries, archives that may have been infrequently consulted in the past have the potential to become far more popular because they can be brought to an international audience, and this is something that will be of great benefit to archive services. The ability to provide remote access to archives is increasing, with born-digital materials and the digitization of traditional materials, and even with just the finding aids available on the Web, we can put researchers in touch with relevant collections that they may otherwise never have discovered. In this way we can increase the use and potentially the prominence of archives and particularly of previously little-used collections.

The reality is that the information world is increasingly online and virtual, and communication and dissemination of information about archives must use the channels that are most effective. We need to re-think our measurement of success in order to include remote users, otherwise we run the risk of seeing static or falling user levels in statistics that do not accurately reflect the true use of the archives. This is analogous to the changes that have taken place in the popular music charts. Up until a few years ago, the charts reflected the music purchased through retail outlets but excluded the ever-growing market for music downloads. Today, the statistics include online digital download stores in order to more accurately reflect user behaviour.

The Sustainability of Finding Aids

Archival descriptions are an investment of time, effort and professional expertise, and they are crucial to make an archive accessible. The technical solutions used to create descriptions, store them, manipulate and disseminate them need to be effective, practical and sustainable. The system that is used to catalogue an archive has important implications that the archivist needs to be aware of. Something that is often overlooked is the importance of the longevity of finding aids. Whilst the collections themselves are the most important priority for preservation, the descriptive information represents a significant investment of time and resources and is crucial for providing effective access to the archives. We should therefore ensure that descriptions are stored in a way that is secure and most likely to ensure their longevity, aside from the means that are used to enable people to access them. Users should have confidence that the descriptions accompanying the archives will continue to be available alongside the archives themselves. Creating sustainable finding aids that can continue to be accessed over time helps to overcome, to some extent, the problems of short-term funding.

Interoperability

Users have increasingly high demands relating to information retrieval. They expect resources to be available on the Web and want to be able to search easily and quickly across a whole range of resources. This can be achieved by ensuring that systems are interoperable. Interoperability can be defined as 'the ability of two or more systems or components to exchange information and to use the information that has been exchanged' (Institute of Electrical and Electronics Engineers 1990).

Interoperability relies on implementing suitable technical standards and providing good documentation. The ability for systems to interoperate is integral to the flexibility required to adapt to future developments in technology and user behaviour. If a system is highly interoperable, it is more likely to be sustainable. The ability to query a whole range of databases and other Web resources can be achieved via a number of protocols, including Z39.50, the Open Archives Initiatives Protocol for Metadata Harvesting (OAI-PMH) and Search/Retrieve via URL (SRU). The National Council on Archives produced an Interoperability Protocol in 2003 which 'seeks to provide a standard of minimum conformity and full compliance, covering data structure, content and technical matters' (NCA 2003). It recommends that standards such as ISAD(G) and EAD should map to other open encoding systems such as Dublin Core and OAI-PMH. This will create the maximum opportunities for sharing archival metadata and searching it along with other cultural heritage resources. Other means to query and retrieve data will undoubtedly be developed: the semantic web is beginning to emerge and we have initiatives underway to enable semantic searching. Implementing protocols in order to enable interoperability requires expertise, and this is the role of programmers and systems developers. For the archivist, understanding the importance of interoperability and the means to facilitate it requires an appreciation of the importance of data structure and the available protocols for cross-searching. A basic understanding of these protocols is important because they each provide different functionality.

Cataloguing Systems

Description is an area where technology has already had a great impact on professional practice, presenting the archival profession with 'the opportunity to transform archival description, to free it from the limits of the print media upon which it has been based' (Pitti 2005). When archivists first started working on a MARC standard for archives (MARC AMC) they began the move away from insular approaches to more standards-based processes: 'Archivists were forced to rethink the ways in which they recorded and presented information about their holdings, and in doing so began to collaborate and develop consensus with their colleagues' (Davis 2006).

The choice of the cataloguing system and the underlying technology used has implications for interoperability and future-proofing. There are arguments in favour of open source solutions, where the underlying code is made available and can usually be used and modified freely. This does give the advantage that the software can be simplified, features can be added and problems can be fixed. Proprietary systems still dominate the market, and most archives use proprietary systems to manage their archive collections. Many proprietary systems do provide the source code, though under restrictive licences, and they often have advantages in terms of offering support and integrated approaches to archives management. But there may be problems with backwards compatibility and with future-proofing and there are usually limitations on how the software can be modified.

Whatever software is chosen, it should provide the ability to exchange and share data between systems in ways that are seamless as far as the user is concerned. For this reason, it is important to ensure that the software provides the ability to import and export content in suitable formats, and particularly in open formats, as the format is the mode of representation of the data. An open format means that the mode of presentation of the data is transparent: 'Open formats are ordinarily standards fixed by public authorities or international institutions whose aim is to establish norms for software interoperability' (openformats.org). Maintaining the data in an open format provides a defence against the unpredictable nature of technical developments. Locking the data into a proprietary format risks making the data dependent upon that system and the company that owns the system. Systems should also support the inclusion of images and links to digital content. The ability, for example, to provide a link from the archival description to a Portable Document Format (PDF) version of a document provides a great advantage for the remote user.

XML and Encoded Archival Description

One option that has many advantages in terms of both the long-term storage of finding aids and interoperability is Extensible Markup Language (XML). Use of XML allows information to be encoded with meaningful structure and semantics that computers and humans can understand. XML is a simple, flexible format that has become widespread, and using XML for data exchange in the UK has become mandated by the e-Government Interoperability Framework (or e-GIF) <http://www.govtalk.gov.uk>. If data is stored in a text-based, structured and open format such as XML, it is likely to be far more secure and far more flexible than if it is stored in a proprietary system.

XML is a meta-language, a grammar for creating a set of rules to create markup languages. The rules are known either as a Document Type Definition (DTD) or Schema. XML has been widely embraced by business, government and academia to become the predominant markup technologies standard. Archivists have created the Encoded Archival Description DTD and Schema (see <http://www.loc.gov/ead>) as the XML application for archive descriptions. EAD originally used Standard Generalized Markup Language (SGML), and can now operate as either SGML or XML. The adoption of EAD offers all the advantages of XML: it is a portable text-based format that provides structure and gives meaning to the data through tags that can be wrapped around different parts of the finding aid to enable machines to identify the title, date, extent, scope and content, etc. This means that the data can be manipulated in many ways, providing different search options and interfaces to it, whilst maintaining the EAD document intact. EAD provides the means to connect the archival description to an electronic representation of the described material, including text, images, audio and video. In addition, formats such as HTML and PDF can be created out of EAD documents, providing appropriate versions for display on the Web and for printing out. This sort of functionality is becoming increasingly important in order to respond to growing user demand. The advantages of adopting EAD are persuasive, and it is possible to use it within a database-driven system, as this provides a suitable means to represent the characteristics of regularized and highly structured data-centric information. Increasingly, commercial database systems offer effective import and export in XML, which facilitates data exchange, as well as the advantages of management functionality and general ease of use. Ideally, EAD finding aids would be searchable using database-driven archive management software: 'It is an opportune time for archivists to begin envisioning archival description that exploits the strengths of both technologies and to continue the process of transcending the limits of traditional print media' (Pitti 2005).

The key issue in terms of archival cataloguing systems is for the archivist to make an informed choice, to think about the benefits of developing a flexible and dynamic archival descriptive system and how to achieve this, to be aware of the issues and understand the importance of enabling interoperability, or be prepared to defend a decision to adopt a system with limited interoperability. The decision made about which system to use is likely to have a long-term impact on the data and how it can be used in the future. The structure and markup used for a finding aid will have implications for how effectively users can search and for cross-searching capabilities. The time and expertise invested in creating finding aids of the highest quality will be compromised if an appropriate technical environment is not used.

I do not propose to enter into a detailed discussion of the pros and cons of different systems and software solutions here. My aim is to argue that whatever the solution chosen, it is a choice that should be made on the basis of firm foundations, with an understanding of the implications. This means that archivists need to have an awareness of issues such as interoperability and sustainability; otherwise the danger is that the choice will be ill-informed or archivists will have to rely too heavily on others with more technical knowledge but less archival understanding to make the decision for them. The archivist has expertise in terms of the management of the archive and should be ideally placed to think about the benefits of a system from both an archival point of view and from a user's point of view.

The Importance of Websites

In the dissemination of the finding aids themselves and the supporting information about the archive, we need to think about using the World Wide Web to the best advantage. The challenge that we are faced with is not just reaching remote users, but also reaching a more numerous and more diverse audience than we previously had. We clearly want to build numbers of distant users, but we need to think carefully about how to communicate with and support such users effectively. The website is increasingly becoming one of the main routes into the archives, operating almost as a virtual reading room. But whilst this analogy is useful to some extent, and can make us think about the various roles a website should play, a website does need a different approach to a physical space, where there is a sense of scale, direction and location. A physical space has physical pointers, lists, indexes, books and other resources, which are arranged in order to facilitate and guide people, and most importantly there are staff on hand to give immediate assistance that is specific to an individual's needs. We can see how people behave and how they work whilst in the reading room of the record office, and we can react to this and improve services based on observation. These physical advantages are not present on the Web, which is a conceptual space. However, the interpretive and supportive role that the archivist plays does not need to be entirely lost simply because the user is remote. It can still, to some extent, be achieved through a well-designed website and appropriately structured collection descriptions. In addition, we can make detailed analyses of online user behaviour and provide a range of support mechanisms so that the online experience is just as rewarding for the user as a visit to the record office.

One of the biggest influences on Web searching behaviours has been the advance of search engines, and most particularly the Google search engine. Increasingly people come to websites through the use of free text searching, and therefore many of them have little or no prior knowledge of the existence or role of archive repositories and are not familiar with the website that they land on. Typically, people glance at each new page, scan some of the text and click on a link that catches their eye or seems closest to the thing that they are looking for. There are usually large parts of a webpage that they never look at: 'Skimming instead of reading is a fact of the Web, and it's been confirmed by countless usability studies. Those who write for the Web must acknowledge this fact and write for scannability' (Nielsen 1999).

Of course, the way that a user sees a webpage depends a great deal on what they have in mind; they may have a definite interest in finding archival sources, or they may just be interested in finding out about a topic and have no particular awareness of archives. For this reason, one of the most important elements in designing an effective website is user testing, as this helps us to appreciate how our users interact with the site. User testing reminds us that not everyone thinks in the same way, starts from the same knowledge base, or uses the Web in the same way.

We should be aiming to keep people engaged with the website and ensure that they find what they are looking for. Visitors to the website will want to know what it is for, whether it is relevant to them and what it enables them to do, and they will want to know this quickly, without having to make too much effort. The site should be as self-explanatory as possible, enabling those with little experience of or understanding of archives to use it successfully, whilst at the same time catering for those with particular interests and requirements. This means that the site needs to be well designed and instantly engaging. It is important to consider the organization of information, the content, functionality, navigation and usability, all of which is often referred to as the 'information architecture' of the website.

When implementing an information architecture there are many features that may be considered and integrated into the site in order to make it more usable and appealing. The homepage is the most important page on the website and should be focused and clear, setting out the nature of the archive institution and the value of the site. Other useful features may include a new users' section, finding appealing and imaginative ways to explain and promote archives, a simple quick search for those who want a straightforward search option and advanced search capabilities for those experienced users who want to carry out more specific searches. The site can provide a site map to help users visualize the structure of the space and navigation that shows the location of a page in the site hierarchy. It can provide more visual content, such as an online exhibition to showcase the rich and diverse holdings of the archive, and it can provide a glossary or other more interactive means to explain archival terms and hierarchical catalogues. The content is likely to be written by the archive professional, yet this is a skill that can be neglected; all too often we do not write content that is appropriate for an online environment, where users tend to scan the page quickly and 'click on the first link that catches their interest or vaguely resembles the thing that they are looking for' (Krug, 2000). There is a danger of providing too much information, cluttering the page with text that users will never read and may find off-putting. In general, content should be precise and broken down into sections with appropriate headings and meaningful linking text. If the site is well designed, with a robust information architecture and carefully considered content, the effect can be substantial. The website is the all important context for the descriptions of archives that we provide, and it is important to ensure that it is effective, usable and accessible.

Finding Aids on the Web

Providing effective access to collections involves the creation of effective finding aids, from brief collection descriptions to full catalogue descriptions with index terms, so we need to think about the finding aids that we create, the ways that we structure the data to make it useful to users and the ways that we then disseminate these finding aids. Archivists have a great deal of experience of cataloguing within a traditional environment, but we now have to ensure that the descriptions that we provide are appropriate for an online environment, and are made to work as hard as possible to reach the widest audience. If technology is harnessed effectively it can be of enormous benefit in this task. We need to think about both the creation of finding aids and the ways in which we can make them available. Finding aids that are suitable for the Web should be appropriately structured for remote searching in terms of the language used, field titles, consistency and general structure. They should be self-explanatory, as the user will not have the archivist on hand to help them interpret the information.

Whilst the website created by the archive institution may provide an important means to access finding aids, as well as plenty of help and contextual information, the future of information retrieval is likely to be in flexible access to a whole range of data sources, so descriptions should be written with a view to facilitating cross-searching. Even if the institution does not have immediate plans to enable cross-searching, it is imperative to create descriptions with interoperability in mind, as this provides the best means to future-proof descriptions. Facilitating cross-searching requires an awareness of protocols, as previously discussed in this chapter, and it also depends upon adherence to data standards. Following widely adopted standards for data creation and structure, and using controlled sources for data where appropriate, will facilitate the development of cross-searching systems.

The skills for website design are in understanding the benefits of a good web architecture, consistent navigation, clear and concise writing, short sections of text, meaningful hyperlinks, good use of colour and spacing and knowing how to design a site that is accessible to people with disabilities. The skills for enabling interoperability are in an awareness of protocols and the importance of data structure and data standards. In essence, the archivist needs to ensure that there is an engaging, usable and accessible website and provide finding aids that are sustainable and suitable for those using the website and those accessing the descriptions remotely, maybe whilst cross-searching a whole range of data sources. However, given the competing demands on the time of the archivist, the most practical approach to this is likely to be for the archivist to work with web designers, web usability experts and IT staff to achieve these goals. For this to be a successful collaboration the archivist still needs to have informed input into the process, in order to ensure that the site functions effectively and the needs of the users are being met. If we relinquish control of the architecture of the website, we are in danger of presenting a website that does not effectively represent the functions of the record office or archive service, therefore an understanding of the principles of good web design are very valuable. If we introduce a cataloguing system but do not ensure that we are fully aware of cross-searching and import/export possibilities then we run the risk of spending time and effort populating a closed system. This can be disastrous if the software vendor goes out of business, as transferring data to a new system will be expensive and time-consuming at best, and in some cases highly problematic if not practically impossible. As well as working with experts in Web technologies, it also pays to use the Web extensively, be aware of sites that are well designed and popular and think about our own good and bad experiences of different websites.

The Changing Web

Users may be accessing the Web through traditional computers, but they just could as easily be using a pen-based, hand-held device, a mobile phone or another portable device. This makes it increasingly important to understand how to design webpages for different screens. As well as the devices, the ways of behaving on the Web are changing. The current tendency is to take a more open, collaborative and social approach, and this is likely to be a continuing trend. Archivists can take advantage of this by looking at different kinds of engagement and communication with users. This participatory approach is characterized by the appearance of a myriad of lightweight tools and applications, many of which are widely used, particularly amongst the younger generation. The term that has come to be used to describe this is 'Web 2.0', coined by O'Reilly Media (see O'Reilly 2005). It has given rise to a whole host of services and tools such as blogs, wikis, social bookmarking, podcasts and syndication feeds. Whilst the term 'Web 2.0' may be a buzzword, and may not remain in common parlance, and indeed the definition of it is open to debate, the behaviours characterized by this concept, and in particular the increasingly participatory nature of the Web, are likely to stay with us. The software, services and tools associated with Web 2.0 are changing the way people think about and use the Web. If we want to use the Web effectively, it is essential to be involved and engaged in this process. New developments are inevitably surrounded by hype, but what is important is the evidence of changes in user behaviour and user expectations. This may be part of the process of the Web maturing: a growing proportion of the population has grown up with the Web and therefore they may view it in a different light from those who have operated in a pre-Web world.

The opportunities to communicate with users and reach new audiences are tremendous, but we will need to take a flexible approach, to understand what users want and to be prepared to change the ways that we work if appropriate. Taking advantage of many of the newer developments on the Web requires the host or creator of the data to relinquish control to some extent, bypassing the concept of the 'professional' as the gatekeeper and controller of their data. The rise of user-driven initiatives and user-controlled or user-generated content is a fundamental shift which is likely to affect the way that we position ourselves in relation to users. We need to open up our data and enable users to have flexible access not only to our descriptions but also information about our services, such as opening times, location, events, training courses and so on, so that they can make use of the information in ways that suit them. I have already discussed the need to think about providing interfaces for machines to access data, which is of central importance, but there are other possibilities for us to promote our services and archives in addition to cross-searching using standard protocols. For example, many users take advantage of personalized homepage services such as Netvibes, Pageflakes and Google homepage. These particular services may not prove to be persistent, but the principle remains that users are increasingly looking to bring the services that they use together into their own environment, and therefore it is incumbent on us to meet these user preferences. If they have open systems, archives can create the means for users to search their collections via this sort of route, enabling the user to place a search facility within their own customized environment. Another possibility that can promote flexibility is the use of microformats, which are open data standards that provide structured, semantic information that can then be re-used in different ways. 'Designed for humans first and machines second, microformats are a set of simple, open data formats built upon existing and widely adopted standards' (microformats. org). The idea of microformats is to make information adapt more readily to people's behaviours whilst keeping things as simple as possible; it is a relatively small step to add microformat markup to existing content, such as to opening times or details of training courses, and this enables the information to be incorporated into other applications. Microformats, personalized homepages and other Web innovations will continue to develop and change over time, so we need to continually assess what is available and what is most beneficial to users, and to ensure that we are working to take advantage of these innovations whilst balancing this against the other competing priorities of our roles and responsibilities.

User-generated content is something that is particularly relevant to archive services, as it is a means to encourage users to become more engaged with archives. We can now provide the facility for users to add content to archive descriptions, enabling us to take advantage of their knowledge and experience. Whilst allowing users to modify our carefully constructed descriptions may be seen as rather too radical, it is perfectly feasible to enable identifiable additions to be made, or simply allow users to add comments, so that the description itself remains under the control of the creator, and the user-generated content is clearly indicated as such. This provides a great opportunity to make users feel involved whilst also enriching the metadata provided about our archive collections. Examples of this type of participatory environment include the 'Your Archives' section of the UK National Archives website (<http://yourarchives.nationalarchives.gov.uk>) and the Polar Bear Expedition Digital Collections, based at the University of Michigan (<http://polarbears.si.umich.edu/>). Providing this sort of service is not without issues, in particular the risks of allowing unvalidated content to be added and the time involved in checking user additions. However, it is something that many websites now provide and it is certainly worth careful consideration. As far as the archivist is concerned, it is something to be aware of and to discuss with technical colleagues, looking at the implications of providing such a facility and possible methods of implementation.

As well as a more open attitude to the data that we provide to users of archives, archivists can also move towards sharing other resources more freely. There are now a number of websites that offer the advantages of sharing resources with others, including sites for sharing images, slides, audio presentations and bookmarks. Putting slides for a presentation on your own site is useful, but it means that people have to visit your site to find them. Putting them on a website along with thousands of other slides means that people can cross-search, tag their favourites and recommend them to others. Equally, social bookmarking allows others to benefit from the bookmarks that you have created. It is important to be aware of the benefits of these social sites and, conversely, of the rights that the website provider may have over your resources if you put them on the site.

It can be difficult to know how far to become engaged with new technologies, and which ones to adopt when developments are so fast-paced. However, there are some advantages to Web 2.0-type tools and services when compared to the more familiar large-scale systems that have been more prevalent up to now. These tools are generally fairly lightweight and user-friendly and designed for people to pick up and use easily and quickly. This is a relative statement, of course, as what is easy for one person is not necessarily so straightforward for another, but in general this type of functionality can be introduced in a relatively short time and without too much technical knowledge. The key to engaging with new technologies is to experiment, to try things out, to sign up to social networks and to look at and use sites for sharing resources. A balance needs to be struck between the time and resources invested in a new feature or new service and the expected benefits that may come from it. What is most important is that archivists are aware of how people are accessing and using information and alive to the possibilities that are available. We need to stay in touch with the ways in which the Web is being used.

The Need to Make Informed Decisions

In the first section of this essay I have looked at the importance of engaging with users via the most appropriate tools and technologies available and of taking an informed approach to the selection and implementation of software and systems. However, it is clear that the majority of archivists do not see themselves as technical and many archivists would not see their roles as being technical other than in a most basic sense of using a computer and working with the front-end of software systems, such as archival management software.

It is understandable that we sometimes feel nervous about engaging with technology and often a little defensive about our lack of knowledge. It easy to be overwhelmed by the dizzying array of applications, formats, systems, standards and protocols that are available. The variety of technical solutions on offer can be problematic, and with so much choice it becomes very difficult to know what to investigate, what to use and what to ignore. When thinking about choosing a cataloguing or management system, for example, it becomes tempting to take the path of least resistance, adopting a proprietary solution that on the face of it promises to do everything that the archivist requires. Equally, there is a danger that the archivist relies too heavily on technical staff to make decisions that require technical awareness. It is not ideal to implement technical solutions where the archivist is ignorant of the pros and cons of the system, the data formats, the capacity for interoperability and the level of future-proofing. So, whilst it is tempting to avoid engagement with technology, this is simply not a tenable position. We need to see the potential of technology as something enabling and liberating and realize that we must engage with it and use it effectively. If we accept that we need some level of technical knowledge to make informed decisions, the issue is then what that level actually is and how we reach it.

Clearly archivists do not need to be, and are unlikely to want to become, highly technical; we do not need to become programmers or software developers. But we do need to be in a position to ensure that this type of work is carried out in a way that is suitable, appropriate and relevant for our aims and for the benefit of our users. We need to play our part, and this requires a level of knowledge appropriate to engage with technology and talk about technical options in ways that can further our goals. We need to be able to enter into dialogues about the merits and drawbacks of using particular systems and services. We may achieve this by a combination of education, training, networking, sharing ideas and information and by ensuring that we have good working relationships with technical colleagues.

Archival Education

There are no widely agreed standards for archival education, but it seems reasonable to assert that a central aim is to build disciplined thinking, based on a firm theoretical knowledge, whilst at the same time connecting learning with the skills that employers require. A key role of the educator is to 'form the mind to the ways of thinking and awareness that will allow the learner to adapt to new circumstances' (Eastwood 2006). The learner needs to feel confident in adapting to meet the changing needs of the profession and of the users. An archive course may provide firm foundations for the student, both theoretical and practical, but it is in the workplace that the skills are developed.

A report by the Society of American Archivists' Task Force on Goals and Priorities back in 1986 urged archivists to develop programs to encourage the use of archival records, to disseminate information about holdings and to increase accessibility. Terry Eastwood describes this area as one of the weakest in archival science: 'Obviously, there are enormous opportunities to facilitate access to and accessibility of archival material in the digital environment, so there is much that educators can do to prepare students with a solid understanding of information technology and its application to these archival processes' (Eastwood 2006).

Archival educators must surely have a role in helping archive students to fully realize the potential of technologies. However, as the range of tasks that archivists take on becomes broader, the challenge to archival education increases. Archivists now have very diverse roles in local and national government, businesses, charities and institutions. The changing role of the modern archivist is reflected in the fact that there are now archivists who do not work with physical collections at all, but who specialize in the gathering, structuring, presentation and dissemination of data for services such as the UK Archives Hub (<www.archiveshub.ac.uk>) and A2A (<www.a2a.org.uk>). Increasingly, some of the more traditional aspects of archival education are less relevant to many archivists in the workplace. An archival education programme may seek to cover a very broad range of themes, from the core professional principles of archives and records management and the importance of records as evidence through to the processes of appraisal, cataloguing and preservation and the use of communication and information technology. The course may well provide a good grounding in archival theory and literacy in a general sense, but if we want to achieve levels of excellence within an increasingly complex environment, we may need to introduce more specialization and move away from the idea of a single profession: 'One key way to cope with an overloaded archival curriculum is to focus on the pressing priorities of the archive profession rather than to stretch and dilute the curriculum to prepare students to become either archivists or records managers or to try to create a single record keeping profession' (Nesmith 2007).

Records management is probably the most obvious example of where specialization may occur. An archive course can provide enough understanding of records management to enable archivists and records managers to communicate effectively, and may produce successful records managers, as the skills required are not dissimilar. However, courses are in danger of becoming increasingly broad and less effectual if we continue to educate students to become record keepers in the most general sense.

The new Information Management and Preservation programme offered by the University of Glasgow, for example, enables students to choose between the digital strand and the archives and records management strand. The core courses that are common to both provide the basic information management components. The emphasis with this course has shifted firmly away from the historic and interpretive elements of a more traditional archives course. This digital strand is about digital curation rather than about the use of technology in the broader sense that this chapter is describing. However, the salient point is that this course is intending to meet the needs of a changing information society and is likely to attract students with a greater interest in technology, and, most importantly, students more willing to embrace technology and use it to the best advantage.

Providing a substantial technical component is probably not appropriate for an archive course, and not practical given the time constraints, but in a rapidly changing environment, the aim of archival education must be to provide the archivist with an understanding of the digital landscape and, probably more importantly, a mindset willing to embrace change and continually learn and adapt to the practical demands of the digital information age. If we do not achieve this, the danger is that there will be an increasing gap between the ways that people work, behave and communicate in the information age and the ways that archivists operate and disseminate information. Equally, the role of the archivist in this area may be taken over by others without archival skills: 'Without an extended academic base, then the job market, with its diversity and range, will be hijacked by non record-keepers, without any natural affinity with the principles of record-keeping' (Procter 2005).

If we, as archivists, do not seek to meet the needs of researchers, with their demands for greater functionality, greater personalization and integration, we may lose this dissemination role altogether. Archival education must play a part in this, co-evolving with changing research and learning behaviours in a new network space.

Workplace Development and Networking

A postgraduate archive course can only play a part in equipping archivists for the technical challenges of the 21st century. It is in the workplace that archivists need to build upon this by continuing their professional development, and indeed it is here that archivists will move from the necessarily more generic archival training to the particulars and specializations of a work role. Education and skill building can be through a combination of networking, training and collaboration.

The rise of digital technologies has, to some extent, brought archives closer to libraries and museums, and indeed to other information professions, in terms of the knowledge and skills required in these areas. Whilst the distinctive theoretical and skills base of archival science is appropriate for core skills relating to record selection, appraisal and administration of archives, we can take advantage of the convergence of the archive, library and museum domains within the virtual environment by learning from others and sharing ideas and innovations. Indeed, in this area of work we can take advantage of initiatives across the broader information community, as we have a common aim of improved communication and effective information dissemination. We should look to take advantage of the support offered and the work being undertaken by centres of expertise in digital technologies and information and communication technology. By collaborating across sectors, we can ensure that we take advantage of initiatives and implement common solutions using common standards. This will work in favour of our users, as they are not generally concerned with the source of the information, whether it is from an archive or library or other repository, but with access to a broad range of information.

The rise of the participatory and social Web may aid us in increasing collaboration and communication with others, taking advantage of wikis, blogs and social networks for online discussion and collaboration. Many services utilize user-generated content, Wikipedia being a notable example, and we can engage with these as users ourselves and ensure that archives are represented on them. By taking advantage of discussions and developments happening across the cultural and heritage sectors, and more broadly in the area of information dissemination, archivists can be involved and be seen to take an active part in this 'community'.

The opportunities for self-learning and shared learning can be combined with training courses that offer a more structured approach to building useful and practical skills. In this area of work we can take advantage of training offered outside of the archive community, rather than being locked into the idea of keeping within our traditional boundaries, and this will ensure that we benefit from the perspectives and experiences of others.

Relationship to Technical Colleagues

Education and professional development can increase the technical awareness of the archivist, but we are still primarily focused on an archival rather than a technical role. We are primarily concerned with the creation, organization and dissemination of data in ways that reflect the content and context of the archives themselves. We need to work with programmers and systems developers to implement technical solutions. It is therefore increasingly crucial that archivists work effectively with these technical colleagues in selecting and developing software, establishing and maintaining a Web presence and disseminating information. We need to see the archives and the technical implementations that we adopt as integral to each other, and this can be achieved by better communication and collaboration with relevant colleagues, taking advantage of the expertise that each party brings to the table. We should work towards a level of mutual understanding so that we can communicate effectively and make choices that take advantage of both archival and technical expertise.

This relationship is analogous to the kind of relationship that archivists have built up with conservators. Whilst the two are clearly separate professions, archivists need to appreciate the issues involved in conserving records and understand the importance of archival storage and environmental controls. We do not see this knowledge as outside of our domain because it is so important to ensure the physical security of archives. Archivists may undertake a certain amount of basic conservation work, but it is conservators who have the detailed, specialist knowledge of conservation. We need to work together to ensure that the physical needs of the archive are properly addressed, and this is the sort of relationship that we should be developing with technical staff.

The New Technical Archivist

There can be no doubt that the traditional skills of the archivist continue to be essential as, whatever the medium, all archives need to be effectively managed, and this requires the ability to select, appraise, catalogue and manage the archives. The demands of the digital age impose new challenges on the archivist and require new skills, and this is problematic when we are already over-stretched and often under-resourced.

The levels of technical knowledge described in this chapter require skills and knowledge that can only be learnt over time and through experience. But with the increasing need for the archivist to cover such broad areas of work, what we may see is the rise of a specialist technical archivist with particular skills, working towards interoperability, maximizing the profile of the archive through the Web presence, looking at new technologies and ensuring as far as possible and practicable that the archive keeps up to date with user behaviours. If the archive profession does not address this need to change and adapt to meet the needs of the new information society, we run the risk of being sidelined in this most crucial area of work. Archivists must avoid the danger of remaining in silos where they are not playing a full and active part in the evolving online world.

References

Anderson, C. (2006), *The Long Tail* (London: Hyperion).

Davis, S.E. (2006), 'How twenty-five people shook the archival world: the case of descriptive standards', *Journal of Archival Organization*, 4 (3/4), 46.

Eastwood, T. (2006), 'Building archival knowledge and skills in the digital age', *Archival Science*, 6, 163–70.

e-GIF, GovTalk, Information on policies and standards for e-government, at <http://www.govtalk.gov.uk/schemasstandards/egif.asp> accessed September 2007.

Institute of Electrical and Electronics Engineers (1990), *IEEE Standard Computer Dictionary: A Compilation of IEEE Standard Computer Glossaries* (New York: IEEE).

Krug, S. (2000), *Don't Make Me Think: a Common Sense Approach to Web Usability* (Indianapolis IN: New Riders).

The Library of Congress, Encoded Archival Description (EAD), version 2002, official site at <http://www.loc.gov/ead/ead.html> accessed September 2007.

microformats, at < http://microformats.org> (homepage) accessed September 2007.

Museums Libraries and Archives Council (2004), *Listening to the Past, Speaking to the Future: the Report of the Archives Task Force*, Annex G: Archives Workforce Study (London: MLA).

National Council on Archives (NCA) Interoperability Working Group (2003), 'Interoperability protocol', at <http://www.ncaonline.org.uk/materials/interoperabilityprotocol.pdf> accessed November 2007.

Nesmith. T. (2007), 'What is an archival educator?', *Journal of the Society of Archivists*, 28 (1), 8.

Nielsen, J. (1999), *Designing Web Usability: the Practice of Simplicity* (Indianapolis IN: New Riders).

O'Reilly, T. (2005), 'What is Web 2.0?', at <http://www.oreillynet.com/pub/a/oreilly/tim/news/2005/09/30/what-is-web-20.html> accessed September 2007.

openformats.org, 'Open vs proprietary formats', at <http://www.openformats.org> accessed September 2007.

Pitti, D. (2005), 'Technology and the transformation of archival description', *Journal of Archival Organization*, 3 (2/3), 21.

Procter, M. (2005), 'On the crest of a wave or swimming against the tide? Professional education in an information-conscious society', *Journal of the Society of Archivists*, 26 (1), 70.

Society of American Archivists (1986), *Task Force on Goals and Priorities, Planning for the Archival Profession: a Report of the SAA Task Force on Goals and Priorities* (Chicago IL: Society of American Archivists).

University of Glasgow and HATII, MSc in Information Management and Preservation, at <http://www.hatii.arts.gla.ac.uk/imp/> accessed September 2007.

Theme III
The Impact of Community Archives

Chapter 6

Other Ways of Thinking, Other Ways of Being. Documenting the Margins and the Transitory: What to Preserve, How to Collect

Andrew Flinn

Only the successful (in the sense of those whose aspirations anticipated subsequent evolution) are remembered. The blind alleys, the lost causes, and the losers are forgotten … I am seeking to rescue the poor stockinger, the Luddite cropper, the 'obsolete' hand-loom weaver, the utopian artisan and even the deluded follower of Joanna Southcott, from the enormous condescension of posterity (Thompson 1981, 12).

The globalised Web has become the most potent weapon in the toolbox of resistance to globalism and the rampant free market (Tony Juniper, Friends of the Earth, quoted in Vidal 1999).

Introduction

If the spectre of communism haunted Europe in the nineteenth and twentieth centuries, other internationalisms now disturb the world. Globalization and its allied 'discontents' are global phenomena which provoke transnational anti-globalization protest and resistance. Both the advocates of globalization and its opponents have embraced the Internet and the digital world to communicate, exchange ideas and information and to mobilize support. The growth of such global oppositional movements and their inherent relationship with digital technologies pose a significant and paradigmatic challenge for the archival profession.

Since the 1950s and 1960s large numbers of people have expressed their commitment to political and social change via an array of single-issue campaign groups, non-governmental organizations (NGOs) and new social movements (NSMs). This commitment has been expressed either in addition to or increasingly instead of participation in orthodox party political organizations. Most notably these have included the peace movement, the women's movement, environmental activism, human rights and anti-poverty campaigns, Third World solidarity and a commitment to equal and sustainable development (Byrne 1997). Since the 1990s these organizations have continued to fracture and proliferate, often adopting the Web as an essential tool for transnational organizing and mobilizing. Some of these groups, though by no means all, have chosen to oppose neo-liberalism and globalism as part of a loose coalition, an anti-globalization movement.

Like previous social movements, these groups are extremely diverse and often differ fundamentally on questions of tactics and ideology but also frequently share a fluid, often spontaneous and non-hierarchical structure, with members cohering around a single or narrowly defined set of issues. These 'loose coalitions, semi-spontaneous mobilizations and ad hoc movements of the neo-anarchist brand' have embraced the Web because their fluidity, horizontal organizing and global interests are reflected in the way the Internet operates:

> The novelty is their networking via the Internet, because it allows the movement to be diverse and co-ordinated at the same time ... The anti-globalisation movement is not simply a network, it is an electronic network, it is an Internet-based movement. And because the Internet is its home it cannot be disorganised or captured (Castells 2002, 140, 142).

The traditional credo of these social movements and campaigns was 'Think Globally, Act Locally' but, as Castells (2002, 143) points out, the impact of online transnational networking has also been to encourage activists to 'Think Locally, Act Globally'.

What should archivists do to document these movements? This may appear an irrelevant problem to those who believe that these movements are beyond the scope of the traditional archival mission. But like Thompson's 'lost causes', many of these movements seek to organize and represent the marginalized and the alternative, the periphery against the centre, the global South versus the global North and in doing so articulate alternative viewpoints to otherwise dominant ideologies and elites. Indeed in the case of environmental and peace movements these ideas are part of the mainstream even if they are not always reflected in the policies of national governments and political parties. The (often digital) traces of these campaigns and networks, as well as other non-elite, non-institutional communities and groups, therefore represent a significant strand in any vision of a more representative, collective social memory and so should not be overlooked or ignored (Logan, 2005).

The principal issue that this chapter seeks to explore is the responsibility of archivists for ensuring that their collections more fully represent all within society, including those from the periphery and the margins and those with alternative or unorthodox opinions, and not just dominant and institutional elements. Taking this responsibility seriously requires archivists to acknowledge their role as active agents in the process of collecting and constructing archival heritage, reliance on passive accumulation or serendipity being particularly unsustainable in this context. In practice this means archivists intervening proactively within a national and perhaps international framework to identify and support the preservation of contemporary collections for future use.

While this article focuses on the records of anti-globalization activists, it could just as equally apply to a whole range of other under-represented groups or cultures. Nor should archivists in their consideration of the justifications for selection and preservation give too much weight to crude measures of the marginality or otherwise of the opinions held by particular groups. Clearly archivists cannot in any way effectively predict which ideas will move into the mainstream in the future nor which of the 'blind alleys, the lost causes, and the losers' will be of interest to future historians or wider society. We should not be too concerned with reflecting success and failure, dominance and marginality within contemporary discourses. Ideas and concepts once considered to be on the fringe often move to the centre of political discourse within a matter of only a few years – witness, for instance, the mainstreaming of identity politics and environmental concerns in recent times. Other once-popular and commonplace attitudes can move in the other direction, becoming more marginal though still being held and articulated by significant minorities. It is the existence of such ideas and the organizations that articulate them that should be of interest and make them worthy of collection, not necessarily the crude numbers who adhere to them. It should not be the responsibility of today's archive profession to decide by omission which ideas and which campaigns should be consigned to the 'condescension of posterity'.

I have argued elsewhere why, from historiographical, democratic and public policy perspectives, the process of seeking to diversify and transform archival collections should be seen as a vital endeavour (Flinn 2007), so this chapter will re-state those arguments only briefly before going on to examine what this democratization might mean for professional practice. Specifically this means considering how archivists might seek to collect the records created by the many groups and individuals who live and organize (sometimes deliberately) on the margins of society and its institutions. The chapter will further examine how the implications of this collecting, both in terms of the technical challenges and the practical professional duties, means that the archive profession must focus increasingly outwards from its repositories and into partnerships with information technology and digital curation experts, and with community and campaigning organizations.

Thirty years on, the need for 'active archivists' and the rejection of archival passivity and narrow selection and collection models which continue to privilege local, national and international elites is as urgent as ever (Ham 1975; Green 2002, 48). Although many archival traces are there to be harvested, the fragility and transitory nature of digital resources means there is no scope for passivity or complacency (Ross 2000). Failure to act will not only impoverish the archival resources available to future historians and others, but will also, in the words of the President of the Society of American Archivists, Richard Pearce-Moses (2007, 16, 22), represent a serious failure in 'our social mandate of preserving the cultural record'.

Inevitably this discussion must also consider problems concerning resources, skills and responsibilities for this work. The latter is perhaps the biggest question of all. Who should be responsible for ensuring that the memory of our society and the archives which store a part of that memory are as comprehensive and representative of the whole of society as possible? Brewster Kahle, founder of the Internet Archive recently suggested that it might be possible to preserve almost everything online in distributed repositories with multiple copies located across the world, although this could only be achieved as a result of a 'large-scale societal effort' and commitment (Kahle 2007, 24). Even if the preservation of the totality of the world's archives is not realizable, the endeavour to create a more diverse and representative archival heritage also requires serious and sustained 'societal effort'. We cannot rely only on national archives services and other national institutions to fulfil this role, although these bodies often do valuable work in terms of practical initiatives and guidance, and perhaps could and should give an even stronger lead in this regard. Some responsibility must also fall on those who work in other public archives as well as many who operate in specialist and non-governmental repositories.

Filling the Gaps and Representing Society?

How then should archivists respond to the gaps or absences in formal, mainstream archives, especially in governmental archives where institutional, administrative and organizational forms are privileged over the citizen and, in particular, over the unorthodox? Active interventions to address these gaps generally take two complementary forms. First, initiatives to revisit and re-describe existing archive collections, whilst necessarily time-consuming, can reveal much that was previously hidden or unremarked in previous descriptions. Second, efforts can be made to ensure collection policies and preservation strategies are more representative and seek to include those on the margins and the periphery and not just the state and the mainstream. In the past this has often meant supporting and perhaps initiating oral history projects and the like but it also means seeking out new contacts and establishing relationships with individuals and non-governmental groups to open up the possibility of preserving and making new collections available. These approaches are practical and important, and there are many examples of both re-description and active collection, though they tend to be local and ad hoc rather than something implemented on a sustained, national basis. Nevertheless their impact can be significant (Flinn 2007, 162–4).

Preserving materials which enable the production of more diverse and inclusive 'thick description' histories, as pioneered by Raphael Samuel following the anthropologist Clifford Geertz, is obviously significant in historiographical terms but it has also implications from public history and public policy perspectives. Exclusions from the national story often reflect broader disenfranchisements in society but conversely the production of genuinely multifaceted and inclusive histories which recount the shared stories of all might also reflect and contribute to more cohesive societies (MCAAH 2005, 10; Hall 2005; Flinn 2007, 159–62).

There are clear resonances here with what are sometimes referred to as Community Archives but this chapter will not dwell on such initiatives as they have been addressed, in the UK at least, by a number of recent contributions to the *Journal of the Society of Archivists* (Flinn 2007, Hopkins forthcoming 2008; Gray forthcoming 2008) and are the focus of ongoing research at University College London (see 'Community Archives and Identities: Documenting and Sustaining Community Heritage', funded by the Arts and Humanities Research Council, at <https://www.ucl.ac.uk/slais/research/icarus/community-archives/>). Instead, this chapter will examine the records of new social movements and campaigning groups with particular reference to how these groups are using the Web and other digital tools to organize, campaign and communicate. Nevertheless it is important to reiterate that, while these are good examples of significant materials and of the problems raised by seeking to preserve and collect them, such challenges are not in any sense unique. One could easily substitute these groups with almost any other community or interest groups and make many if not all the same points with regard to the professional challenges and responsibilities that collecting their records pose.

Organizing, Campaigning and Inhabiting a Digital World

> ... the Net is more than an organising tool – it has become an organising model, a blueprint for decentralised but cooperative decision making. It facilitates the process of information sharing to such a degree that many groups can work in concert with one another without the need to achieve monolithic consensus (which is often impossible, anyway, given the nature of activist organizations). And because it is so decentralised, these movements are still in the process of forging links with their various wings around the world, continually surprising themselves with how far unreported little victories have travelled, how thoroughly bits of research have been recycled and absorbed (Klein 2000, 396).

Since Naomi Klein's *No Logo* was published, the numbers of activists and campaigning groups using the Internet and Web-based applications at the heart of their activities have continued to rise. In common with many other organizations, these campaigning groups and networks have recognized the Web as a powerful tool for organizing and mobilizing like-minded individuals locally, nationally and even internationally. Recognition of the utility of the Web for campaigning activities has not just been confined to the large and longer-established political organizations and trade unions. Indeed many of these organizations were slow to realize the opportunities offered by digital technologies and initially tended to use the Web to replicate their traditional communication and organizing techniques (Norris 2001, 21). By contrast the smaller, more autonomous campaigning activist groups (of the left and the radical right) tended to be early and innovative adopters of the Web in their activities. Both Castells and Norris identify human rights, women's, environmental, labour, religious and peace movement groups as being amongst the most active and prominent users of the Web for campaigning purposes, enabling 'mobilizing, publicity and interaction', often on a transnational, global scale.

In the mid-1990s one of the first movements to come to wide public attention was the Zapatista movement from Chiapas in Mexico. The Zapatistas and their supporters made effective use of the Internet and other electronic communications to circumvent traditional media channels and directly address and build a global support network for what was essentially a regional conflict (Castells 2002, 138; Norris 2001, 21, 171). By the beginning of the 21st century such was the range and variety of social movements and other campaigning groups on the Web that Norris likened it to 'a virtual Hyde Park Corner where a plurality of multiple actors can and do find opportunities to network, organise and express their viewpoints' (Norris 2001, 190). Among the most dynamic and significant examples of these global radical networks are the World Social Forums (<http://www.forumsocialmundial. org.br>) and the various local and regional Social Forums. These networks bring together virtually and in physical meetings different radical groups with many varying interests under the banner 'Another world is possible'. Similar initiatives and interactions between real and virtual campaigning are to be found in the campaigns to build an international consensus against the war in Iraq and the war on terror (Carty and Onyett 2006).

Those protesting against globalization and the global exploitation of workers and resources realized at an early stage that the global exchange of information upon which much of the pro-globalization rhetoric rested was also a tool for opposing and organizing against globalization. The Web and newer web-based collaborative technologies allowed these movements and networks, usually widely distributed, loosely-formed, horizontally organized and often profoundly ideologically non-hierarchical, to disseminate information, news and tactics across regional and national boundaries in ways that did not just circumvent traditional media and governmental structures but actually out-manoeuvred them and challenged their legitimacy: 'Hierarchical communication channels, typical in bureaucratic organizations like government departments and international agencies, are less effective and slower mechanisms of information transmission than horizontal networks shared by informal coalitions of alternative social movements' (Norris 2001, 20).

However, for many of these groups, in particular those networks who wished to organize or campaign on an international basis against multinationals or to mobilize against the war in Iraq, the Web was more than just a tool for the independent dissemination of information, it was also central to their organizing and mobilizing strategies and was even a site for inventive political action and protest itself (Rolfe 2005; Carty and Onyett 2006).

Among early and innovative users of the Internet in 1990s were anti-corporation groups such as Stop Esso, the Boycott Nestlé campaign, the anti-Nike activists' Global Exchange and other anti-sweatshop movements (Carty 2002). One of the most influential campaigns in this regard, both in terms of the content and the role that the website played was the McLibel Support Campaign which supported Helen Steel and David Morris's defence against the McDonald's libel writ for distributing the leaflet 'What's wrong with McDonald's'. The McSpotlight website was launched in 1996 and quickly became well known amongst anti-globalization activists and others worldwide as the site for information about the case and the coordination of local actions across the UK and the world. Crucially the site also developed as a notice-board and portal for information about and links to other similar campaigns on the Web, as a network and discussion forum bringing together dispersed but otherwise like-minded individuals and as a source, most tellingly, for the unhindered downloading and worldwide dissemination of the original and very low-circulation London Greenpeace leaflet over which McDonald's originally had sued. In 1998 included among the many hundreds of sites McSpotlight pointed to were ones supporting anarchist politics, animal rights, anti-nuclear campaigns, climate change and environment issues, civil liberties and human rights campaigns, corporate watch organizations, direct action campaigns, first nations, left-wing socialist and labour organizations, independent and alternative media organizations and anti-poverty campaigns (Vidal 1997, 177–8, 326).

Subsequently the Web helped to enable the formation of transnational networks and global coalitions of many of these groups into a significant international movement directed against global capitalism and its institutions. The scale of developments were first discerned clearly at a national UK level with the coordinated disturbances in the City of London in June 1999 and then more significantly in the international demonstrations in Seattle in December 1999. In Seattle, the size of the protests and the breadth of the assembled coalition, which included NGOs, labour unions, religious groups and direct action groups coordinated by the Direct Action Network (DAN), took the authorities by surprise and closed down the scheduled meeting of the World Trade Organization (see the pictures and the diary entries posted by Stephanie Zimmerman at World Trade Organization – Seattle Protests, <http://www.zmedia.org/WTO>). These events, at least partly coordinated through the Internet and then documented in real time by new independent and alternative media structures such as the Seattle Independent Media Centre, kick-started a series of international anti-globalization protests in Washington, Prague and Genoa and the establishment of a global movement of alternative online media outlets (<www.indymedia.org>; Castells 2002, 141–42; Della Porta and Diani 2006, 163–5, 193–7).

These campaigns were very high-profile and sought to harness the Internet to mobilize and connect internationally, but other campaigns and groups, including localized and autonomous environmental networks such as Reclaim the Streets and Earth First!, also used the Internet, e-mail, chat rooms and (more recently) blogs, text and instant messaging from the mid-1990s onwards to organize locally. Of particular interest was the use of technology to coordinate acts of civil disobedience which resulted in the rapid mobilization of people (flash mobs or swarming) at specific locations or targets without the advanced knowledge of the authorities. Few if any past records of the day-to-day activities of these groups are likely to exist and traces of their activities and campaigns may only subsequently be recorded within the police and state files or in brief media reports.

Similar patterns of activity remain discernable in 2008. Blogs, wikis and other Web 2.0 social networking sites allow groups of people to interact, collaborate and disseminate information quickly and widely without needing further outside mediation. These technologies are used not just for social purposes but also in business, education and by campaigning organizations, allowing individuals to discuss and work together remotely in either open or closed forums (Dearstyne 2005 and 2007). The inherent collaborative, disintermediated and disruptive nature of these technologies makes them attractive to anti-globalization campaigning groups. These 'new social tools' improve 'shared awareness and group coordination' and this potential for enabling collective action makes them 'inherently political' and subversive (Shirky 2008, 186–7).

This was true of the Make Poverty History (MPH) and the G8 protests in July 2005. The activities of the majority, mainstream campaign partners had a high profile and were well documented. However, a substantial fringe presence at the protests in Edinburgh was drawn from anarchist and direct-action-inclined groups who rejected the MPH's alliance of mainstream politicians, celebrities and the state and saw the activities of the G8 as a fundamental cause of world poverty rather than as a potential solution. The activities and analysis of these groups is barely documented or recognized. The MPH campaign is exploring the possibility of depositing its records with a mainstream archive repository, and a selection of G8-related websites, which include 'G8 Alternatives' but generally emphasize the mainstream, is maintained by the UK Web Archive Consortium (<http://www.webarchive.org.uk/col/c8150. html>). For those unorthodox and direct action groups which organized themselves via chat rooms, text, e-mail and password-controlled sites, any archival traces of their protest and articulation of an alternative position on anti-poverty campaigns have probably already largely disappeared.

As a consequence of the transitory nature of many, particularly local, campaigns even those groups who are not deliberately seeking to avoid detection and surveillance are likely to slip into obscurity without leaving much trace except perhaps on independent media sites and perhaps in the local press. Protests against a local planning decision, a mobile telephone mast or the settlement of asylum seekers in a local area may be marked by an official response or by media reports but these rarely privilege the voice of those who organized or supported the campaign. Once the campaign is finished, the traces of it (increasingly digital, a website not maintained, minutes and e-mail stored electronically and then deleted, a discussion list or electronic petition closed down) will frequently be left to deteriorate and disappear.

In addition to being used to organize, plan and mobilize protests and campaigns in the real world, the online world has also been an arena for protest itself. Cyber-activism or 'hacktivism' has included 'cyberpetitions, virtual protests, virtual blockades, gripe sites, email bombs, web hacks and computer viruses' (Rolfe 2005, 66). Groups such as the Electrohippies Collective, Adbusters and Culture Jammers have been active since the 1990s in combining online and offline acts of environmental, anti-consumerist protest and subversion; and latterly the anti-war movement, particularly in the US, has been exploring the potential of social networking (including the 'Campaigns Wikia' at <http://campaigns.wikia.com/wiki/Campaigns_Wikia>) for organizing effective online political action (Mobbs 2002; Carty 2002, 135–44; Carty and Onyett 2006, 240–245). In 2007, in the virtual world of Second Life there were a number of demonstrations and protests against the presence of racist and neo-fascist groups; social protest groups such as Second Life Left Unity were established and in September 2007 virtual strike action was organized against IBM by Italian trade unionists in association with their global union federation, UNI.

New technologies give individuals and groups the ability to record and disseminate their opinions and experiences with an ease and range which was unimaginable in earlier eras. Citizen journalism and the blogosphere may create much which is ephemeral and lacks the controls on quality that might be expected from more mediated traditional publishing but the best also democratizes the processes of knowledge creation and exchange in ways not seen before. One only need think of the generations of researchers who have used the logs and diaries of the Mass Observation archive to imagine what riches await those who study the blogs and web-diaries of our age. The public, communal and interactive nature of most of these online diaries differs from the private space that traditional diaries gave entry to, but the new technologies seem to be blurring many of the barriers between the real and virtual and the private and public (O'Sullivan 2005, 68). All this suggests that potential sources for local, national and in some cases international histories are being created without a clear strategy to manage them and to prevent them from being to lost through neglect. Does this matter? Are these losses important? Are these traces, these individuals, organizations and activities significant?

There are two ways of giving an affirmative answer to these questions. First, for social historians and other researchers these movements and the traces thereof, (however apparently marginalized and transitory, however peripheral to present dominant cultures and political discourses) are the authenticate expressions of the ideas and feelings of a segment of society. As such they are as potentially important for any understanding of the late 20th and early 21st centuries as other marginal and alternative movements were to the history of earlier periods. It is only with hindsight that we will be able to tell which, if any, of these movements might in years to come turn into something really significant. In any event, leaving aside questions of long-term significance, in terms of the dialogue between the South and the North, the centre and the periphery (epitomized by the Social Forums and New Social Movements), and in relation to social credit arguments about whether or not democratic participation has declined in contemporary societies or whether conversely people have sought to express their associational activities through local, cultural, single-issue groups and activities, these materials may well represent something very important indeed.

Second, if you liken the records of the political and campaigning organizations described here to the materials of other community organizations (as defined by place, ethnicity, gender, religion, sexual orientation or just a shared interest), many if not all of the same arguments concerning the contribution these traces might make to a shared and more representative memory of our society and the fragile and transitory nature of those materials, and hence that memory, would be equally relevant. This loss and forgetting is simply not sustainable or justifiable for public sector archivists charged with preserving (by selection and collection) the memory of society.

These justifications do not just apply to what might be described as 'politically correct' organizations and causes but must also logically include right-wing, racist organizations, radical or militant religious groups or sects, and nationalist or other terrorist organizations. Perhaps it might also include even those individuals who, as a consequence of their beliefs and actions with regard to themselves or others, break the norms and taboos of society and so are 'forced to operate underground' but who also use the web to organize and sustain themselves as individuals or communities (Della Porta and Diani 2006, 133). Evidence of these groups and their activities may also have to be retained for future research but if there is to be an 'archive of the taboo' it will have to be administered and managed with the appropriate sensitivities and controls regarding security and access in place.

The real urgency of this responsibility is, of course, dictated by the comparative fragility of digital records. Without appropriate and early intervention by record-keepers and the establishment of a record-keeping framework, this material and our potential to understand and interpret it deteriorates rapidly – much more so than the deterioration of letters and diaries neglected and abandoned in a filing cabinet or in an attic (Bearman, 2006). The essential unstable nature of digital materials must be factored in with the rapidity with which web pages change and disappear and the often short-lived nature of the groups and campaigns themselves.

Of course, the groups or individuals who create these materials do so in the course of their day-to-day activities with little consideration or interest in any long-term value or heritage. Indeed, in many cases they may not wish to see such material preserved at all or they may have very serious concerns over the potential legal and physical consequences of such materials being made available. These concerns will raise difficult ethical and practical issues in terms of selection, preservation and access. If this material is to be retained, it will be necessary for there to be early and direct intervention by archival and information technology professionals and for that intervention to be based on a relationship of trust with the creators in which the archivists' knowledge, reliability and experience in the field has been previously established.

How to Respond? Some Suggestions for Documenting the Margins

The simplest response to the challenge of seeking to preserve the records of marginal or hard-to-locate social movements, or community organizations seeking to tell their own story, or indeed any individual or collective initiative outside the mainstream governmental or commercial environment, particularly when the activities of these individuals and groups take place in the digital environment, is to do nothing. The archive profession could throw up its hands in protest at the sheer scale of what this might entail, argue that it is impossible given the present levels of staff and resources available and conclude that archivists should concentrate on the core records of the State and its institutions and perhaps a small number of selected, important private organizations and individuals.

In terms of the campaigning organizations under discussion in this chapter (though not for other types of community organizations), such passivity might be justifiable if other existing records contained sufficient information. The records of the state can usually be used to reveal something of those marginalized or on the periphery, however slight or unrepresentative these references might be. This is certainly the case with regard to those groups, organizations and individuals (such as anti-globalization or peace movement activists, or nationalist or religious radicals) which attract the attention of the security forces. The records of state security forces, as attested to in both the UK and in more authoritarian states elsewhere, can be very revealing and sometimes are the only records of dissent. In a country like apartheid South Africa the formal archival record of the majority of the population and of their political, industrial and liberation organizations from the apartheid period was extremely partial, limited and 'distorted' (McEwan 2003). But even amongst these biased and flawed state archives, the anti-apartheid activist, human rights lawyer and Constitutional Court judge, Albie Sachs was able to find the official record of his torture. By accessing and reading the preserved record of his resistance and protest against that torture, Sachs was able to reclaim some dignity from what had otherwise been a 'total personal humiliation' and the 'worst moment in my life' (Sachs 2006, 4–7).

Less dramatic but equally revealing is the question of what you should do and where you should go to study the history of the UK Communist Party between 1920 and the end of Second World War. With the exception of the personal papers of some leading figures, the party's official archives in the Labour History Archive and Study Centre in Manchester contain relatively little from that period. Many of the party's official organizational records were either burnt in anticipation of police raids or taken away in the course of such raids. Much better and more extensive collections are to be found both in Moscow, amongst the records of the Communist International to which the party sent regular deposits of its records and publications, and in The National Archives (TNA) at Kew where Home Office, Secret Service, Special Branch and police informants' records contain much that is valuable and (in the opinion of historians) reasonably reliable about the activities and organization of British communists in this period.

Valuable as such material appears, there are significant problems with relying on the records of state organizations. First, it remains the case that such materials (particularly those that originate with the state and the security services rather than those seized from the groups under surveillance) are produced by the state and for a particular purpose. Their accuracy cannot be necessarily guaranteed and there are several obvious reasons why a police surveillance report or an informer's account of events might be exaggerated or falsified. Even allowing for readings against the grain, the state's records of oppositional organizations or campaigns are not the same as those records which originate with the individuals or organizations themselves. The record of Albie Sachs's torture and his subsequent protest at his treatment is persuasive and powerful but it is a direct record of the interaction between an individual and the state, albeit an extreme interaction. It remains the case that otherwise the records of the liberation struggle in South Africa which are held within the formal state archives were and are extremely partial. Second, even if the materials which originate with the state are a useful source for the study of such individuals and organizations, there is no guarantee that this material will be preserved or whether it will be made available to the public. For understandable reasons, any material which relates to the security services and surveillance activities will take a long time, if ever, to be released for general access.

Finally, the possibility of using state records 'against the grain' only really exists for those organizations and ideologies that are really perceived to be genuinely a threat to national interests or public safety. Those organizations and campaigns which are not perceived in this way are unlikely to receive close attention from state agencies and so find their way into the national archives. If we cannot rely on the state's records alone then alternative ways to document these groups need to be found and archivists will have to develop ways of dealing with the mass of digital material in spite of the resource implications.

There are a number of current initiatives trying to address the challenge of identifying and preserving the predominantly digital records of political and social movements. For instance the International Association of Labour History Institutions (IALHI), the International Institute of Social History (IISH, Netherlands) and the Amsab-Institute of Social History (Amsab-ISH, Belgium) have all begun to explore making provision for the paper and digital archives of the anti-globalization movement. In 2005, a symposium at IALHI's 36th annual conference was held on the topic of 'Anti-Globalism'. The meeting included contributions on documenting and researching the movement and resulted in the publication *Inside Outside* (Mestrum and Weber 2006). Among the contributors was Piet Creve from the Amsab-ISH who outlined the beginnings of a 'strategy for the archives and documentation of the anti-globalization movement' based upon the Belgian experience (Creve 2006). Creve and Kwanten have both stressed the necessity for collecting institutions to be proactive in this regard, seeking out and building relationships of trust with social movements and campaigning groups, developing capacity and expertise within the archival institution by trying to 'keep a finger on the pulse of the anti-globalization movement.' This pro-activity and institutional expertise is particularly important in this context, because (as has already been noted) these movements are often organizationally and structurally very fluid and non-hierarchical and so not burdened with a bureaucratic structure which routinely produces and retains records. Indeed, the preservation of records may be entirely contrary to the usual practice of these organisations. Furthermore, as has been noted, much of their communication, organization and mobilisation is done digitally and thus requires a more deliberate policy of intervention and activity to ensure the preservation of their records (Creve 2006, 20–22; Kwanten 2006, 126).

In the UK important mapping work has been done by DANGO (the Database of Archives of Non-Governmental Organizations, <www.dango.bham.ac.uk>). This Arts and Humanities Research Council (AHRC) project, based at the University of Birmingham, sought to raise awareness of the importance of non-governmental organizations ((NGOs) broadly defined and including all manner of non-commercial and non-mainstream political organizations and campaigns) in the UK since 1945 (McKay 2006). As of November 2007, the project had identified 3,900 national NGOs in the UK and had established a database of nearly 2,000, giving details of activities and, where available, archives for research. Whilst DANGO was not an archiving project itself, it did seek to find out from groups such as the direct-action Earth First! collectives whether they had any records. In some cases DANGO staff sought to facilitate a relationship between a campaign group (for instance Make Poverty History) and an archive repository (University of Warwick Modern Records Centre). The work completed by DANGO is a useful starting point for identifying those campaigns and organizations whose records and activities should be preserved.

Pearce-Moses (2007) outlines three potential professional responses to the digital environment. He believes that two of these (retaining the status quo and seeking to deal with the problem of digital preservation by narrowing the definition of the record and of what ought to be collected, and the worst-case scenario of ignoring digital records completely and focusing traditional skills and attention on paper records) will result in the loss of 'interesting, valuable materials' and represents an ethical abrogation of professional responsibility. In his best-case scenario he describes the profession embracing the need for new skills and a new proactive, strategic and cooperative role along with other information professionals and record creators to ensure the long-term preservation of society's digital heritage.

National archives services and professional bodies should play a leading role in each country in promoting Pearce-Moses' positive professional response and not just for official, government records but for the cultural record of the whole of society. In a number of countries including Canada, South Africa and Northern Ireland, the national archive services have responsibility not only for government or public records but also have broader mandates which include taking responsibility for important private collections and to some extent for documenting the whole of society. In these circumstances, rather than narrowing the focus of appraisal to evidence of business and organizational transactions which privilege elites and bureaucratic forms whilst excluding other more marginal voices, archivists should engage in the 'messy', contingent and subjective business of appraisal and selection (Moss 2006, 236–40; Green 2002, 48). Unfortunately in the UK, without new archival legislation mandates for similar broader concerns, TNA cannot play that expanded role with regard to collecting non-official, non-public records, although through its sponsorship of research and good practice in digital preservation and through its advisory services it can at least support other appropriate repositories in implementing Pearce-Moses' preferred strategy.

In this context, the widespread use of Web 2.0 technologies by these transnational networks and social movement groups to disseminate and mobilize will pose new problems for those archivists who seek to capture them. Like websites, the wikis, internal blogs and social networking sites used by campaigning groups are essentially dynamic, always changing and evolving. They have no fixed form and can be constantly added to and altered by members, representing a potentially continuous conversation inside the group. At what point should the archivist seek to capture or fix this conversation for posterity (Dearstyne 2007, 28–32)? It may be possible to arrange only for snapshots of these conversations to be taken, but it indicates again the necessity for a close relationship between the collecting archivist and the record-creating group, as well as the acquisition of new professional skills and expertise (Uricchio 2007). Reflecting on these new challenges, Brown writes of a

> … cultural shift that will be required of collecting organizations, in order to transform their curatorial traditions … In the future, web archiving will itself need to transform into 'web information management', a comprehensive approach to managing and sustaining the information assets that form the very essence of the world wide web (Brown 2006, 193–5).

With regard to the preservation of digital records belonging to individuals, there have been some useful research projects which have implications for archivists dealing with social movements and individual activists. The JISC-funded PARADIGM project (2005–07, <www.paradigm.ac.uk/index.html>), run by the Bodleian Library at the University of Oxford and the John Rylands University Library at the University of Manchester, studied the challenges of managing personal digital records (in this case the private papers of MPs), including websites, blogs and e-mails, and then sought to develop best-practice models for digital preservation of such papers. Writing up the project's findings Thomas and Martin (2006, 35–6) recommended that if these records are to survive and to be useable, involvement in this field requires active and early intervention in the record creation and preservation process. Cooperation and collaboration are central to success in this area. Such a role can only be undertaken if the archivist establishes an effective working partnership with information technology specialists and a relationship of trust with the record-producing community. Although the PARADIGM team focused on the digital papers of individuals, their recommendations can be applied more widely, including to the records of small, non-mainstream community and social movement organizations:

'This is particularly true of short-lived campaigns such as those connected to the anti-globalisation movement. Not only are such records predominantly based on the Internet technologies but as they transcend national boundaries they fall outside of national collecting remits' (Thomas and Martin 2006, 52 n48).

Similarly the AHRC-funded Digital Lives Research Project (2007–09, <www.bl.uk/digital-lives/index.html>), jointly run by the British Library, University College London and the University of Bristol, looks at the management of personal digital collections and their relationship to digital repositories, and is expected to produce results of interest to all concerned with the preservation of individuals' digital collections.

As far as the public Web is concerned there are a number of national and international Web archiving initiatives which impact on the preservation of the traces of non-official or otherwise marginal groups. The most ambitious of these is the Internet Archive (<http://www.archive.org/index.php>) which since 1996 has employed web crawlers to capture regular snapshots of the whole available Web and to then make the sites available for use via 'The Wayback Machine'. Though there are problems in terms of what is not collected (the deep Web), of material that disappears between the snapshots and the ethics of preservation and access without permission, this is still an remarkable resource, for instance allowing researchers to trace 10 years of developments on the McSpotlight site. The Internet Archive's founder Brewster Kahle believes that this technology may well be able to create a digital repository of all human endeavours, though he acknowledges that achieving this would require a massive commitment on the part of wider society (Kahle 2007).

Other national initiatives such as 'Pandora' (National Library of Australia, <http://pandora.nla.gov.au/>), 'Minerva' (US Library of Congress Web Archives, <http://lcweb2.loc.gov/diglib/lcwa/html/lcwa-home.html>) and the UK Web Archiving Consortium (led by the British Library, <http://www.webarchive.org.uk/>) are selective, subject-based approaches. These often work with web creators or other partners to ensure that with the appropriate permissions, all content within particular selected fields is captured and preserved but external content and links cannot be relied upon to remain unless they have been preserved elsewhere (Brown 2006, 8–40). As is the case with the UK Web Archiving Consortium, it is possible that a selective and internationally collaborative approach which included thematic or subject areas that covered the groups and networks discussed in this chapter would be a positive step forward in the preservation of traces of their activities. New legislation with regard to the legal deposit of published electronic content makes the British Library responsible for preserving open, public websites (including some blogs) but this would not address the issue of those closed or private digital resources generated by the individuals or organizations under consideration here. Any initiative to capture more than just the public face of these networks would need to work closely with groups concerned to ensure that closed and otherwise hidden materials were also preserved, and to satisfy any concerns over the short-term use and accessibility of the material.

Challenging and Changing Professional Practice

It is clear that involvement with both digital archives and with community or otherwise marginal or transitory campaigning groups fundamentally challenge the notion that the archivist can afford to be merely a passive recipient of these records. The threats to digital materials even in official and more stable environments are well known, so when dealing with informal campaigns and networks archivists cannot wait to preserve the material until it comes into the possession of the archives. Indeed, in a non-custodial environment, where ownership and custodianship remains with the creator, such collections may never enter the archive. Passivity and inaction will only result in this material being lost or made unreadable.

In the not-too-distant future it may be that long-term preservation formats of digital materials may be guaranteed by developments amongst software companies or by open source software initiatives but both Bailey (2007) and Kahle (2007, 30) remain sceptical and recommend continued active archival involvement. In any event it is likely that such long-term solutions will be of greater application in more formal, mainstream organizations. In the meantime, if contemporary social movement and transnational network materials are to be preserved and contextualized then the archivist must identify which materials or which creators of materials are worthy of selection and, ultimately, preservation as early as possible, and seek to build a relationship with that individual or group which aims at providing the framework for the eventual preservation of the material. In cases where the group or campaign in question may be very short-lived and transitory this will require rapid action and specialist knowledge.

As has been suggested, many of these networks and groups will be organizing, mobilizing and perhaps actively campaigning not just in the real world and not just by relatively fixed and well-understood digital forms such as e-mail, websites and word-processed documents but also via dynamic and evolving media such as instant messaging, social networking sites, wikis, blogs and other virtual, participatory and collaborative mediums. The skills and expertise required by the archivist working with groups to capture and understand these interactions will have to be significantly enhanced. William Uricchio has characterized the changes and challenges posed by social media thus:

> Decentralized, networked, collaborative, accretive, ephemeral and dynamic … these developments and others like them bear a closer resemblance to oral cultures than to the more stable regimes of print (writing and the printing press) and the trace (photography, film, recorded sound) … and like oral cultures, they seem to evade the preservation frameworks that we have put in place in our institutions of memory, built as they are around tangible media. And yet despite these conditions, these collaborative efforts also enjoy embodiment as digital text … They can be apprehended, but the question is, at what point? What constitutes a sufficient 'capture' in a dynamic and fast-evolving distributed network where any of the nodes is capable of change? (Uricchio 2007, 20–21).

If we are to enable the preservation of an archival heritage which reflects the full diversities and complexities of contemporary society, then these are the problems and questions that archivists and others will have to solve. Indeed, Uricchio (2007,

24–5) suggests that the very effort to understand and solve these questions might also suggest solutions to the unrepresentative nature of the traditional archive.

Piet Creve's (2006, 22–5) strategy for documenting anti-globalization movements does not explicitly address these new social technologies but he does propose an archivist's toolbox for use in addressing the archives of social movements and transnational networks. The acquisition of technical skills and expertise are an important component of the toolkit but are not the only elements. He also suggests that building trust and effective, mutually beneficial partnerships with the organizations, and raising awareness of the importance and value of their archives are of equal importance.

As fundamental as the technological challenges that must be faced and the partnerships with IT specialists that must be forged, archivists must also change their attitudes to how and where they carry out their professional responsibilities. Increasingly this will not just be in their repositories but also in the wider community; not just becoming involved when the records are deemed to be of archival, cultural and historical value but close to the point of their creation whilst they are still very much part of the group's campaigning or day-to-day activities, offering advice on appropriate formats and frameworks which will maximize the chances of future preservation. These relationships will not necessarily be easy to establish and it will require skill and diplomacy (and include a realization of the possibility of failure) to build a working relationship to convince a group of the value of engaging with their archives. The aim must be to overcome any suspicion of the archivist's motives and to reach the position where the profession is seen less as a representative of the state and rather as a servant of the whole community's future histories and culture. To some extent this will depend on the archivist's connections within and knowledge of the 'colourful world of the anti-globalization movement' (Creve 2006, 25) but this may not always be enough. Some records of the original social movements (CND, Amnesty, various women's movement organizations) have been deposited with mainstream archival repositories, and the World Social Forum has shown some concern with its future memory, setting up its own Living Memory website (<www. memoria-viva.org/indexen.htm>). However, other smaller, more militant and more autonomous networks such as Earth First! groups or animal rights activists are likely to remain more suspicious and difficult to engage with the process.

Again, as is the case with community archives, concern with the records of these movements also implies changes in what is defined as an archive, and what values and criteria are used in their selection for eventual preservation. Notions of professional objectivity are thoroughly undermined but the question of how these selections are to be carried out remains. It is difficult, but seeking to more fully represent the diversity of society including all its viewpoints and to democratize archival culture is an important starting point. It requires honesty and transparency about the reasons for selections, collection and description. The criteria upon which the judgements about what and who is to be remembered and who and what is to be forgotten should be openly acknowledged and discussed by wider society.

Ultimately it is also a matter of setting priorities, identifying and allocating the appropriate resources and deciding who has responsibility for these initiatives. It would be helpful to see national institutions such as TNA, particularly through its advisory services, playing a more prominent role in this matter, and already the

British Library is taking responsibility as part of the UK Web Archiving Consortium for 'sites of cultural, historical and political importance'. Ultimately specific digital repositories may be required to look after all our digital preservation requirements but in the meantime there is a role for specialist repositories, perhaps operating from within the higher education sector and collaborating as part of a national, indeed international network, to deal with the traces of campaigning movements and organizations. Knowledge of both the technical requirements and of the transnational networks and anti-globalization movements themselves will be essential if these repositories are to act as centres of expertise for archives of these movements. Given the autonomous and federal nature of some of the groups as well as the global focus of many of the networks and protests, both the local and the international frameworks will be important considerations in this type of work.

Records of campaign groups and new social movements are already held by institutions like the Modern Records Centre at Warwick University, the Labour History Archive and Study Centre in Manchester, the Brynmor Jones Library at Hull University, the London School of Economics, and the Women's Library at London Metropolitan University. Having already demonstrated an interest in these type of organizations and having some experience of collecting and processing comparable material, and by building upon the mapping already done by the DANGO project and the experience and network being coordinated through IALHI, it is possible that these institutions or other similar ones might succeed in building sustainable relationships with anti-globalization movements to ensure that the present-day equivalents of both the Chartists and the 'deluded follower of Joanna Southcott' are rescued from the 'enormous condescension of posterity' (Thompson 1981, 12).

Concluding Thoughts

Initiatives to democratize the archives and to ensure that they become more representative of all shades of opinion and activity, of ordinary citizens and of unorthodox or marginalized concerns, pose fundamental questions about the role of the archival profession and its responsibility in the construction of the archive. The partiality of the archival heritage is not accidental; it flows directly from professional participation in the processes of deciding what is important and what is not, what should be kept and what should not and what properly constitutes a record and hence an archive and what does not. Initiatives to democratize the archive recognize the subjectivity of the existing process and seek to acknowledge and work within that subjectivity to establish local, national and even international frameworks which seek to re-balance collections and selection policies.

Part of the logic of the globalizing process has been to question the continued importance of national governments and national boundaries, with real power and influence shifting towards transnational governmental bodies and commercial organizations. If this process continues, where should the archives of these institutions reside and how should they be made accessible to all the citizens that they affect? Furthermore, if the importance of national governments and their records are declining, what then is the future role for national archives services? Looking beyond the duties of care for their existing holdings, one possible responsibility would be to take the lead in enabling the preservation of a more representative digital archival heritage for the whole of society rather than just the record of governance. What should be done, however, if the archive state does not or will not recognize its opponents? What if, like the Chartists, the suffragettes and even the environmental activists of the 1960s and 1970s, contemporary campaigns against neo-liberalism, climate change and poverty are the antecedents of future political orthodoxies, how will the present-day archive profession ensure that the stories of their challenges can be told? In thinking globally and acting locally, we will have to think and act creatively to ensure that this legacy is preserved.

References

Bailey, S. (2007), 'Taking the road less travelled by: the future of the archive and records management profession in the digital age', *Journal of the Society of Archivists*, 28 (2), 117–124.

Bearman, D. (2006), 'Moments of risk: identifying threats to electronic records', *Archivaria*, 62, 15–46.

Brown, A. (2006), *Archiving Websites. A Practical Guide for Information Management Professionals* (London: Facet).

Byrne, P. (1997), *Social Movements in Britain* (London: Routledge).

'Campaigns Wikia', at <http://campaigns.wikia.com/wiki/Campaigns_Wikia> accessed 13 April 2008.

Carty, V. (2002), 'Technology and counter-hegemonic movements: the case of Nike Corporation', *Social Movement Studies*, 1 (2), 129–46.

——— and Onyett, J. (2006), 'Protest, cyberactivsm and new social movements: the re-emergence of the peace movement post 9/11', *Social Movement Studies*, 5 (3), 229–49.

Castells, M. (2002), *The Internet Galaxy* (Oxford: Oxford University Press).

'Community Archives and Identities: Documenting and Sustaining Community Heritage', at <https://www.ucl.ac.uk/slais/research/icarus/community-archives/> accessed 13 April 2008.

Creve, P. (2006), 'Towards a Strategy for the Archives and Documentation of the Anti-Globalisation Movement', in Mestrum, F. and Weber, D. (eds).

Database of Archives of Non-Governmental Organizations (DANGO), at <www.dango.bham.ac.uk> accessed 13 April 2008.

Dearstyne, B. (2007), 'Blogs, mashups and Wikis. Oh, my!', *The Information Management Journal*, July/August, 24–33.

——— (2005), 'Blogs. The new information revolution?', *The Information Management Journal*, September/October, 38–44.

Della Porta, D. and Diani, M. (2006), *Social Movements: an Introduction*, 2nd edn (Oxford: Blackwell).

Digital Lives Research Project, at <www.bl.uk/digital-lives/index.html> accessed 13 April 2008.

Flinn, A. (2007), 'Community histories, community archives: some opportunities and challenges', *Journal of the Society of Archivists*, 28 (2), 151–76.

'G8 Alternatives', Web Archive Consortium, at <http://www.webarchive.org.uk/col/c8150.html> accessed 13 April 2008.

Gray, V. (forthcoming 2008), '"Who's that knocking on our door?": Archives, outreach and community', *Journal of the Society of Archivists*.

Greene, M. (2002), 'The power of meaning: the archival mission in the postmodern age', *The American Archivist*, 65 (1), 42–55.

Hall, S. (2005), 'Whose Heritage? Un-Settling "The Heritage", Re-Imagining the Post-Nation' in Littler, J. and Naidoo, R. (eds).

Ham, F.G. (1975), 'The archival edge', *The American Archivist*, 38 (1), 5–13.

Hopkins, I. (forthcoming 2008), 'Places from which to speak', *Journal of the Society of Archivists*.

Independent Media Centres, at <www.indymedia.org> accessed 13 April 2008.

Kahle, B. (2007), 'Universal access to all knowledge', *The American Archivist*, 70 (1), 23–31.

Klein, N. (2000), *No Logo* (London: Flamingo).

Kwanten, G. (2006), 'The Role of Private Archival Centres in Storing, Preserving and Providing Access to Political Records in Belgium' in Procter, M. et al. (eds).

Littler, J. and Naidoo, R. (eds) (2005), *The Politics of Heritage: the Legacies of Race* (London: Routledge).

Logan, D. (2005), 'The globalization of public and private economy and its impact on the Information Society', *Comma*, 4, 1–2. [*Comma* is the journal of the International Council on Archives.]

Lusenet, Y. and Wintermans, V. (eds) (2007), *Preserving the Digital Heritage. Principles and Policies* (The Hague: UNESCO).

McEwan, C. (2003), 'Building a postcolonial archive? Gender, collective memory and citizenship in post-apartheid South Africa', *Journal of Southern African Studies*, 29 (3), 739–57.

McKay, J. (2006), 'DANGO: Database of Archives of UK Non-Governmental Organizations since 1945', *Record Keeping*, Autumn, 14–15.

Mayor of London's Commission on African and Asian Heritage (MCAAH) (2005), *Delivering Shared Heritage* (London: GLA).

Mestrum, F. and Weber, D. (eds) (2006), *Inside Outside. Past and Future of the Anti-Globalization Movement. Proceedings of the International Colloquium on Anti-Globalism, Ghent, 9 September 2005* (Ghent: IALHI Amsab-ISH).

'Minerva', US Library of Congress Web Archives, at <http://lcweb2.loc.gov/diglib/lcwa/html/lcwa-home.html> accessed 13 April 2008.

Mobbs, P. (2002), *Campaigning Online. Using the Internet to Get your Point Across* (GreenNet: Civil Society Internet Rights Project).

Moss, M. (2006), 'The Function of the Archive' in Tough, A. and Moss, M. (eds).

Norris, P. (2001), *Digital Divide. Civic Engagement, Information Poverty and the Internet Worldwide* (Cambridge: Cambridge University Press).

O'Sullivan, C. (2005), 'Diaries, on-line diaries, and the future loss to archives; or blogs and the blogging bloggers who blog them', *The American Archivist*, 68, 53–73.

'Pandora', National Library of Australia, at <http://pandora.nla.gov.au/> accessed 13 April 2008.

PARADIGM (Personal Archives Accessible in Digital Media) project, at <www.paradigm.ac.uk/index.html> accessed 13 April 2008.

Pearce-Moses, R. (2007), 'Janus in cyberspace: archives on the threshold of the digital era', *The American Archivist*, 70 (1), 13–22.

Procter, M., Cook, M. and Williams, C. (2006), *Political Pressure and the Archival Record* (Chicago IL: Society of American Archivists).

Rolfe, B. (2005), 'Building an electronic repertoire of contention', *Social Movement Studies*, 4 (1), 65–74.

Ross, S. (2000). *Changing Trains at Wigan: Digital Preservation and the Future of Scholarship* (London: NPO Preservation Guidance Occasional Papers).

Sachs, A. (2006), 'Archives, truth and reconciliation', *Archivaria*, 62, 1–14.

Shirky, C. (2008), *Here Comes Everybody. The Power of Organising without Organisation* (London: Allen Lane).

Thomas, S. and Martin, J. (2006). 'Using the papers of contemporary British politicians as a testbed for the preservation of digital personal archives', *Journal of the Society of Archivists*, 27 (1), 29–56.

Thompson, E.P. (1981), *The Making of the English Working Class* (Harmondsworth: Penguin).

Tough, A. and Moss, M. (eds) (2006), *Record Keeping in a Hybrid Environment. Managing the Creation, Use, Preservation and Disposal of Unpublished Information Objects in Context* (Oxford: Chandos).

UK Web Archiving Consortium, at <http://www.webarchive.org.uk/> accessed 13 April 2008.

Uricchio, W. (2007) 'Moving beyond the Artefact: Lessons from Participatory Culture', in Lusenet, Y. and Wintermans, V. (eds).

Vidal, J. (1999), 'Modem warfare', *The Guardian* 13 January.

——— (1997), *McLibel: Burger Culture on Trial* (London: Macmillan).

World Social Forums, at <http://www.forumsocialmundial.org.br> accessed 13 April 2008.

World Social Forums, 'Living memory', at <www.memoria-viva.org/indexen.htm> accessed 13 April 2008.

Zimmerman, S. (1999), 'World Trade Organization – Seattle protests', at <http://www.zmedia.org/WTO> accessed 13 April 2008.

Chapter 7

Archives of Exile: Exile of Archives

Andrew Prescott

I can't but say it is an awkward Sight
To see one's native land receding through
The growing waters; it unmans one quite,
Especially when Life is rather new;
I recollect Great Britain's Coast looks white,
But almost every other Country's blue,
When gazing on them, mystified by distance,
We enter on our nautical Existence.
Byron, *Don Juan*, Canto II, 12

How do archivists do theory? The frequent use of the word 'theory' as a catch-all phrase to describe the whole range of new philosophical and critical approaches which have emerged since the Second World War gives the misleading impression that they comprise a single homogenous philosophy which can be readily grasped and exploited. This impression is reinforced by references to the 'application' of theory. This phrase conveys the idea that the new theoretical insights are a toolkit containing a range of critical spanners, screwdrivers and wrenches which, once mastered, can be used to dissemble texts and reveal the hidden cogs within them. The unhelpfulness of the suggestion that theory can be 'applied' is illustrated by the use made of the work of the Russian critic Mikhail Bakhtin. Among Bakhtin's most influential works was *Rabelais and his World*, which explored the cultural history and significance of the carnival, presenting it as a time when hierarchy was suspended and new aesthetic and cultural alignments forged (Bakhtin 1984). Bakhtin's work has been 'applied' to a enormous range of subjects from medieval misericords to vaudeville and burlesque. The theories of Bakhtin are frequently cited or described at second hand and there is a limited engagement with his original work. Bakhtin, who was a challenging and provocative scholar, has become domesticated and familiar, prompting a group of Bakhtin specialists to comment:

> That domestication, although it has been resisted in some quarters, persists in more: carnival, dialogism, heteroglossia, and the rest continue to roll off the tongues, and out from under the keyboard-caressing fingers of scholars and graduate students who find in them a useful analytical framework which does not in itself need to be interrogated ...
> At the very least, 'using' or 'applying' Bakhtin has become difficult, if not impossible, to distinguish from 'exploiting Bakhtin ...' (Barta et al. 2001, 10).

The case of Bakhtin emphasizes the enormous diversity of theory. Bakhtin worked in the Soviet Union long before the development of many of the major strands of modern literary theory: 'Bakhtin was certainly not a feminist, a deconstructionist, or a poststructuralist (though he was a post-Sausurrean). Such labels represent cultural anachronisms and ideological impossibilities in the world of Soviet life and thought' (Barta et al. 2001, 2). The use of the term 'theory' is convenient precisely because the range of new theoretical approaches and insights is so widespread and diverse that it is impossible to find any other single term to refer to them. If we adopt for, example, the term 'postmodern', as does Callum Brown in his *Postmodernism for Historians* (2005), there is a risk of excluding key figures such as Bakhtin and of misrepresenting others such as Foucault who declined to label his work as postmodern. In such a confusing terminological situation, it is not surprising that the Wikipedia entry on postmodernism currently (April 2008) carries a banner lamenting that 'This article or section is in need of attention from an expert on the subject'.

Since postmodernism emphasizes diversity, variety and heterogeneity and stresses the significance of personal perspectives, it is impossible to define a body of theory which can be 'applied'. It is not feasible for archivists to receive a training course in theory to bring their academic training up to date. It is necessary rather to engage with individual theorists through reading, debate and discussion. This does not mean that it is necessary to master the whole field of critical theory. I personally find some theorists more helpful than others. For me, the works of Roland Barthes are a constant source of new insights and fresh perspectives, possibly because of their emphasis on the cultural function of text and its multiplicity of meanings. As somebody who researches medieval revolts and insurgencies, I find myself constantly returning to Barthes's essay on *les événements* of 1968, 'Writing the Event' (Barthes 1986, 149–54). On the other hand, while Derrida's essay, *Archive Fever*, has played a central part in drawing the attention of archivists to developments in theory (Derrida 1998), I personally have found it less helpful in considering how new theoretical approaches affect our view of the archive. Derrida forcefully illustrates how the archive is itself a reflection of both the archive keeper and the power structures of which the archive keeper is a representative. However, this is something of which archivists are often already conscious, so Derrida's comments are less exciting for those who are already familiar with how archives work behind the scenes. In other words, it is not necessary to swallow theory whole; it is a varied and multifaceted area, and precisely the attraction of modern theoretical writing is in the varied intellectual approaches offered to the reader.

In this chapter, I would like to try and illustrate further such an approach and to sketch – briefly, superficially and idiosyncratically – how engagement with a theoretical discussion might help change our perspectives on archives and reshape our understanding of some familiar collections and archives. The resulting discussion questions our definition of what an archive is and how it might be created. The theme is exile. Somebody who comes across the title of this essay in Google might anticipate that it should contain a short survey of interesting papers and records relating to exiles in UK archives, the sort of article that has been a staple of journals such as *Archives* or the *Journal of the Society of Archivists*. Classically organized archives, which reflect the structure of the administration which produced them, are not very suitable for finding information about particular subjects. The nature of documents in archives makes a subject-based arrangement impracticable, so the usual approach has been to create subsidiary guides and surveys, usually at a cross-institutional level. The various guides produced by the Historical Manuscripts Commission are excellent examples. While these are at a practical level very useful, they do not tell us very much about how a theme such as exile in expressed in the archives. Is the exile a central figure in our archives or at their margins? What do the records tell us about the experience of exile or how it is culturally conceived?

This is of course the type of study which is undertaken from the archive, but the concept of the guide or survey is shaped by a particular type of methodology, an empirical approach in which these questions can be answered by accumulating a sufficiently large amount of data. The assumption is that the answers will become obvious if we accrue enough information by trawling through a sufficiently large number of archives. An alternative approach might be to concentrate on individual documents and to look at the different layers of information they reveal, at their multiplicity of meanings. Such a method would be more fragmentary but would convey a greater sense of the cultural connections of the subject. The effect would be very similar to the essay by Barthes on 1968. 'Writing the Event' contains very little hard information about what actually occurred in 1968, but by defining the 'three fashions, three writings' of speech, symbol and violence which carried forward the revolution of 1968, Barthes conveys in just six pages a greater sense of the nature of *les événements* than many longer accounts packed with far more facts.

Barthes begins his essay on 1968 by immediately (but deftly, as the information is tucked away in a footnote) defining his own relationship to *les événements*. He notes how one of his memories was of 'streets filled with motionless people seeing nothing, looking at nothing, their eyes down, but their ears glued to transistor radios, thus representing a new human anatomy' (Barthes 1986, 149). Barthes places himself as somebody who was sympathetic to the protests but whose experience of theme was mediated by the broadcast media – a new form of participation, he suggests (Barthes 1986, 150). The short passage in Barthes illustrates the importance of reflexivity, an awareness of the way in which the personal experiences of the author or researcher affect such issues as the questions asked, the information used and the texts which result from the research.

Why should I be interested in exile? I am a London-born UK citizen from families with deep roots in Somerset (on my father's side) and Essex (on my mother's). I have little experience of the wider world beyond the UK. As an academic, exile has not previously impinged much on my interests prior to this essay. The reason for my interest lies in humdrum elements of my professional experience. In 2000, I edited with Elizabeth Hallam a book called *The British Inheritance* which was a collection of pictures of documents from the National Archives, the British Library, the National Archives of Scotland and the National Library of Wales. I was very struck in the course of preparing this book by the way in which the key documents selected by the National Archives in Edinburgh and the National Library in Aberystwyth were items which would be unfamiliar to the English audience. They suggested that each library and archive embodied competing narratives of UK history which spoke of very different senses of British identity. This made me very interested in issues of identity.

The emphasis on reflexivity means that issues of identity are of great significance in theoretical discussion. I was working by this time at the University of Sheffield, and in 2004 Professor Martial Staub was appointed as Professor of Medieval History at Sheffield. Martial has published studies of the medieval church in Germany, including a detailed study of the role of the church in the urban culture of Nuremberg. This has helped foster an interest in forms of memory and group identity in medieval cities. This encouraged Martial to become fascinated by exile as an overarching theme of Western culture. Martial is deeply interested in the individual experience of exile, but also stresses the importance of an imagined experience of exile as a recurrent cultural motif. It is striking that such myths of exile, whether the Israelites in Babylon, the legend of the Trojan origins of the settlement of Britain or the parallel claims to Trojan origin in France or Germany, are an important component of many of the medieval foundation myths, as a study by Susan Reynolds has illustrated (Reynolds 1983). It is paradoxical that mythologies of exile, an enforced departure from home, should form a central part of the legends which buttressed the formation of nations and accounted for their appearance in national homes. Martial sees this process of imagining exile as a theoretical insight which can potentially transform our understanding of the nation, which remains one of our fundamental cultural building blocks.

Naturally, Martial and I found a great deal to talk about when he arrived in Sheffield. He illustrated the richness of exile as a connecting theme in the study of medieval history in his inaugural lecture at Sheffield, 'Exiling History'. On meeting him, I quickly found out why he should be interested in exile as an aspect of identity. Martial is a member of an old family from Alsace. This of course is a region of Europe which has been at the heart of the modern struggle over national identity. He studied in France, but has worked in Germany, and writes and teaches in both French and German. Yet one could imagine that he might have felt a sense of having been an exile in his own country. And now, having moved to Sheffield, he is in actual (though evidently very congenial) exile. In conversation about exile as an important intellectual theme, we naturally contemplated the question of archives. Since archives are based on governmental structures, ultimately rooted in the nation, this makes it difficult for them to encompass exile, which inherently cuts across governmental structures. Martial was keen to develop an archive of exile, possibly using digital means to draw together disparate materials in new configurations, but what form would such an archive take? Would it indeed be an archive?

The exile is a challenging figure, and he or she challenges our concept of the archive. The archives of the two *départements* of Bas-Rhin and Haut-Rhin which form Alsace-Moselle illustrate the way in which a conventional archive structure, by stressing official structures and continuities, minimizes traumatic and disruptive issues. It is striking how the structure of the archives elides over the traumatic events of the history of this region between 1870 and 1945. The website for the *archives départementales du Bas-Rhin*[1] apologetically notes that, after 1870, it was impossible to continue the archival series as found in other *départements*. To deal with this unusual situation, two extra series had been established. After 1945, the series return

---

1 <http://archives.cg67.fr/ > accessed 14 April 2008.

to their conformity with the standard French pattern. The structure and description of the archives gives the impression that this was a passing but regrettable episode in the history of a solidly French region. There is no suggestion that material relating to the area can be found in other national archives. However, as David Allen Harvey has recently described, as a result of the fact that many Germans had moved to the region during the period and suspicions felt by the French government about the loyalty of some Alsatians, there was a traumatic process after 1918 by which a group of Triage commissions assessed the nationality of the inhabitants of the region with a view to deporting those of German origin (Harvey 1999). According to Harvey:

> By the end of October 1919, at which time the Triage Commissions were formally disbanded (many of them had already ceased their functions), they had examined tens of thousands of individual cases and left a lasting mark on the social structure and the collective memory of the province. A total of about 150,000 Germans were expelled or emigrated of their own accord from Alsace and Lorraine to Germany in the period following the end of the first world war. This figure, while considerable, represented less than a third of the Germans residing in the former Reichsland as of November 1918. Many of the rest eventually received French nationality through marriage or were authorized to remain as foreign residents in the provinces. For those forced to leave, however, expulsion meant starting again in a nation devastated by war and revolution (Harvey 1999, 549–50).

For many of those expelled, this was a form of exile; for others who stayed by assuming French nationality, this was another form of exile. Each of the cases considered by the commission represented a different kind of relationship to experiences of national identity and the possibility of exile. The *archives départementales* contain the detailed records of the proceedings of the Triage commissions, but these are placed in the series AL, one of the anomalous, non-standard series devoted to specifically to Alsace-Lorraine during the period 1870–1945. The treatment of this series thus conveys the idea of exile and the possibility of exile as anomalous, extraordinary and disruptive. Yet here this traumatic experience was at the heart of the formation of the identity of this region and the entire episode was significant in the development of modern French, German (and ultimately European) identity.

This is how experience of exile tends to appear in the archives: as an anomaly, with fleeting and transitory individuals and groups seeking help or posing problems. Since conventional archives represent an institutional view, and generally an institutional view from the national or regional centres, the exile is a passing and ephemeral presence. A characteristic example from the UK occurs in an archive on which I have been working in recent years, that of the United Grand Lodge of England, deposited in the Library and Museum of Freemasonry. Among the many fascinating items in the historical correspondence in the Library and Museum of Freemasonry is a letter from the officers and members of the Lodge of Love and Unity at Dover to the Grand Secretary in London, dated 26 April 1816 (HC 9/A/50). The Dover lodge wrote to the Grand Secretary to solicit assistance from the Grand Lodge on behalf of one Segunda Correa, a Spanish officer, who had landed in Dover on the ship from Calais with no money, little English and few contacts. Correa was, however, a Freemason, so his first action was to go to the local masonic lodge. Correa explained to the Dover brethren that his father had been a gallant military officer who had supported the king at the time of the uprising against Ferdinand VII. However, Correa's father had mildly suggested some modest political reforms and as a result had been thrown into a dungeon without trial and had been sentenced to servitude in the galleys. The aim of Correa in undertaking the hazardous journey to England was to seek support from the British government for the release of his father. Moved by the Spaniard's story, the masonic lodge took a collection on his behalf, paid for a carriage to take him to London, and wrote to Grand Lodge to ask for its support for the young man in his 'filial and very praiseworthy undertaking'.

How Correa was received in London, what happened to his father and whether he eventually returned to Spain, we do not know. We simply see him passing through Dover, making contact with one organization and then moving on. The exile is invariably an anomaly in the archive. This archival sense of the exile as a marginal outsider is evident even with very large groups. Following Louis-Napoleon's coup in France in 1851, many French exiles appeared in the Channel Islands. Perhaps the most celebrated of these refugees was Victor Hugo, and nothing perhaps illustrates the way in which the theme of exile can unsettle our national preconceptions than the fact that Hugo spent so much of his literary career in the Channel Islands. Indeed, *Les Misérables* can be viewed as one of the great achievements of British literature, and our understanding of its powerful depiction of Paris is transformed by seeing it as writing in exile. Yet this large group of French refugees, who had their own newspapers, social clubs and book shops, left a surprisingly small trace in the UK's official archives. There are a few nervous police reports (for example, the National Archives HO 45/4547A), but little which enables us to understand their society and culture. For this, we are largely dependent on memoirs and autobiographies of both French and British radicals. Paradoxically, the activities of the French exiles left more evident traces in French archives, since the French police were convinced that they operated a secret network throughout France and there are many French police reports of supposed subversive incidents (Payne and Grosshans 1963). The French exiles produced books and publications, but often these do not survive in UK libraries and archives. A periodical published by an exile group called *La chaîne d'union* began publication in London, but copies of the London printings only survive in French libraries – the periodical only appears in UK libraries after publication was transferred to Paris.

Although the exile appears in the institutional archive as a marginal figure, examining the interaction between institutions and exiles can transform our perception of the character of the institution. This in turn might unsettle our view of the character of that institution's archives. To return again to the example of Freemasonry (chosen only because it is a subject on which I have recently been working), it provides a good example of a social institution in which the study of exile opens up new perspectives. The creation of a masonic Grand Lodge in London in 1717 appears superficially as an institutional and social expression of the Hanoverian settlement, and much early English masonic activity and literature seems to have a strongly Whig flavour (Jacobs 2003). It is tempting to relate the early growth of Freemasonry to the development of a self-consciously British identity claimed by Linda Colley for the period after the Union (Colley 1992). However, much of the early ideology of Freemasonry was shaped by two exiles. The first printed *Book of Constitutions* of the Freemasons was prepared by a Scottish Presbyterian clergyman James Anderson, exiled to London (Stevenson 2002). In shaping this *Book of Constitutions*, Anderson apparently drew extensively on Scottish practice. In his work, Anderson was deeply influenced by another exile, Dr John Theophilus Desaguliers, a scientist and popularizer of Newton, who emerges as one of the leading ideologues of early Freemasonry (Weisberger 2000). Desaguliers was a Huguenot who as a small child had been forced to flee with his family from La Rochelle. Desaguliers's stress on Freemasonry as an institution in which men of every type of religion could mix together in concord and harmony seems very much like an attempt to create a social force which would soothe those religious tensions which had led to Desaguliers's own exile. There was a prominent Huguenot component in early Freemasonry, which suggests that providing exiles with a sense of identity and access to the élites of their new home was a major element in early Freemasonry. Yet our understanding of early Freemasonry needs to be triangulated with another group of exiles, the Jacobites in France who brought Freemasonry with them from Scotland. Figures such as the Chevalier Ramsay developed in exile a form of Freemasonry which harked back to the medieval chivalric orders and was to prove very influential on the continent.

Superficially, early Freemasonry appears as a loyalist Hanoverian institution, but the role of different exiles in Freemasonry and their differing relationship to it suggests further unsuspected dimensions to the institution. Again, this is not readily apparent in the archives of early Freemasonry, which focus on institutional and administrative issues such as the mechanism by which local lodges were established. The early minute books of Freemasonry suggest a movement spreading out from London; the sense of a cross-connection between different groups of exiles which emerges from a study of the individuals involved is absent. These themes continued to be prominent in the history of Freemasonry. National Grand Lodges were developed across Europe, and it is natural in investigating the growth of Freemasonry in particular countries to turn to the records of the national Grand Lodge. But, in considering the development of Freemasonry in Sweden, it is surprising to find that as many Swedes became Freemasons in England as in Sweden (Prescott, forthcoming). This theme carries through to the nineteenth century. Roger Burt in his detailed analysis of the membership of Cornish Freemasonry in the late nineteenth century has shown how membership was valued by Cornish miners forced to seek work in the gold and metal mines of America, South Africa and Australia by the collapse of the Cornish mining industry (Burt 2003). It provided them with a means of making social and business contacts on arrival in a strange country. A characteristic document from the archives of a Cornish masonic lodge is a letter to the lodge at Calstock from a Cornish miner living in Colorado and sending money to support the building of a new hall for the lodge.

In unsettling our view of the history of individual institutions, exile can also provide us with new perspectives on the history of libraries and archives and thus give us new critical insights into the material in them. It is now a commonplace that the creation of national libraries and archives can be related to the process of articulation of national identity in the eighteenth and nineteenth centuries. One of the first actions of the newly independent Greeks was to found a national library; likewise the creation of a National Library in Bulgaria was closely bound up with the complex twists and turns of the emergence of an independent Bulgaria at the end of the nineteenth century. Closer to home, the National Library of Wales in Aberystwyth and the National Museum in Cardiff are two of the most concrete achievements of the *Cymru Fydd* movement for greater Welsh autonomy in the late Victorian and Edwardian period (Jenkins 2002). Similarly, the creation of the British Museum in 1753 can be seen as an expression of that craze for so-called British institutions in the middle of the eighteenth century. Yet the process by which the British Museum Library emerged as one of the foremost libraries in the world and the early hub of the information infrastructure in the UK was very much the product of the middle of the nineteenth century. The determination that the British Museum Library should '… unite with the best English library in the world the best Russian library out of Russia, the best German out of Germany, the best Spanish out of Spain, and so for every language, from Italian to Icelandic, from Polish to Portuguese' (Harris 2004) may at a superficial level be read as an imperial statement – a view that the capital of the greatest empire in the world must inevitably have as one of its attributes the greatest library in the world.

Yet, of course, this imperial library was the creation of an exile – Antonio Panizzi, the Principal Librarian of the British Museum from 1856 to 1866 (Miller 1967). Panizzi had fled as a young man from a sentence of execution imposed on him as a Italian nationalist in Naples. Panizzi's Italian revolutionary activities remain in many respects mysterious, but it was said that he remained sufficiently nervous that he had an emergency escape route protected by a bullet-proof door built into his office. This was evidently a man constantly conscious of his exile, and perhaps his British Museum Library should be seen not so much as a library of empire as a library of exile. It perhaps reflected Panizzi's own impatience with a host community that appeared oblivious to European culture. It was a library which enabled the remarkable community of exiles which gathered in London after 1848 to continue in their exile to have access to the intellectual inheritance of their lost countries. It is telling that the most famous user of Panizzi's celebrated reading room was the exile Marx.

The creation at the same time of a Public Record Office in London may at first sight appear to be a more firmly nationalistic activity, driven by directly national concerns – the reliance of English law on precedent and the need to have ready access to documents supporting precedent, an increasing pride in the lines of continuity of the English constitution, a concern with the antiquity and antecedents of such bodies as the peerage and parliament, and so on. The whole concept of the Public Record Office and the British approach to archival science which flowed from it appears bound up with a particular Victorian view of the English constitution and English constitutional history. Yet one of the driving forces behind the creation of that remarkable repository in Chancery Lane, Sir Francis Palgrave, was a Jew and deeply anxious about his relationship to his family history and precedents. As Geoffrey Martin has pointed out (Martin 2004), there were strong parallels in outlook and character between Panizzi and Palgrave, and it is perhaps that awareness of exile, what Lukacs called a 'transcendental homelessness', which links not only Palgrave and Panizzi but also the institutions they created in Great Russell Street and Chancery Lane. The very site of the great repository in Chancery Lane, on the ancient *Domus Conversorum*, reflects a connection with themes of exile.

If the theme of exile can give us fresh perspectives on the history of particular libraries and archives, similarly archives themselves can be subject to exile – the exile of archives. At the simplest level, of course, this is straightforward repatriation, an issue with which we are increasingly becoming familiar. To revert to the history of Freemasonry, this is a subject of major significance at present following the recovery by the French Grand Lodge of more than 750 boxes of masonic archives seized during the German occupation of Paris in the Second World War (Grimsted 2001; 2008). These were sent back to Berlin by the German occupiers to glean information about alleged masonic conspiracies. After the fall of Berlin, the archives were seized by the Soviet Army and taken to Moscow, where they were very carefully sorted, boxed and catalogued by Russian archivists. Their existence in Russia remained unknown and unsuspected until Patricia Kennedy Grimsted tracked them down. Representations were made by the French government for their return, and they were duly returned to Paris in 2004. The exile of such an archive poses issues for the archivists who recover them, such as the way in which the story of the Russian sojourn of this archive should be preserved in the classification and cataloguing of the documents, and the extent to which components of the archive seized from other national grand lodges should be disentangled from it.

Fascinating though this story is, since the survival of this archive was unknown until very recently, it adds little to our understanding of the cultural significance of the exiled archive. More intriguing from this point of view are those exiled archives whose existence is well-known and which exercise continued fascination in the home country. Obvious examples are candidates for restitution such as the 350 Ethiopic manuscripts seized by Napier's forces in the sack of Maqdala in 1868 which are now in the British Library. There are even archives exiled within their own country. The Lindisfarne Gospels, displayed in splendid surroundings in the British Library's new exhibition galleries in London, are sometimes depicted as a manuscript in exile from the north-east of England. The only substantial medieval manuscript from the Isle of Man, the Chronicle of the Kings of Man, also languishes in the British Library. One might also think of the records of the eighteenth-century London Welsh societies in the Department of Manuscripts of the British Library, deposited there by the London Welsh School (Additional MSS.14866–14956). These manuscripts are vital records of a key moment in Welsh language and literature. Currently housed less than ten minutes' walk from the Welsh School which was such a focus of this movement, there seems to be little argument for actual repatriation of these manuscripts. Yet they continue to exercise a fascination for students of Welsh literature, and, by having to use them in London, the Welsh-speaking scholar in a way shares something of the experience of the Welsh exiles in London in the eighteenth century.

Sometimes archives are in exile simply because they were not viable in their home country. The British Library, for example, has a major collection of *samizdat* and printed ephemera associated with the Solidarity movement in Poland.[2] This was systematically collected from Poland in the 1980s (often at great personal risk to the curators involved) because it was not clear at the time that the movement would be successful and that the material would be preserved. The successful collection

---

2 <http://www.bl.uk/collections/easteuropean/polish.html> accessed 14 April 2008.

of underground Polish material prompted similar activities by the British Library elsewhere in Eastern Europe as the Soviet bloc collapsed. In particular, the British Library built up the one of the best collection in the world of books, pamphlets, bulletins, newspapers and documents from all sides involved in the Balkan crisis of the early 1990s.[3] The collection covers the wars in Croatia and Bosnia-Hercegovina, the crisis in Kosovo and NATO bombing of Yugoslavia, and the conflict in Macedonia. The survival of this material was not assured in the countries involved, as the destruction of the Bosnian National Library demonstrates. It is ironic that a key source of information on the traumatic ethnic cleansing and associated population movements in the former Yugoslavia should be an archive that is itself in exile. Many of the items in this collection comprise 'grey literature' which is frequently not regarded as formal archival material, but a more difficult question is the relationship between these archives and the bodies which helped generate them. Is it archivally valid to assemble archives in exile in this way? Do they have any status as archives if they are geographically so far removed from the corporate entity they represent?

In developing the kind of 'archive of exile' envisaged by Martial Staub, one possible model is *Forced Migration Online*, a digital resource developed by the Refugee Studies Centre of the University of Oxford.[4] However, at the heart of *Forced Migration Online* is a digital library comprising over 9,000 full-text items. These are chiefly printed 'grey literature' – reports, offprints, conference proceedings and so on – which were collected by academic staff of the Refugee Studies Centre on an ad hoc basis. Can such an apparently serendipitous collection form an archive? It has not the systematic legacy of a sustained administrative activity. There is no single corporate body responsible for it. Yet it is an enormously rich resource for investigating and understanding the experience of exile, richer than many administrative archives with their transitory shadowy exiles. Very quickly, in investigating exile we are forced to recognize the value of sources of information which seem very different from conventional archives. Consider the case of the Marranos, Portuguese and Spanish Jews who underwent a process of forced conversion. On the surface, they appeared as conventional Christians, but behind closed doors they retained their loyalty to the Jewish religion and practised it in secret. In conventional archives, there is by definition no trace of this hidden identity. The French anthropologist Nathan Wachtel has shown how, in order to recapture the hidden history and remembrances of these groups, it is necessary to cross-reference early modern inquisition records and interviews with surviving Marrano-Jews from Latin America (Wachtel 2001). Remembrances of ritual, of family traditions and inter-connections with individuals may all be significant. Oral history is of immense importance, but it is only one component. Archives engaged in gathering together the memories of such groups, such as that at the Institute of Marrano-Anusim Studies at Gan Yavne in Israel,[5] are very different from a conventional archive in their mixture of reminiscence, ritual, books and artefacts with conventional documentary material.

---

3 <http://www.bl.uk/collections/easteuropean/balkan.html> accessed 14 April 2008.

4 <http://www.forcedmigration.org> accessed 14 April 2008.

5 <http://www.casa-shalom.com> accessed 14 April 2008.

Since exiles by definition transcend governmental boundaries, a conventional archive, focused on a government body or other administrative unit, excludes exiles. To follow the exile, we must go outside the Record Office doors. To invite the exile into the archive, we need to widen our concept of the archive. Oral history is of immense importance in this pursuit of the exile, as are family photographs and papers. These are the type of informal materials which form the focus of many community archive projects. Community archives assume that archives can be created not only by institutions but also put together by informal groups which simply have shared experiences and interests. In their diverse, informal and 'bottom-up' approach, community archives represent one of the most striking and innovative responses to new critical theories – although many of the participants in community archives would hardly see themselves as theorists in action. The great growth in community archives in recent years has been fostered by the support offered by such activities as the Archives 4 All programme at the National Archives[6] and the Community Archives Development Group of the National Council on Archives.[7] These have assisted community archives in accessing funding from the Heritage Lottery Fund and elsewhere. A portal to community archives, <communityarchives.org.uk>, has been established.

Many of the community archives which can be accessed through <communityarchives.org.uk> relate to distinct and identifiable ethnic communities. We have memories of Italian immigrants from Emilia-Romagna and Sicily living in the Lee Valley north of London. We have an Indian community centre archive in Belfast and a history of the Asian community in Tyne and Wear. There is the Cypriot Diaspora Archive, based in Haringey in north London where there is a large Cypriot community and the first attempt systematically to record experiences of Cypriot migration to London. Characteristically many of these archives consist of a mixture of oral history interviews, photographs and a few scanned documents. The Cypriot Diaspora Archive[8] is certainly one of the most impressive of its type but the question is immediately raised as to what should be in the archive. In addition to interviews, photographs and other documentation, there is a description of a book which is not available via the website. There are also web pages describing a play developed as part of the project. If the website is a community archive, it would seem logical that the content of both the play and the book should have been represented in some way. More disturbing is the ephemeral character of some of the archives: for example, the domain name for the Chinese in Newham website has not been maintained, so that it now points to an advertisement for surveillance equipment.[9] Links to a number of other archives in the directory are broken. Should greater stability be expected of an archive? Is the key characteristic of an archive not precisely that stability in time?

---

6 <http://www.nationalarchives.gov.uk/partnerprojects/a4a/> accessed 14 April 2008.

7 <http://www.ncaonline.org.uk/community_archives/terms_of_reference/> accessed 14 April 2008.

8 <http://www.cypriotdiaspora.com/> accessed 14 April 2008.

9 <http://www.hidden-histories.org/Esch_pages/Chinese_link.html> accessed 14 April 2008.

However, perhaps even stability is not a feature of the archive. At the time of writing, Facebook included over 500 groups whose title includes the word 'exiles'. These groups provide very direct testimony as to the structure, contacts and experience of exiled groups. They include, for example, Malta Gay Exiles, a group established to argue the case for greater equality for gays, lesbians and transsexuals in Malta.[10] The group offers the following definition of exile: 'In this case the use of the term "exile" refers to voluntary absence from the country and/or a certain level of psychological distancing from an anti-GLBT culture'. Since the Facebook group campaigns to improve conditions for gays in Malta, it draws in many who are simply supporters of the campaign and not themselves physical exiles, but nevertheless the Facebook group provides direct evidence of the way in which anti-gay legislation has driven many out of Malta. Facebook also contains many groups populated by straightforward exiles of particular nations or regions. The exchanges on these groups provide immediate evidence of the contemporary experience of exile and must surely be regarded as archives, but the very nature of Facebook means that the information in these groups is not stable in time. The archive of exile here becomes a flux, and starts to mirror the experience of exile itself.

Many of the immigrant communities in <communityarchives.org.uk> are not exiles and would not see themselves as such, but community archives nevertheless illustrate how, in developing archives of exile, we need to extend our view of the content of archives. Following the overthrow of Salvador Allende in 1973, a large group of Chilean exiles settled in South Yorkshire. These Chilean exiles set up various organizations to denounce human rights abuses in Chile and Latin America and in 1987 the Chile Sports and Cultural and Development Association (CSDC) was set up to coordinate solidarity campaigns, and to develop self-support mechanisms to bring the community more closely together. The website of the CSDC[11] richly documents the activities of this community. One of the chief means by which these exiles have recorded their experience of exile has been through the creation of *arpilleras*, a form of patchwork. These patchworks show:

> the coupe against the elected Salvador Allende in 1973, and the rusulting [sic] oppression.
> the violence and torture
> military coupe
> the 'disappeared'
> exile
> resettlement in the UK.
> The object of the work is to show thier [sic] history and that after thier exile, they are now part of the UK.

Even the misspellings of words like 'rusulting' are telling evidence of the experience of exile. These patchworks are among the most striking expressions of the Chilean experience of exile in South Yorkshire. Clearly, in developing an archive of exile, we move quickly beyond the purely textual and encompass material objects. A recent

---

10 The website for this group is <http://www.gayexiles.com> accessed 14 April 2008.
11 <http://www.chilescda.org> accessed 14 April 2008.

display at the Millennium Galleries in Sheffield was *Migrations*, part of a multi-stranded project being developed by Belfast Exposed exploring different experiences of migration.[12] Among the works displayed were *My Lovely Day* (1997) by Penny Siopis, which comprised:

> ... spliced sequences of 8mm home movies that the artist's mother shot in the 1950s and 1960s in South Africa with sound and visual text which tell an elemental story of migration, displacement and exile. The words (narrative) are those of Siopis' maternal grandmother telling her grandchildren of her emotional and literal journeys between Europe, Greece and South Africa in the early part of last century. The moment of her telling is apartheid South Africa, as are the scenes captured on film, yet her references to social turmoil and catastrophe are those of an earlier time – the 1922 Greco-Turkish conflict in Smyrna, World War I and World War II. The sound combines traditional Greek music and song, with Siopis' mother's voice singing 'My Lovely Day', made as a 78 record in 1955.

Another work in the display was *Refugee Talks* (1998) by Andrea Lang, which consisted of nine sequences, each one featuring a person or group of people singing a song. Each song was recorded by an inmate of a refugee reception centre in Oslo and was chosen to reflect their experience. The catalogue comments:

> Andrea Lange's works are involved with the human drama of community. For her, issues of displacement, assimilation and difference revolve around the central point of communication, inclusion and understanding. In a range of profound projects over a number of years she has investigated the situation of confrontation, incarceration, and commemoration to reveal the complexities inherent in the idea of placing the self inside the system of the other.

The phrase 'the complexities inherent in the idea of placing the self inside the system of the other' expresses perfectly the way in which an engagement with the theme of exile can disrupt and challenge our understanding of and engagement with archives. And it is helping to discover and investigate complexities of precisely this kind that an engagement with theory can transform our understanding of archives.

References

Bakhtin, M. (1984), *Rabelais and his World* (Bloomington IN: Indiana University Press).

Barta, P. et al. (2001), *Carnivalizing Difference: Bakhtin and the Other* (London: Routledge).

Barthes, R. (1986), *The Rustle of Language* (Oxford: Blackwell).

Brown, C.G. (2005), *Postmodernism for Historians* (Edinburgh: Pearson).

Burt, R. (2003), 'Freemasonry and business networking during the Victorian period', *Economic History Review*, 56, 657–88.

---

12 <http://www.belfastexposed.org/exhibitions/index.php?exhibition=36&show=past&year=2006> accessed 14 April 2008.

Colley, L. (1992), *Britons: Forging the Nation, 1707–1837* (New Haven CT: Yale University Press).

Derrida, J. (1998), *Archive Fever: a Freudian Impression* (Chicago IL: University of Chicago Press).

Grimsted, P.K. (2008), 'Displaced cultural treasures as a result of World War II and restitution issues: a bibliography of publications by Patricia Kennedy Grimsted', at <http://www.iisg.nl/archives-and-restitution/bibliography.php> accessed 14 April 2008.

———— (2001), *Trophies of War and Empire: the Archival Heritage of Ukraine, World War II, and the International Politics of Restitution* (Cambridge MA: Harvard University Press).

Harris, P. (2004), 'Thomas Watts 1811–1869', in *Oxford Dictionary of National Biography* (Oxford: Oxford University Press).

Harvey, D. (1999), 'Lost children or enemy aliens? Classifying the population of Alsace after the First World War', *Journal of Contemporary History*, 34 (4), 537–54.

Jacobs, M. (2003), *The Radical Enlightenment*, 2nd edn (Los Angeles CA: Temple).

Jenkins, D. (2002), *A Refuge in Peace and War: the National Library of Wales to 1952* (Aberystwyth: National Library of Wales).

Martin, G.H. (2004), 'Sir Francis Palgrave [formerly Cohen], 1788–1861', in *Oxford Dictionary of National Biography* (Oxford: Oxford University Press).

Miller, E. (1967), *Prince of Librarians: the Life and Times of Antonio Panizzi of the British Museum* (London: Secker & Warburg).

Payne, H.C. and Grosshans, H. (1963), 'The exiled revolutionaries and the French political police in the 1850s', *American Historical Review*, 68 (4), 954–73.

Prescott, A. (forthcoming), 'Relations between the Swedish and English Grand Lodges in the eighteenth century'.

Reynolds, S. (1983), 'Medieval *origines gentium* and the community of the realm', *History*, 68, 375–90.

Stevenson, D. (2002), 'James Anderson: Man and Mason', in Weisberger et al. (eds).

Wachtel, N. (2001), *La foi du souvenir: labyrinthes marranes* (Paris, Seuil).

Weisberger, W. (2000), 'John Theophilus Desaguliers: promoter of the Enlightenment and of speculative Freemasonry', *Ars Quatuor Coronatorum*, 113, 65–96.

Weisberger W. et al. (eds) (2002), *Freemasonry on Both Sides of the Atlantic, Essays concerning the Craft in the British Isles, Europe, the United States, and Mexico* (Boulder CO and New York: Columbia University Press).

Theme IV
Archival Use and Users

Chapter 8

Users, Use and Context:
Supporting Interaction Between Users
and Digital Archives

Andrea Johnson

Introduction

The first chapter in our third theme, 'Archival Use and Users', is essentially a work
in progress: it gives a detailed overview of the author's doctoral research carried out
over four years, in six countries and engaging over 500 users. The chapter examines
those challenges which users face when searching and using primary sources in a
digital format and identifies the main problems users encounter when searching this
complex archival domain. The lengthy search for a methodological framework is
discussed, as is the development of a contextual model of interaction; other ongoing
studies of the use of technologies to support specific aspects of the interaction process
are also considered. The chapter concludes with a summary of key findings to date
and an examination of how best to manage raised user expectations in the wake of
search engine dominance and TV programmes like *Who Do You Think You Are?*.

So What is the Problem with Digital Archives?

Over the past five years there has been a large investment in digital archives but
early evaluations have shown that many of these projects have not lived up to the
overarching expectation of 'access for all' (Economou 2002; Education for Change
2005). The research to date has shown that users continue to find digital archives
difficult to navigate and search.

My undergraduate thesis involved undertaking a summative user-centred
evaluation of a large archival digitization project (Johnson 2004). This research
resulted in the identification of several problems areas, three of which provided a
particular basis for further investigation; they are summarized as follows:

- *Search behaviour.* Specific types of search behaviours resulted in varying
  search strategies which had a direct effect on search results and user
  satisfaction. Searches which focused on the location of a specific item often
  ended unsuccessfully.
- *Navigation.* Many users found the site difficult to navigate, with 29 per cent
  of users stating they did not find the site easy to use. (These users had average

or above-average IT experience.)

- *Context.* The principal aim of the project was to improve access to archives; however 70 per cent of participants stated they would not visit their local archive. The main reason for this appears to have been a lack of understanding that the digital object represented a 'real' object that could be accessed locally. As users did not associate the digital object with a 'real' object, contextualization of the object within a wider perspective was poor.

These research findings have been echoed across the digital archive environment. Where user-centred principles have been applied in the design process, projects boast a superior interface design; however, there remains a complexity in navigation and a difficulty in contextualizing the digital object. Initial research led me to examine non-user groups with an aim to design interfaces that supported their specialist requirements (Johnson 2005).

To extract the information that would facilitate interface design for specialist user groups, an initial study of the digital archive environment was undertaken in order to gain a 'snapshot' of the current position. During this study it became apparent that there is a distinct lack of fundamental concepts and models regarding users and how they interact with the system. To illustrate this point: in *Theories of Information Behaviour*, the comprehensive ASIS&T research guide (Fisher et al. 2005), only one of the 72 theories listed in the text examine searching archival material. Archives seemingly are the 'poor cousins' compared to libraries in the information science domain or are not seen by the information sector as being separate from libraries.

Having consulted with various user groups, archivists and academics across disciplines, it is evident that the real challenge of digital archives lies in understanding user behaviours, developing robust conceptual models based on this evidence, building systems and utilizing technologies. Conceptual models of users and their interaction are seen as prerequisite to transforming this problem domain. Findings from this initial study have led to a revised research agenda.

To date systems have been designed primarily with archival description and arrangement in mind. Whilst this has proved satisfactory for many professionals, it leaves many users lost and confused in the hierarchical arrangement of the digital object. So how can this situation be rectified? Is there a solution?

Professor of Archival Research at Glasgow University, Michael Moss believes the solution lies in actively engaging with other disciplines that use, handle and exploit information in all its different guises. He states: 'There is nothing to be gained from remaining in an archival gulag except extinction.' Professor Moss has witnessed the benefits of this type of collaboration on a visit to the Inter-Faculty Information Initiative at the University of Tokyo which brings together specialists from many disciplines to address a raft of information needs and user seeking behaviours. An interesting feature of this initiative is that it pulls information professions out of their 'institutional comfort zone' into the hurly-burly of intellectual discourse, forcing them to look at their services from different perspectives and explore radically different technical opportunities.

If the archival domain is to respond to its users constructively and successfully it needs to know them in far more detail. 'User-pulled', 'bottom-up design' and 'user-centred design' are all terms that describe a philosophy of design based on a significant understanding of the user and how they actually use the technology under investigation. This is now widely recognized as a design approach that is more likely to result in high-quality, user-accessible systems. The in-depth, ethnographic approach taken in this research is intended to reflect this, but I have encountered some criticism from the archive community for adopting this methodology. There are professionals within this domain who truly believe that they know 'what is best' for the user and that undertaking real user consultation is a waste of precious resources. However, I do not support this view and firmly believe that however thorny the discussion may become, 'user-led' design holds the solution to the lofty aim of 'access for all'.

A Research Agenda

In order to provide an overarching context for the findings detailed in this chapter, it is helpful to establish the main research questions that form the basis of my enquiries:

- *The user.* Who uses digital archives and for what purpose? What are the motivational factors?
- *The information-seeking and retrieval process.* How do users currently seek and retrieve information within a dynamic digital environment?
- *A model of contextual interaction.* How do we model the interaction between the user and the digital archive, capturing the multidimensional context that exists in each interaction?
- *Translation of information.* How do we support the user in translating information to meet her/his own specific information need?
- *The wider perspective.* How do the findings from this specialist problem domain fit into the wider theoretical debate within the information science field?

In order to begin to answer these questions a comprehensive study of the domain has been undertaken; this started in summer 2004 and continues to date.

In Search of a Conceptual Framework

For two years I struggled to find a guiding conceptual framework that 'fitted' this domain. This quest for rigorous intellectual support acutely highlights the need for conceptual models and methods for the archival domain when examining users, use and their interaction with archival material, whatever the form.

Allan et al. have identified 'Global Information Access' and 'Contextual Retrieval' as the two great challenges for information retrieval and seeking research (Allan et al. 2003). The problem of contextual retrieval in a digital archive environment remains relatively unexplored. The problem I encountered from the outset was that current information-seeking and retrieval models that could be applied to digital archives would only capture a small amount of the complex contextual factors that exist in this specialist domain. The model of contextual interaction had to facilitate the incorporation of a robust user model. The problem was further compounded by the fact that there are no universally recognized user models for this domain. The model would also need to include elements such as user goals and context.

An extensive literature review of information-seeking models was undertaken in order to identify key areas of analysis and development; particular attention has been given to Bates (1989), Ellis et al. (1993), Marchionini (1995), Kuhlthau (1993), Dervin and Nilan (1986), Yang (1997), Vakkari (2001a; 2001b), Ingwersen and Järvelin (2005) and Savolainen and Kari (2006).

In an attempt to find a suitable conceptual framework I have undertaken a comprehensive review of conceptual models across disciplines. Kuhlthau states that collaboration across disciplines is essential for future research (Kuhlthau 2005). She proposes four imperatives for fostering collaboration and continuing to develop the conceptual frameworks; this research incorporates all four of the points in its long-term aims and objectives:

* Stay with a problem long enough to verify findings and draw concepts from the findings.
* Apply the broad conceptual frameworks to inform the findings of one's studies.
* Develop research projects that incorporate concepts of interest to more than one area of the field.
* Design application of the concepts for implementation into systems and services.

As a result of this transdisciplinary approach, Cognitive Work Analysis was identified as a framework to support a comprehensive design and evaluation process (Rasmussen et al. 1994; Pejtersen 1989). Cognitive Work Analysis is an analysis that examines the constraints which shape information behaviour. It investigates behaviour in context; individual studies provide results which are applied to the specialist domain under investigation. Cognitive Work Analysis facilitates this by evaluating the systems already in place and developing recommendations for future design.

On implementing Cognitive Work Analysis, it soon became apparent that a single researcher cannot apply it to a satisfactory standard. The same can also be said of Contextual Design techniques (Beyer and Holzblatt 1998). Contextual Design is a powerful design tool but many of its processes need to be undertaken by design teams as opposed to a single researcher. Rapid Contextual Design techniques will be implemented later this year with another researcher during the design process for Archifau Cymru: Archives Wales, a programme for a national virtual archive for Wales.

Discourse Analysis was also investigated as a means for facilitating the analysis of discourses in the archival domain, providing a practical insight into how discourses can affect the initial information need, the information-seeking process and the resulting use of archival resources. To date there have been similar investigations into the digital library sector (Talja 2005), but no such investigations have been made in the archival sector. It was decided that this conceptual framework was too far removed from mainstream computer science and would be viewed with a certain amount of suspicion, and may be better applied to the archivist community than to the user community.

After nearly two years searching for a conceptual framework that would fit this domain, I attended a conference entitled *Information Use in Information Society* at Bratislava in October 2006, where Professor Tom Wilson introduced Activity Theory as a conceptual framework for rethinking information behaviour research (Wilson 2006). Following this and further to a vigorous investigation of Activity Theory and interaction design, Activity Theory was adopted as the conceptual framework through which the remainder of the research would be undertaken.

Activity Theory and Digital Archives

Activity Theory is a general conceptual framework; it is not a highly predicative theory. It is a psychological approach based on cultural-historical psychology and was a dominant theory under communism in the Soviet Union. It seems fitting that I spoke about the application of Activity Theory in the development of twenty-first century digital archives in the place of its birth at a conference in Moscow earlier this year.

The main rationale for adopting Activity Theory is that it focuses on the activities of people using technology rather than on human-computer interaction (Kaptelinin and Nardi 2006). This focus on activities enables researchers to extend the scope of their analysis to include higher-level, meaningful tasks.

According to Leontiev interaction between human beings and the world is organized into functionally subordinated hierarchical levels (Leontiev 1978). He identified three levels: activity, actions and operations. Activities, identified in this research as the interaction between the user and the digital archive, are undertaken to fulfil a motive.

In Activity Theory, 'activity' refers to a specific level of interaction, the level at which the object has the status of a motive. A motive is an object that meets a need of the subject – the ultimate cause behind any human activities is need. The object of activity, which is defined by Leontiev as the 'true motive' of an activity, is the most important attribute differentiating one activity from another. 'Thus the concept activity is necessarily connected with the concept of motive. Activity does not exist without a motive ; "non-motivated" activity is not activity without a motive but activity with a subjectively and objectively hidden motive' (Leontiev 1978).

This concept of motive helped to crystallize an area of key findings from the longitudinal study. The users' goals or needs were found to be of hierarchical arrangement, with high-level goals driving the user more than low-level goals. For example, a user searching for crucial documents to support a legal claim against the State has a higher motivational context than a user who is browsing for details of their house history.

Preliminary findings are indicating that the user's motivational context may provide the key in identifying 'user-pulled rather than technology-pushed' design solutions. Identifying the motive for use early in the interaction process provides designers with an opportunity to place the user on a pathway that others with similar motives have travelled and have found useful. The idea of pathways to common sources of information based on the user's motivational context has been well received by a number of national repositories and will be developed over the coming months. It is hoped that a taxonomy of motivational factors will be produced as part of this research.

Another major factor in adopting Activity Theory was its recognition of a special status for culturally developed artefacts or tools, considering them to be fundamental mediators that relate human beings to the world and to human culture and history (Vygotsky 1978). The tools usually reflect the experience of other people who have tried to solve similar problems before and invented or modified the tool to make it more efficient and useful; an example of this would be a cataloguing system. This concept of tool mediation plays an important role in digital archives, especially with reference to archival context.

The use of tools within the digital archival domain can be seen as an accumulation and transmission of archival knowledge. In this research, technology is regarded as a tool that mediates the interaction between the user and the digital object. Emphasis is placed on contextual factors which exist in the domain and on the interaction between users and the digital object via their system environment.

Because tool mediation is such an important aspect of Activity Theory it also takes into account long-term developmental changes in users, technology, their interaction and the overall context of the domain. Once again this long-term development aids in setting the scene for what has gone before in terms of tool development, what has taken place during the study and preparing the way for what may happen in the future.

Collecting the Behaviours of Digital Archive Users

Since 2004 I have conducted a longitudinal study of the information-seeking behaviours of digital archive users. The main areas under investigation have been these:

- How do users with a lack of knowledge search this complex information space and contextualize information?
- How do expert users search this complex information space and contextualize information?
- What are the common problems encountered by both sets of users?
- How do archivists and other information professionals design and evaluate these systems?

The study has encompassed various sites across Europe and North America utilizing a multi-method approach to data collection. The primary source of qualitative data has been provided via ethnographic observation techniques, supported particularly through individual or group interviews. Weblogs, questionnaires and user diaries have also been utilized. In addition to this a series of evaluations have been undertaken in order to gain an insight into the behaviours of digital archive users and produce a pool of data on which the model of contextual interaction could be built. In addition to this a process of contextual inquiry has been undertaken in order to understand the domain and users' mental models, with the production of hierarchical task analysis, domain models and personas.

At the start of the research the findings were available from a small number of studies which had been undertaken to examine digital archive users and their information-seeking behaviours (Duff et al. 2004; Duff and Johnson 2002). In addition to this, the data from the Public Service Quality Group of the National Council on Archives' *Survey of Visitors to UK Archives 2006* was also available. Public Service Quality Group provides a 'snapshot' of user behaviour when visiting an archive.

This multi-method approach to the study has ensured a rich and vibrant snapshot of the domain. It is hoped that this detailed inspection of users and their interaction will yield some suggestions on how best to evaluate digital domains. At present baseline metrics and methodologies that can be shared across digital projects are uncommon (Harley et al. 2006).

As the author is a member of AX-SNET (Archival eXcellence in Information Seeking Studies Network), this study feeds into the work of an international group of researchers whose overarching aims are to improve access to primary sources and explore the ways users seek information in archives. The research group is currently making recommendations on the establishment of metrics that support shared data-gathering and data sets.

AX-SNET is also investigating the development of an online analytical tool that could provide a detailed account of remote user behaviour. This is a challenge recognized across the domain: various national repositories are trialling analytical tools and the Public Service Quality Group have this year piloted an online survey with a view to capturing data on remote users.

Analysing the Behaviours of Digital Archive Users

It became evident very early on in the study that there are three main problems continually encountered by users; these are considered below.

Where Shall I Look?

> *P068:*[1] 'I really have no idea where to start this search; I've typed my question in Google and had no joy. I don't know where to look – that's the problem.'

A common starting point for inexperienced or novice users are search engines such as Google. Without the knowledge or experience to locate archival sources, the user will often become frustrated at this early point in the interaction process. Expert users often rely on provenance to structure their search by identifying the function of the archive and its intended audience.

As Beth Yakel states:

---

1 Prefix denotes the unique ID number that each participant has been allocated.

The importance of entering any archives with a place to begin cannot be overstated. This appeared to be a means by which researchers established a modicum of control over the environment ... creating a space from which to reconnoitre the archives on one's own terms by providing a safe harbour or known place from which to begin (Yakel and Torres 2003, 71).

What Shall I Say?

> *P049:* 'I know I'm not asking the right question, I'm just not asking it right as I know the document is there as I have actually seen it. What do I need to type in that box to get the result?'

It may seem like stating the obvious, but asking the right questions is a prerequisite to getting the right answers. Asking questions or mediation is an essential part of the interaction process in a face-to-face encounter between user and archivist. Having observed many hours of this type of interaction two points are apparent. Firstly, in many cases users can be reluctant to ask questions as they do not want to appear stupid:

> *P106:* 'I want to ask her [the archivist] but I feel right daft and that fella at the desk now, he looks like he knows what he's doing ... I'll wait a bit and see if I can do it myself.'

Secondly, the reference archivist employs a strategy of 'step away from that question'. This first became clear at an observation session at the National Archives, Kew, in 2006. I had asked the Customer Relationship Manager to explain what processes he went through when dealing with users on the telephone. During this session he explained:

> You have to get them to step away from the question, it may be it's not what they want to know but it's how they have framed the query. By getting them to step away from the question you can start to establish what it really is they are looking for and help them locate information.

Given that mediation is so important in a face-to-face interaction, how is this then translated into a digital environment? Butterworth states that digital archive use disintermediates (Butterworth 2006). Disintermediation happens where the role that the archivists play in supporting users to make the best use of archival resources is removed. He advocates that digitizing archival materials and putting them online does not solve this disintermediation: in fact it compounds the problem. He suggests ways of repairing the disintermediation gap through the provision of online tutorials and annotation stating what the collection can be used for as opposed to the standard archival description

What is That?

> *P032:* [laughs] 'I have no idea what that is, it wasn't what I was expecting, put it that way. My goodness, I was hoping for a copy of a Birth Certificate of my great-great-aunt, I now need to decipher all this information. I have no clue where to start.'

Having successfully navigated the search environment and yielded results, the user can still be thwarted at this stage in the interaction process, as they cannot contextualize the information without support. The need by the user for interpretation and translation is further examined below under the heading 'The user's active construction of meaning and archival context'.

These three problem areas encountered by users are common throughout the research findings. They form the basis on which any design recommendations are based: does this system support the user to find, ask and make sense of archival material in a digital environment?

Whilst collecting the behaviours of digital users it became evident that areas such as use of language, the use of technology, the hierarchical arrangement of the archive and the archival expertise of the archivist play a key role in supporting archive users. These areas do not neatly transfer over into the digital environment, where the problem is further compounded by deep data structures and an innate difficulty in understanding the representational relationship between the surrogate and the primary source.

> *P025:* 'I know if I was at the archive I could find this document; it's just so confusing when you are sitting here on your own without their [the archivist's] help. Look at that ... what on earth does that mean? You need a degree to understand this stuff.'

The problem with digital archives seems to be that users lack the support of archivists in formulating queries, identifying archival sources and interpreting and contextualizing the search results. This is corroborated by a recent survey at The National Archives, England (2002), which reported that 98 per cent of their onsite users find information that is useful to them, once they sought out archival expertise. This piece of research is significant in that it indicates that it is a lack of archival intelligence, as opposed to technical skill, that leads to users seeking mediation. It makes sense then to examine how archivists mediate the interaction between the user and primary sources, with a view to seeing how this can be translated across into a digital domain.

> *P078:* 'I come here [to the archive] to do my research as experience has taught me that I do not do well at home on my own. Some days I will not approach the staff once, other days I can be at the desk six or seven times. They know where the records are and what is appropriate for my research interest. I wish I could transfer all their knowledge on to a computer and take it home with me. They say a lot of this is now online, that's all fine and good if you know what it is you are looking for.'

By collecting the behaviours of digital archive users it is hoped that this 'bottom-up' approach, based on a deeper understanding of how users actually seek and use digital archival resources, will inform system design within the domain and aid professionals in providing services that users require in order to effectively use digital archival resources.

The model of contextual interaction, detailed below, is based on this 'bottom-up' approach and is a direct result of over four years of user behaviour observation. This is one example of how I have used the rich and multifaceted data gleaned from the continuing longitudinal study of digital archive use.

The data will also be applied to provide a searching and retrieval environment that could be easily accessible, actively supporting user orientation and the presentation of contextual information. A recent study by the Arts and Humanities Research Council found that archives, museums and libraries are the most trusted information sources; however, it was the easily accessible sources which are least trusted, such as the Internet, newspapers and television, that were used most (Usherwood 2005).

The User's Active Construction of Meaning and Archival Context

What makes searching digital archives different from any other type of exploratory search? Why do users encounter the 'What is that?' problem? The answer lies with the archival context.

Primary sources are complex objects; they necessitate contextual interpretation and analysis by the user. This interpretation and analysis requires knowledge of record form by the user and knowledge of the purpose for which the records have been kept: this is a prerequisite to a successful outcome. Documents cannot be retrieved without an understanding of their creation and context. An archival document is born out of a function or activity, it has relationships with other documents. These links or bonds are given a special term in Canada: here they are called the 'archival bond'. These links need to be transparent; this relationship to others through the archival bond forms the basis of archival context. The following quote illustrates this: 'The object itself represents the tip of a very large iceberg: the tip is visible above the water only because there is a large mass of complex social relationships "underneath" it – that generate, use and give meaning to, the digital documents' (Rehberger et al. 2006).

A professional genealogist, for example, will know where all major collections relevant to genealogy are located. These collections, whose records provide a rich source of information to the family historian, were originally gathered for purposes quite other than those for which they are now used. The novice user, however, will not know which collections are rich sources for family historians. Having no knowledge of archival sources and no grasp of the significance of related records, and unaware of both the original purpose and the modern potential of these records, the novice will not know where to start.

In a digital format the archival context is system-dependent, as it is through the system that the user begins to understand and analyse the archival value of the digital object. This need for interpretation and translation by the user is in direct conflict with the whole principle of provenance and archival description; that is, non-interpretation by the archivist.

The problem of archival context is further compounded by system provision: all systems are not created equally, some facilitate archival context better than others, a fact which has been highlighted during the evaluation of a number of digital archives.

The evidence suggests that a digital object's meaning is socially constructed through use. Thus one way to begin to understand an object is to understand how people interpret and use the object at a particular point in time. This proposition lies at the heart of my research.

When observing user behaviour it became apparent that users actively construct the meaning of a digital object through a strategy of 'translation'. This strategy is one whereby the user has identified an information 'gap' and so has an information need. The user is required to define and articulate this need in order to search the digital archive; this requires translation of the information need into language that matches both the archival domain and the search interface. At this early stage many users encounter the problem of 'Where shall I look?' and 'What shall I say?'. Once the source and language of the search have been successfully navigated the user can begin the search process. This is where a further process of translation takes place, where the context of the digital object, provided by the system, is identified by the user who then distils and transforms this into a format that 'makes sense' to them and their specific information need.

If the user cannot contextualize the digital object, the 'What is that?' problem occurs. In order to combat this, users consistently and almost without fail actively seek out sources of expertise to aid them in translating the information they discover during their search. The sources of 'expertise' range from tapping the shoulder of the person who happens to be sitting next to them, to seeking out archival expertise via digital reference or through the archivist sitting at the reference desk.

In effect the translation is an explicit contextualization of information intended to meet a defined and articulated individual need. The level of expertise required to support the contextualization of data has a direct correlation to the perceived complexity of the information seeking task by the user. From the results of the study to date it is apparent that there is very little research being undertaken to discover how users employ this strategy of translation in actively constructing their meaning of the digital object. How users could be supported in this process is a key part of this research, with social computing, discussion forums, online expertise and intelligent help systems all being investigated.

A Model of Contextual Interaction

One of the main outputs of my doctoral research is a model of contextual interaction between the user and the digital archive, see Appendix 1.

Created as a direct result of collecting the behaviours of digital archive users, this 'bottom-up' approach is based on a deeper understanding of how users actually seek and use digital archival resources. As noted earlier under the heading 'In search of a conceptual framework', the creation of the model was undertaken with no primary conceptual model/framework in place; however it was identified from the outset that the concept of archival intelligence was a key concept through which the model could be developed (Yakel and Torres 2003).

Based on the archival intelligence (AI) study there are three forms of knowledge required to work effectively with primary sources and become an expert user. These are: domain (subject) knowledge, artefactual knowledge and archival intelligence.

AI refers to the knowledge about the environment in which the search for primary sources is being conducted; AI is a researcher's knowledge of archival principles, practices and institutions, such as the reasons underlying archival rules and procedures, how to develop search strategies to explore research questions and an understanding of the relationship between primary sources and their surrogates (Yakel and Torres 2003).

Archival intelligence can be categorised into *three dimensions*; within each of these three areas, the study has identified characteristics that reveal expertise:

- knowledge of archival theory, practice and procedures
- the ability to develop strategies to reduce uncertainty and ambiguity
- intellective skills.

Each of these areas has been mapped across the model of contextual interaction. The concept of archival intelligence, along with the results of the user behaviour study, provided a robust basis on which the model was designed.

Testing and Evaluation of the Model of Contextual Interaction

The testing and evaluation of the model of contextual interaction is being coordinated through the application of the activity checklist, which Kaptelinin et al. (1999) described as 'a tool for representing the "space" of context'. The application of the activity checklist is one of the ways I have ensured that Activity Theory is applied throughout the remainder of the research. One of the by-products of this application will be a robust questionnaire based on the activity checklist criteria that can be used by other researchers in this domain.

The testing and analysis is being undertaken in a series of evaluations and tests which encompass:

- *user studies:* variety of user types with different motivational factors
- *user panel:* consisting of all major stake-holders
- *usability testing:* including thinking-aloud observation
- *interviews:* both semi-structured and time-line
- *contextual inquiry:* to understand domain and mental models
- *questionnaires:* both online and paper
- *weblogs.*

During the initial stages of testing it became clear that central themes were emerging which could be attributed to specific use types. Following this discovery, personas were identified as a means of presenting and analysing this information. Personas are a powerful tool for understanding and communicating user behaviours, needs, desires and contexts (Kuniavsky 2003; Pham and Greene 2003). They are archetype representations of actual groups of users and their needs, based on research with real people.

Personas serve as a critical design and analysis tool as they allow for a greater understanding of users, their goals and behaviours as they position the user at the centre of the design process.

The development of personas has been a three-part process: identifying target segments; conducting qualitative research; and analysing the research results and developing personas (Pham and Greene 2003).

The data from the testing of the model of contextual interaction was analysed to identify goals, patterns and needs within and across user segments. From this, primary and secondary personas have been identified. Primary personas drive design and reflect the group most difficult to design for. A project that satisfies the needs of the primary persona will likely meet the needs of the secondary persona. Conversely, a project designed around the needs of secondary personas are likely to frustrate and confuse the primary personas. (Each project should have between three and seven personas.)

The primary persona is Bob, our 'TV hobbyist' presented in Appendix 2. He represents very distinct needs, motivations, expectations and technology implications. The decision to make Bob the primary persona was made very early on in the analysis process, influenced by the research findings to date of novice users struggling with digital archival material. This, coupled with the prospect of the continuing popularity of family and local history and an ageing population in the UK, makes this user segment a primary design aim. Further analysis and testing of the persona Bob, our TV hobbyist, is planned for 2008.

The Formation Process: How to Introduce Bob to the Archive Domain

It is clear that early intervention will aid the user in problems of 'Where shall I look?' and 'What shall I say?'. There is very little low-level help available to users like Bob who need this type of support. Virtual reality tours and animation, speech interfaces, multimedia provision and visualization techniques are currently all under investigation as ways of aiding Bob to introduce him to the archive domain.

> *P096:* 'I don't use help. Tell you what, I'd like a kind of idiot's guide to archives, written in plain English for those who have never used them before ... now that's not rocket science is it?'

During the testing users have offered an insight into the types of supports they would consider useful; these range from virtual tours of the archive and an 'idiot's' guide to finding sources to access to chat rooms (asking for helpful pointers to get started) and case study examples of how others have undertaken similar problems. It is interesting to note that novice users do not consider themselves 'researchers' and tools such as 'research guides' will not appeal to this type of user as they do not identify themselves in this way.

Bob Wants to be an Active Participant, not a Passive Consumer

Based on the findings to date there is a strong body of evidence that many non-users see the top facilitators to accessing an archive to be:

- accessing via the Internet
- tools that support contributing content
- making content relevant to them
- promotion of the extent of archival material available
- provision of tools and aids that support them
- making records easily searchable with digital content.

These facilitators to access indicate that we are witnessing a paradigm shift from:

Passive consumer → Active participant

This shift from passive consumer to active participant can be illustrated through the popularity of sites that proffer the opportunity of user-generated description and content, such as the BBC website. Whilst the idea of user-generated description makes many archivists very nervous, social computing technologies may offer alternative ways of providing users with information in a way that requires less specialist knowledge or skills, supporting them in their active construction of meaning of the digital object. Various genres of social computing are currently being tested to see what fits the domain and at what stage in the interaction process they should be introduced.

The 'Your Archives' Project (2007) at the National Archives (England, Wales and the UK) and the Polar Bear Expedition Digital Collections (2007) are two examples within the archive domain of user-generated description and content.

How Does Bob Seek Help? Expertise Online

Users have offered an insight into the types of expertise they would consider useful. These range from the online specialist clinics where users could ask an archivist questions on a specific topic to chat facilities with peers, whilst at the other end of the scale automated help processes based on personalization, similar to Amazon's recommendation systems, and the application of artificial intelligence and the concept of the 'virtual archivist' were also suggested.

An interesting point to note here is that very few novice users have asked for the 'virtual archivist'; it is only once a user has experienced the archivist–user mediation process that they put a value on this. Many experienced users requested the 'virtual archivist' based on their experience of the archivists' expertise.

How can we support Bob and close the disintermediation gap? Facilitating a range of expertise online is one way to do this, ranging from simple semi-automated processes using datasets to 'ask the archivist' sessions and the application of artificial intelligence agents. Discussion groups and the application of collaborative software are also being investigated.

Provisional work has been undertaken with a national repository in investigating ways that this could be introduced. As part of this work it is essential to examine how archivists mediate the interaction between the user and primary sources, with a view to seeing how this can be translated across into a digital domain.

Conclusion and Future Work

The main findings from the study to date are summarized below, along with areas for further research.

Identification of the Three Most Common Problems Encountered by Users

The identification of the three most common problems encountered by users and, more importantly, at what stage they encounter them during their search has been fundamental to the study, as we saw under the heading 'Analysing the Behaviours of Digital Archive Users'. Based on this information current archival systems are currently being redeveloped to support the user.

Users' Active Construction of Meaning of the Digital Object

This process has not been previously examined in the archival domain prior to this study, as we noted under the heading 'The User's Active Construction of Meaning and Archival Context'. This study seeks, as a first step, to expand our knowledge here, to investigate of how different types of technology can mediate the process of construction of meaning at different stages.

A Model of Contextual Interaction

Prior to this study there has been no attempt to model the interaction between the user and the digital archive. The model of contextual interaction was introduced to archival professionals at two of their major conferences in the UK and Canada in 2006. It was well reviewed and I was invited to a number of further meetings in order to discuss its development in further detail. The model is now the basis on which I am investigating digital archive use across three national repositories. The remainder of the study will be spent testing and analysing the model, both qualitatively and quantitatively, applying the results of the testing iteratively to it. The development of the model is an ongoing process.

Identifying and Producing Sets of Personas

The findings to date have been analysed to identify goals, patterns and needs within and across user segments. From this, primary and secondary personas have been identified. The primary persona Bob will drive design and reflect the group most difficult to design for. How to support Bob in his introduction to archives, his need for help and expertise, his use and reuse of digital objects and his desire to be an active participant are all currently under investigation.

Tracking User Behaviours

Since the inception of the study in the summer of 2004, there is evidence of major changes in user search behaviours. An example of this is iterative searching: at the beginning of the study users would search iteratively for a maximum of two or three times; today as users are experienced in Google-type search they will search iteratively for five to seven times. Whilst the search is not sophisticated, with Boolean terms hardly ever being used, users will change their search criteria in response to search results.

As the study of the domain has been longitudinal in nature, such changes in behaviour have been identified and continue to be monitored on an ongoing basis. Activity Theory has and will continue to support the analysis of these developmental changes. It is my intention to continue to study users within this specialist domain as an element of my post-doctoral research.

Horses for Courses? The Application of Technology

Clearly the application of different types of technology at different stages of the interaction process will be of great benefit to users of all types. Different types of technology, such as animation, speech interfaces and collaborative social software, are all being tested at present to see what effects they have on different types of users during different stages of the interaction process.

How Will Bob Use and Reuse Digital Objects?

A two-part study is planned that asks the users, on ending a session using digital archives, a series of questions surrounding intended use, motivational factors and satisfaction. A follow-up session a month later asks the users how exactly they used the information and if their original goal was realized. To date no such study has been undertaken in the domain ascertaining use, user satisfaction and the users' motivational factors. Something similar has been undertaken in the digital library domain by Pomerantz and Luo (2006).

The Fruits of a Transdisciplinary Approach

Working across disciplines such as computer science, archival science, information science, information retrieval, interaction design, human–computer interaction (HCI), psychology, ethnography and archival intellience has been challenging; however, this has enabled a rich and panoramic view of the problem domain. I have attempted to translate this into a robust multi-method approach to my research and the application of its results in the domain. One area of planned future development is to emphasize the transdisciplinary nature of this work by creating a set of tools that supports researchers from any discipline when investigating the use of digital archives.

Conclusion

As previously stated, I firmly believe that, however thorny the discussion may become, 'user-led' design based on solid evidence holds the solution to the lofty aim of 'access for all'. During the course of this study I have witnessed two major phenomena that have affected user behaviour in the archive domain; the rise of Google and the major success of the television programme *Who Do You Think You Are?*.

The establishment of Google as 'the' way to search, and the user expectations surrounding this behaviour, have already been referred to. More critical for the archival domain, however, is the further impact this has on user expectations. When presented with 'Google-like' interfaces users expect the results to mirror that of Google, and in many cases within the archival domain, this does not hold true. Are we setting users up for a fall by doing this? Searching and exploring archival material in a digital environment are, after all, complex processes requiring multi-level searching and repeated interaction. It may then be misleading to present both search and results in a simple 'Google-like' guise.

User expectations are an important factor in the design of systems. The advent of the TV hobbyist, following the TV programme *Who Do You Think You Are?*, has heralded a major shift in user expectations:

> *P112:* 'Well, they find out all they need to know in an hour; here I am digging away and have not even found mammy's mammy yet! I didn't think it would take so long or be so hard.'

The result of the success of the TV programme, now in its fourth season, and the growing popularity of family history has manifested itself in a large number of new and inexperienced users accessing online digital archival material, making the need to know more about their behaviour more urgent than ever.

So how do we support the interaction between the user and digital archival material? How do we manage these high expectations? The first crucial step towards this is gaining evidence of, and understanding of, user behaviour through empirical studies combined with agreed research agendas and conceptual framework. Based on this evidence we will be able to develop the systems and tools that will link users and their diverse interests with a wealth of archival material.

I hope that this chapter has demonstrated some ways in which this can be done. Unlocking the potential of the archive is inextricably bound up in unleashing the potential of our users, terrifying as this may seem to some: the possibility of it all provides the impetus for us to forge ahead. Perhaps 'access for all' may not be so far away after all?

References

Allan, J. et al. (2003), 'Challenges in information retrieval and language modeling: report of a workshop held at the Center for Intelligent Information Retrieval', *ACM SIGIR Forum* [Association for Computing Machinery Special Interest Group on Information Retrieval], 37 (1), 31–47.

AX-SNET (Archival eXcellence in Information Seeking Studies Network), at <http://www.si.umich.edu/ArchivalMetrics> and <http://www.axsnet.org> accessed 1 October 2007.

BBC (British Broadcasting Corporation), at <http://www.bbc.co.uk/> accessed 28 January 2008.

Bates, M.J. (1989), 'The design of browsing and berrypicking techniques for the online search interface', *Online Review*, 13 (5), 407–24.

Beyer, H. and Holzblatt, K. (1998), *Contextual Design: Defining Customer-Centred Systems* (San Francisco CA: Morgan Kaufmann).

Butterworth, R. (2006), 'The "Accessing of our Archival and Manuscript Heritage" Project and the Development of the "Helpers" Website', *Technical Report: IDC-TR-2006-001* (Interaction Design Centre, School of Computing Science, University of Middlesex), available at <http:///www.cs.mdx.ac.uk/research/idc/techreports.html>.

Dervin, B. and Nilan, M. (1986), 'Information Needs and Uses', in William, M.E. (ed.), *Annual Review of Information Science and Technology [ARIST]*, 21, 3–33.

Duff, W., Craig, B. and Cherry, J. (2004), 'Historians' use of archival sources: promises and pitfalls of a digital age', *The Public Historian*, 26 (2) (Spring), 7–22.

Duff, W. and Johnson, C. (2002), 'Accidentally found on purpose: information-seeking behaviour of historians in archives', *Library Quarterly*, 42 (4), 472–96.

Economou, M. (2002), 'User evaluation: report of findings', *National Council on Archives and National Archives Network User Research Group* (NANURG), at <http://www.ncaonline.org.uk/materials/nanurg.pdf> accessed 19 April 2005.

Education for Change (2005), 'Evaluation of the Big Lottery Fund ICT content programmes. Interim report', at <http://www.biglotteryfund.org.uk/assets/ICT_content_prog_eval.pdf> accessed 7 April 2005.

Ellis, D., Cox, D. and Hall, K. (1993), 'A comparison of the information-seeking patterns of researchers in the physical and social sciences', *Journal of Documentation*, 49, 356–69.

Fisher, K.E., Erdelez, S. and McKechnie, L. (eds) (2005), *Theories of Information Behaviour* (Medford NJ: Information Today).

Harley, D. et al. (2006), *Use and Users of Digital Resources: a Focus on Undergraduate Education in Humanities and Social Sciences* (Berkeley CA: Centre for Studies in Higher Education).

Ingwersen, P. and Järvelin, K. (2005), *The Turn: Integration of Information Seeking and Retrieval in Context* (Dordrecht: Springer).

Johnson, A. (2004), '"The Mersey Gateway Project: how was it for you?" A user-centred evaluation of an archival digitisation project', B.Sc. thesis, Edge Hill College, Lancaster University.

Johnson, A. (2005), 'Are targeted user-centred interfaces the key in facilitating the conversion of the traditional non-user to a user of archives?', paper presented at the Conference of the ACH/ALLC (Association for Computers and the Humanities/Association for Literary and Linguistic Computing), Victoria (British Columbia), 14–18 June. Available at <http://mustard.tapor.uvic.ca/cocoon/ach_abstracts/xq/pdf.xq?id=122> accessed July 2007.

Kaptelinin, V. and Nardi, B. (2006), *Acting with Technology: Activity Theory and Interaction Design* (London: MIT Press).

Kaptelinin, V., Nardi, B. and MacAuley, C. (1999), 'The activity checklist: a tool for representing the "space" of context', *Interactions*, 6, 27–39.

Kuhlthau, C. (2005), 'Towards collaboration between information seeking and information retrieval', *Information Research*, 10 (2), at <http://www.information.net/ir/10-2/infres102.html>.

───── (1993), 'A principle of uncertainty for information seeking', *Journal of Documentation*, 49 (4), 339–55.

Kuniavsky, M. (2003), *Observing the User Experience: a Practitioner's Guide to User Research* (San Francisco CA: Morgan Kaufmann).

Leontiev, A. (1978), *Activity, Consciousness, and Personality* (Englewood Cliffs NJ: Prentice Hall) (originally published in Russia 1975).

Marchionini, G. (1995), *Information Seeking in Electronic Environments* (New York: Cambridge University Press).

Moss, M. and Johnson, A. (2007), 'Breaking out of the archival gulag', abstract submission for special issue of the *Journal of Personalization Research*.

The National Archives (2002), *Measuring Impact* (Richmond UK: The National Archives).

The National Archives (2007), 'Your Archives Project', at <http://yourarchives.nationalarchives.gov.uk/index.php?title=Homepage> accessed 1 October 2007.

National Council of Archives Public Services Quality Group (2006), *Survey of Visitors to UK Archives 2006*, at <http://www.ncaonline.org.uk/research_and_development/survey/> accessed 24 May 2006.

Pejtersen, A.M. (1989), *Modelling User Needs and Search Strategies as a Basis for System Design* (Roskilde, Denmark: Riso National Laboratory).

Pham, D. and Greene, J. (2003), 'Creating and using gs and scenarios to guide site design', presentation at the New York meeting of the Usability Professionals Association, 20 May 2003. Available at <http://www.nycupa.org/past_events/razorfish-2003>.

Polar Bear Expedition Digital Collections, at <http://polarbear.si.umich.edu/> accessed 1 October 2007.

Pomerantz, J. and Luo, L. (2006), 'Motivations and uses: evaluating virtual reference services from the users' perspective', *Library & Information Science Research*, 28, 350–73.

Rasmussen, J., Pejtersen, A.M. and Goodstein, L. (1994), *Cognitive Systems Engineering* (New York: Wiley).

Rehberger, D., Fegan, M. and Kornbluh, M. (2006), 'Reevaluating access and preservation through secondary repositories: needs, promises and challenges', paper presented at the European Conference on Digital Libraries (ECDL 2006), at Alicante, 17–22 September; published in Gonzalo, J. et al. (eds), *Research and Advanced Technologies for Digital Libraries* (Berlin: Springer), in the series *Lecture Notes in Computer Science* [*LNCS*], vol. 4172, pp. 39–50.

Savolainen, R. and Kari, J. (2006), 'Facing and bridging gaps in web searching', *Information Processing & Management*, 42, 519–537.

Talja, S. (2005), 'Users' Library Discourses', in Johannsen, C.G. and Kajberg, L., *New Frontiers in Public Library Research* (Oxford: Scarecrow), pp. 307–27.

Usherwood, B. (2005), *Perception of Archives, Libraries and Museums in Modern Britain* (Sheffield: Department of Information Studies, University of Sheffield).

Vakkari, P. (2001a), 'A theory of the task-based informational retrieval process; a summary and generalization of a longitudinal study', *Journal of Documentation*, 57 (1), 44–60.

Vakkari, P. (2001b), 'Changes in search tactics and relevance judgements in preparing a research proposal; a summary of findings of a longitudinal study', *Information Retrieval*, 4 (3/4), 295–310.

Vygotsky, L. (1978), *Mind in Society; the Development of Higher Psychological Processes* (Cambridge MA: Harvard University Press).

Wilson, T.D. (2006), 'A re-examination of information-seeking behaviour in the context of activity theory', *Information Research*, 11 (4), at <http://informationr. net/ir/11-4/paper260.html> accessed July 2007.

Yang, S. (1997), 'Information seeking as problem-solving using a qualitative approach to uncover the novice learner's information-seeking process in a Perseus hypertext system', *Library & Information Science Research*, 19, 71–92.

Yakel, E. and Torres, D.A. (2003), 'AI: archival intelligence and user expertise', *The American Archivist*, 66 (Spring/Summer), 51–78.

Appendix 1

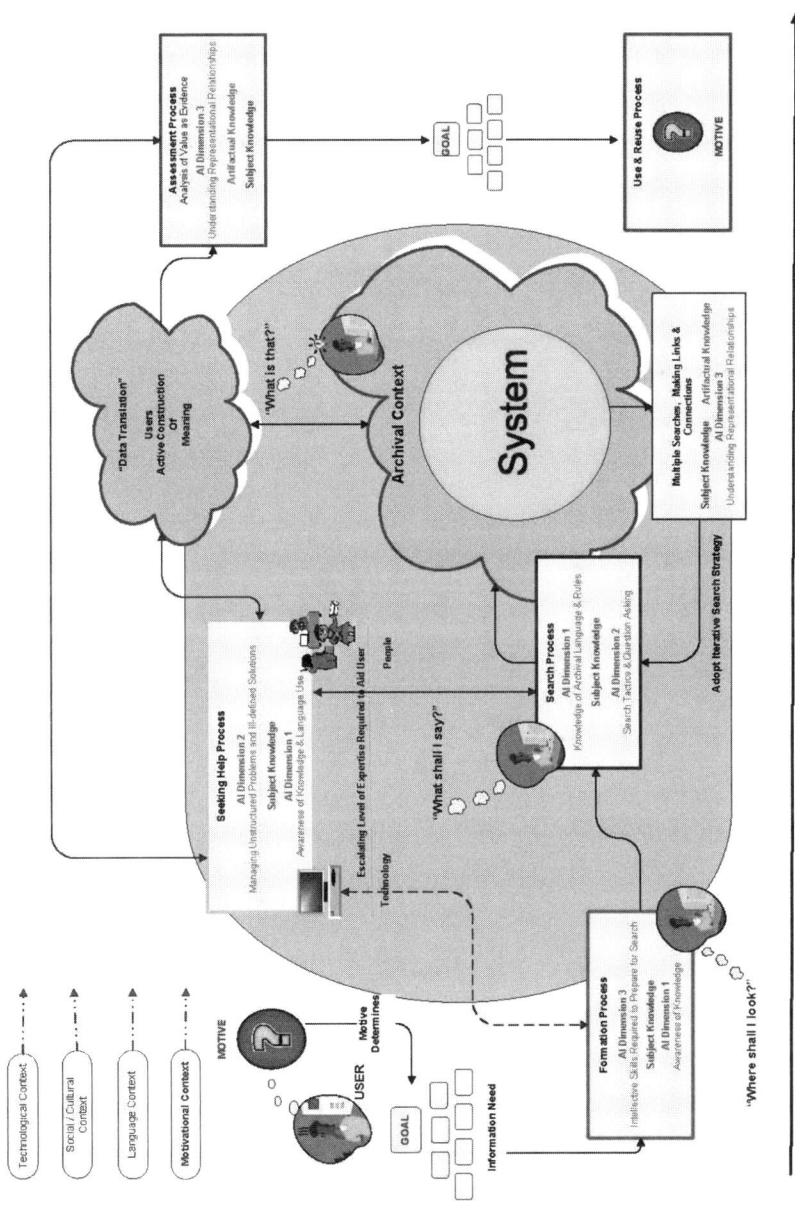

Appendix 2

BOB, OUR TV HOBBYIST 'I don't know where to start'	• Unrealistic expectations • Requires access to introductory tools and resources • Wants to be able to contribute content	
Personal profile Bob likes a challenge, something he can get his teeth into (and they are all his own, he says). He has watched the programmes on TV and has decided to start tracing the history of his house; 'it looks easy enough and it will keep me from under the Mrs's feet'. He has never used archival material before but, if this goes well, 'me and the Mrs are going to do the family history together'. His son bought him a laptop for Christmas and he attended the local community centre to do 'IT for beginners'. He is not worried about his beginner's skills as he is sure it will all be easy enough once he gets his bearings. Bob wants a 'one-stop shop'; he does not want to be hopping from one site to another as he gets lost easily. Bob has vision impairment and likes the text size to be a minimum of 20pt.		**Personal information** *Profession:* Retired ambulance driver *Age:* 60 *Location:* Liverpool, Merseyside *Home life:* Married with 2 children and 1 grandchild *Personality:* Bubbly, friendly, likes a challenge
User goals Bob wants to be able to: • discover how to access material over the Internet; he wants the 'idiot's guides' • set up his own account that can help him 'keep track of things' • add content, and to add comments to existing content • access help online from others and archivists if he needs it • access digitized content • find out about his local history following events at the 'Capital of Culture 2008' • see the text without strain	**Our objectives** We want Bob to: • visit archives often • register for e-mail alerts and online newsletters • recommend archives to others • obtain the skills required to access archival content • feel prepared for a visit to his local archive • contribute content and add comments	**Internet use and skills** *Internet experience:* Beginner (1 year) *Primary uses:* Finding information, e-mail and looking at sport and travel information *Favourite sites:* Everton FC, BBC Sport, Expedia and Wikipedia *Search engine:* Google *Social networking:* Friends Reunited

Chapter 9

Permitted Use and Users: The Fallout Shelter's Sealed Environment

Gerard P. Collis

What are archives for? Who are archives for? And what is the difference between archives and museums? We shall explore some extreme archives: the caves at Lascaux, the UK National Nuclear Archive and nuclear waste repositories. Beyond the fundamentals of preservation and access, this essay is exploratory.

Prologue

Walter M. Miller Jr (1923–96) was an American science-fiction writer, whose only novel *A Canticle for Leibowitz* was published in 1960. This was a reworking of a series of short stories which had originally appeared in *The Magazine of Fantasy and Science Fiction*, 1955–57. The novel won the prestigious Hugo award at the 1961 World SF Convention (Clute and Nicholls 1993, 809).

The Special Collections and Archives department at the University of Liverpool is home to the Science Fiction Foundation Collection.[1] This Collection includes an extensive reference library and papers and manuscripts of many well-known science-fiction writers. Ten years ago I was Assistant Librarian for the Collection, cataloguing both printed books and archival material. One lunchtime I was reading Miller's novel while minding the Special Collections and Archive service desk. An academic researcher noticed the cover of the book when he came over with an enquiry unrelated to science fiction. He told me that he had read the novel when it was first published and had read it again every year since. As a result, I too have made a point of doing so each year.

Miller was a veteran of the Second World War, having served in the US Army Air Corps. In February 1944 he took part in the bombing of the Abbey of Monte Cassino (Miller 1993, preliminary page), which had been founded in the early 6th century (CE) by St Benedict.

A German medical officer stationed in southern Italy initiated the rescue of many of the Abbey's historical treasures, which the German army evacuated to the Vatican. This not only included artworks but also the Abbey's archives and library, as well as the collections of Naples archaeological museum and the national gallery which had been placed in the Abbey for safe-keeping (Hapgood and Richardson 2002, 15).

---

1 Online as the SF Hub website, at <http://www.sfhub.ac.uk/> (home page), accessed February 2008.

The American airmen who flew in the bombing raids had been told that the Abbey was fortified and being used for German artillery emplacements. In fact, the German forces had made a point of not using the Abbey which was occupied by at least a thousand Italian civilians. The Abbey was reduced to rubble. It is estimated that several hundred refugees were killed in the attack (Hapgood and Richardson 2002, 199–211).

The subtitle of this chapter is taken from Miller's novel, which is set centuries after a nuclear holocaust, where a monastic community devotes itself to the preservation of the few written documents that have survived.

Behind the Curtain

What do we know about archives users? Can our user profiles help us understand them any better? After all, how much can we really predict about the interests of others or understand their motivations? Few of us would expect construction workers to take an interest in avant-garde art, for example.

Christo was born in Bulgaria. Jeanne-Claude was born in Morocco. They have been based in New York since 1964, and work together under the shared name Christo as environmental artists making temporary interventions in buildings and landscapes. They are perhaps best known for their *Wrapped Reichstag* of 1995, where the entire German parliament building was wrapped in silver fabric.

In 1970–72 Christo and Jeanne-Claude created *Valley Curtain* in Rifle Gap valley, Colorado. This involved the construction of a curtain across the narrow valley, using a quarter of a million square feet of orange fabric (Chernow 2002, 213).

Initial reactions to the plan for the artwork were mixed, with comments from locals such as 'I don't get the real point of the thing' and that the artist must be 'off his rocker' (Chernow 2002, 207). However, the project had the support of local businesses, including the owners of the golf course that would overlook the giant artwork. The golfers themselves were 'not very impressed' (*Christo's Valley Curtain* 2004).

The final week of the project in August 1972 was recorded by celebrated documentary film-makers Albert and David Maysles. One of the construction workers, Donald Jenkins, can be seen in the film, awestruck at the unfurling, saying 'I've never seen anything so beautiful in all my life' (*Christo's Valley Curtain* 2004). These rugged, tattooed workers celebrated, cheering and hugging each other.

The Maysles brothers' film *Christo's Valley Curtain* was nominated for an Oscar in 1973. David Maysles wanted to invite Donald Jenkins to the awards ceremony, but the organizers refused to allow access to an outsider. Jenkins had risked his life in the construction of *Valley Curtain*.

Jeanne-Claude later commented that the construction workers 'had never worked on a work of art before and they loved it' (*Christo's Valley Curtain*, 2004). One local councillor stated that thanks to *Valley Curtain* the town of Rifle had become 'a community of artists' (Chernow 2002, 216).

Does a visit to an art gallery mean that somebody is keen on art? The Tate Gallery opened its northern England annex in Liverpool in 1988, displaying works from its modern art collection. There was considerable interest in the new gallery, not least from local people, and there was a large number of visitors during the gallery's opening weeks. Among the first exhibitions was the Rothko Room,[2] a chapel-like alcove designed for the quiet contemplation of nine large paintings by the artist Mark Rothko (1903–70). Visitors often left the Rothko Room in particular visibly puzzled or audibly amused,[3] and some of these visitors may well have been attracted to the gallery for purely sardonic reasons.

This certainly was not a repetition of the hugely successful exhibition of 'degenerate' modern art held by the Nazis in 1937 at several German galleries (see Ascherson 1995, 69–83), and such responses from visitors to the Tate Liverpool must have been disappointing and perhaps unexpected. Regardless of this, the visitor statistics will have looked very impressive.

In 1972 Rifle Gap valley was already suffering radioactive contamination from the uranium processing plant ten miles away (Chernow 2002, 210), and a year later, just 35 miles away, an underground nuclear detonation[4] was carried out (Chernow 2002, 208).

Nuclear Archives

When the treasures rescued from Monte Cassino were ceremonially presented to the Vatican in 1944, there were press, radio and newsreel reporters ready to record the event. Nazi propagandists had taken this opportunity to portray the German army as preserving European culture (Hapgood and Richardson 2002, 56, 70–71).

Archives play an essential role in our cultural heritage. Prompted by the conflicts in the Middle East, the International Committee of the Blue Shield issued a statement on threatened cultural heritage: 'Cultural property is priceless and irreplaceable, of vital importance not only to each community, but also to humanity'.[5]

But we also need to preserve archives for our own survival.

The world's first commercial nuclear reactor[6] was ceremonially opened at Calder Hall in West Cumbria in 1956. The decommissioning process for the reactor began in 2003. The UK Nuclear Decommissioning Agency plans to develop the site as a museum and national nuclear archive, although the decommissioning process and the clean-up of the site are expected to take a century to complete ('Nuclear Future' 2005, 8).

The National Nuclear Archive is intended to act as the key source of information for the long-term management of radioactive waste. The Archive itself will undertake

---

2 Currently on display at Tate Modern, London.

3 As observed by the author during visits to the gallery.

4 See 'Rio Blanco nuclear test site', Center for Land Use Interpretation website, at <http://ludb.clui.org/ex/i/CO3130/> accessed 15 June 2007.

5 'Statement by the International Committee of the Blue Shield on threatened cultural property in the Middle East conflict (ICBS)', International Committee of the Blue Shield website, 24 July 2006, at <http://www.ifla.org/VI/4/admin/icbs-MiddleEast072006-en.htm> accessed 15 June 2007.

6 Although this claim is disputed (Croall and Sempler 1980, 34).

the task of managing the records of a number of agencies. It will be necessary to preserve this information for centuries.

The UK Atomic Energy Authority (UKAEA), with the radioactive waste agency Nirex, have recently undertaken a pilot study to assess information management and preservation needs (Wise et al. 2005, 24–7). The study examined a subset of the records of the Windscale Advanced Gas-Cooled Reactor (WAGR). The decommissioning of this reactor began in 1983.

These were records created in diverse media over the 20 years of the reactor's active life. These records concerned the low-level and intermediate radioactive waste which will remain at the site for another 50–100 years, until transfer to permanent storage at the planned national radioactive waste repository (Wise et al. 2005, 25). A site for this repository has yet to be established.[7]

The study led the UKAEA to the conclusion that access to radioactive waste management information would be best served in the long term by copying records to microfilm and acid-free 'permanent' paper. Electronic records would also be printed in this way, which currently presents the most viable solution for preserving digital information (Wise et al. 2005, 25).

Research cited by the Committee on Radioactive Waste Management (CoRWM) has found that, on average, people in Britain live about 26 miles away from a radioactive waste site of some kind.[8] The UKAEA's records project manager, David Gray, is one of the authors of a journal article which stated: 'In many applications a small number of failures may be acceptable but the preservation of radioactive waste does not fall into this category' (Wise et al. 2005, 27).

The International Council on Archives (ICA) published a report in 2006 on the issue of preserving radioactive waste information, with the recommendation that the International Atomic Energy Agency should establish and manage an international archive of radioactive waste disposal records (Macarthy and Upshall 2006, 14).

However, the approach of the nuclear industry and oversight agencies in Britain has predominantly been short-term and overly secretive (Edwards 2005, 12), with political and commercial issues apparently taking priority over long-term issues of public safety, and evidently over the issues of public awareness and consultation.[9], [10] In contrast, the ICA report stresses the importance of access to radioactive waste archives and 'open networked public knowledge', in an attempt to ensure no less than 'intergenerational knowledge transfer' (Macarthy and Upshall 2006, 4).

---

7 See for example Press Association, 'Peers attack nuclear waste plans', *Guardian Unlimited* website, 3 June 2007, at <http://www.guardian.co.uk/uklatest/story/0,,-6679643,00. html>.

8 'CoRWM compiles provisional shortlist of waste options', website of the Committee on Radioactive Waste Management, 4 April 2005, <http://www.corwm.org.uk/content-594 >.

9 *New Scientist* magazine's editorial comment was: 'It would be difficult to think of a worse way to decide where to put your nuclear waste. First, conduct the process in secret … ' ('A Very British Burial' 2005, 3). The magazine obtained details through the Freedom of Information Act.

10 See also Press Association, 'Peers attack nuclear waste plans'.

A Monumental Task

Gregory Benford has been Professor of Physics at University of California, Irvine for almost 30 years.[11] Benford is also a science-fiction writer and a co-editor of anthologies including *Nuclear War* (1988). In the early 1990s Benford joined other scientists, along with anthropologists, linguists and historians, consulted by the US Department of Energy on its Waste Isolation Pilot Plant (WIPP) project,[12] with its waste repository located in a disused salt mine near Carlsbad, New Mexico. This has since become the world's first underground repository for radioactive waste from the production of nuclear weapons (Palmer 2006).

Benford was involved in the development of a system of permanent warning markers, which must not only physically survive for thousands of years, but also still convey a coherent message (Benford 1999). Redundancy of form was seen as essential for transmitting messages: conventional warnings in present-day languages and conventional hazard symbols were supplemented with specially devised, highly iconic symbols. This system has been adopted for the proposed repository for spent nuclear fuel at Yucca Mountain, Nevada.[13]

Nevada's Grand Basin National Park is the site for the Clock of the Long Now, sited in a chamber hollowed out of a mountainside, designed to be in operation for 10,000 years, and intended to inspire long-term thinking.[14] The Long Now Foundation has also instigated the Rosetta Project to create an online archive of all documented human languages.[15] Of the world's 6,000 languages, half are under threat of extinction.[16]

The UK's Acts of Parliament are recorded on vellum, a medium with a proven longevity of at least a thousand years, and copies in this form are kept in the care of The National Archives. But specialist palaeographic and linguistic skills are required today to read and understand documents written in the English of a thousand years ago.[17] For how long will the language of today's written documents be readily accessible?

Gregory Benford describes a visit to a 1960s nuclear test site in New Mexico, simply marked with a small plaque which reads: 'THIS SITE WILL REMAIN DANGEROUS FOR 24,000 YEARS' (Benford 1999, 50–51).

---

11 See 'Gregory Benford', UC Irvine Department of Physics and Astronomy website, 23 May 2005, <http://www.physics.uci.edu/faculty/benford.html> accessed September 2007.

12 See US Department of Energy Waste Isolation Pilot Plant website, <http://www.wipp.energy.gov/> (home page), accessed 3 July 2007.

13 'The monumental task of warning future generations', US Department of Energy Office of Civilian Radioactive Waste Management website, January 2005, at <http://www.ocrwm.doe.gov/factsheets/doeymp0115.shtml>, accessed January 2006.

14 The Long Now Foundation website, at <http://www.longnow.org/> (home page), accessed January 2006.

15 The Rosetta Project website, <http://www.rosettaproject.org/> (home page), accessed July 2007.

16 'International Mother Language Day', UNESCO Education website, at <http://tinyurl.com/pchfr>, accessed 3 July 2007.

17 See, for example, Trask 1999, pp. 91–6.

Documents

The walls and roofs of many caves in south-west France are covered in drawings, paintings and engravings made during the last Ice Age. This region of France has been a UNESCO World Heritage Site since 1979. The best-known example is the group of caves at Lascaux in the Dordogne region, discovered by chance in 1940, by children at play. The cave paintings at Lascaux are at least 17,000 years old, and show many detailed, realistic images of large animals, among other, more puzzling images. Lascaux has received some media attention recently (for example Connor 2006, 3), after the installation of new air-conditioning equipment in the caves led to dramatic degradation of the paintings.[18]

In the 1950s, the librarian, writer and philosopher Georges Bataille (1897–1962) visited Lascaux to research a monograph on the caves and the art there (Bataille 1955). He explored the site at night, in order to avoid the tourists. There were almost 1,200 tourists entering the caves every day.[19]

The writer André Malraux (1901–76) closed the caves at Lascaux. He had led a brigade of French Resistance fighters in 1944 and then served in France's first post-war government as minister of cultural affairs. In 1961 Malraux initiated a long-term programme for the protection of heritage sites (Cate 1997, 391). The caves were closed to the public in 1963, with access restricted to five academic researchers a day. Since 1983, replicas of two areas have been open to the public, the 'Great Hall of the Bulls' and the 'Painted Gallery'.

We cannot claim to understand what these cave paintings were meant to convey. There are certainly competing theories. For example, an area known as the Shaft includes an image of a dead man, which is most often interpreted as the depiction of a hunting accident, not least by Bataille. However, it has also been suggested that the prone body was intended as a warning to visitors of a pocket of lethal carbon monoxide gas (Eshleman 2003, 36–7).

How can we even begin to interpret the paintings in the caves at Lascaux? Bataille wrote of Lascaux as 'the birth of art', but others such as Eshleman have argued that caves pre-date any notion of 'art', and instead seek other ways of describing the paintings. Such apparently basic notions nevertheless lend themselves to investigation and competing interpretations. Notions of the 'document' were surveyed by Michael K. Buckland in the late 1990s. Buckland observed that 'not all phenomena of interest in information science are textual or text-like' (Buckland 1997, 804). For example, placing the emphasis on function rather than form, the librarian and 'documentalist' Suzanne Briet (1894–1989) argued that access to evidence is crucial to the definition of a document: 'any physical or symbolic sign, preserved or recorded, intended to represent, to reconstruct, or to demonstrate a physical or conceptual phenomenon' (Buckland 1997, 806).

---

18 See International Committee for the Preservation of Lascaux website, at <http://www.savelascaux.org/>, accessed July 2007.

19 See 'The Cave of Lascaux', Ministère de la culture et de la communication website, at <http://www.culture.gouv.fr/culture/arcnat/lascaux/en/>, accessed 3 July 2007.

The writers Bataille and Malraux each recognized the paintings in the caves at Lascaux as documents, and the actions undertaken by Malraux in effect established the caves as an archival repository.

Access Restrictions

We are used to archival repositories restricting access to reading rooms and, especially, to secure document stores. When the caves at Lascaux were closed to the public, this was because the sheer number of visitors was putting the Palaeolithic documents at risk.

We expect public museums, in contrast, to provide open access and put objects from their collections on display to visitors. But access may not always be so easily defined or so straightforward:

The Museum of London

The Museum of London turns away as many as 5,000 visitors from its Roman London Gallery every year (Hall and Swain 2000, 88). Visits to the gallery are always fully booked, and it is not possible to accommodate all the visits from school parties. Access here is restricted by circumstances, an issue of practicality.

The Smithsonian Institution

The US Army Air Force's B-29 Superfortress bomber *Enola Gay* was used to drop the atomic bomb on the Japanese city of Hiroshima. The Smithsonian Institution's National Air and Space Museum planned to display the bomber's fuselage as part of an exhibition for 1995 marking the 50th anniversary of the attack. The exhibition was also to include objects recovered from 'ground zero' and photographs of the aftermath. A first draft of the exhibition's 'script' was leaked to a veterans' organization, provoking widespread outrage and the cancellation of the planned exhibition. The fully-restored *Enola Gay* was finally exhibited at the museum, with a video showing interviews with the aircrew, and another showing the story of the aircraft's restoration. Although the museum has preserved and restored the *Enola Gay* and made it accessible for public viewing, the museum's display denies their visitors access to the contextual information needed to interpret this complex artefact and its contentious history (Dubin1999). It seems many Americans are proud of the *Enola Gay*'s place in their national heritage and demand that their national museum reflects this, especially since 'anything [the Museum] says is official history', as a member of the American Legion commented (Dubin 1999, 222).

The aircraft itself would not be at any more risk if it were part of a display which suggested an alternative view of its history, but this would be perceived as a risk to the authority of those espousing canonical history.

Australian Museums

Australian museums have adopted 'culturally sensitive curation'. Access to certain artefacts created by indigenous cultures may be restricted: 'handling and visual inspection may be limited on the grounds of gender', to avoid 'offence or distress to actual or cultural descendants' (Simpson 2005, 14). Access is restricted to privileged members of the public. The majority of the public may be perceived by some as putting such an object at risk, but this risk is metaphysical rather than physical.

Archival Repositories

It is not unusual for individual archival documents or an entire archival collection to have access restricted by embargo, perhaps for as long as a century or more in the case of some government records. It is also not unusual for a collection's donor or lender to make a requirement that the archival repository only allows access to individual researchers who have received prior permission directly from them. Here the risk is not to the physical survival of the documents. The content of the documents themselves is perceived as presenting a potential risk in certain circumstances, either to their creators or associates of their creators.

By contrast, the UKAEA's pilot study on radioactive waste records has recommended restricted access to original archival materials simply as a way of increasing their longevity, without attempting to define which researchers may or may not be permitted such access (Wise et al. 2005, 26).

Access – How Open?

The Archives Hub is an online union catalogue of descriptions for collections held at higher education and further education institutions in the UK, but also includes a small number of descriptions for collections held in other institutions which may be of interest to academic researchers. Access to the Archives Hub website is open, and free of charge to users. It is a condition of publication that collections must be available for use by researchers in further and higher education.[20]

Many collection descriptions published on the Archives Hub simply state that access is open, without qualifying this in any way. There are occasional exceptions, such as demonstrated here:

> Accessible to bona fide researchers who should make advance application stating the nature of their research, the use to which it will be put, and enclosing a letter of recommendation (if appropriate) from their supervisor. Before granting access, the University must be satisfied that the documents are needed as a serious and necessary source of information.[21]

---

20 'Archives Hub: collection policy', Archives Hub website, 16 May 2006, at <http://www.archiveshub.ac.uk/arch/ahcp.shtml>.

21 From a collection description published on the Archives Hub website.

The popular BBC television series *Who Do You Think You Are?* has greatly increased the public profile for archives in recent years, but before this increase in family history research, perhaps such stringent requirements may well have been just what inexperienced members of the general public would expect from such 'socially exclusive' institutions.

The poet Clayton Eshleman has been able to visit the Palaeolithic caves at Lascaux several times over the years. He reports a remark made by a science writer: 'What is a *poet* doing in the caves?' (Eshleman 2003, xi). Would Eshleman's work have been considered 'serious and necessary'?

But this level of restriction is not typical of publicly funded archival repositories. For example, the website for the Lancashire Record Office states that 'anyone is welcome'.[22] This is reminiscent of Miller's novel, where a priest explains how the community of monks views access to its priceless documents: 'They aren't particular about who reads their books, as long as he washes his hands and doesn't deface their property' (Miller 1993, 113).

Museums and Archives

What then are the differences between archives and museums? Archival collections often include objects and artefacts, and museums often hold archival material, perhaps at least their own records. Museums often display textual documents as well as documents in a wider sense. Both archives and museums are responsible for the safe-keeping of these collections and also for providing access to them. The difference between these institutions cannot be located simply in generic differences in the material in their care.

The Museum of London holds an archival collection, the London Archaeological Archive, with records of over 3,000 excavations in addition to thousands of boxes of artefacts. The museum aims 'to make 100 per cent of the Museum's core collections physically available and interpreted in an accessible and enlivening way'. However, for the archival material, the museum has found it to difficult to provide public access to 'some very complicated records' (Hall and Swain 2000, 88).

The Lancashire Record Office does also state that 'a reader's ticket is required for access to original documents', and this of course is standard practice for archival repositories, but something that is seldom required by public museums.

Museums are open to the public; they present material from their collections for public display. The material on display may be still a certain distance from visitors behind barriers of some kind or within protective display cases. Visitors to the Louvre view the *Mona Lisa* through bullet-proof glass.

Museum displays are overwhelmingly visual, which is something immediate, instantaneous (Büchler et al. 1990, 14). A Soviet tank from the Second World War may still impress very young visitors although they would be very unlikely to be familiar with any history of the Soviet Union or even of the Second World War.

---

22 'Planning a visit', Lancashire Record Office website, at <http://www.lancashire.gov.uk/education/record_office/planning/>, accessed 1 September 2006.

Museums and galleries have an 'aura' about them. The German philosopher and literary critic Walter Benjamin (1892–1943) suggested that an artwork's aura is generated by its uniqueness and by the maintenance of a certain physical distance from the public (Benjamin and Arendt 1999, 211–244). At the same time, a mystique may, of course, be generated for many individual artworks by the widespread availability of reproductions. The *Mona Lisa* is a very familiar image, as famous as a film star.

Even as children we know that museums are special places where treasures are kept and that we should behave accordingly. Their aura provides a degree of security for the material on public display, in addition to the care of the invigilators employed by the museum.

The 'graffiti artist' known as Banksy has on several occasions been able to insert his handiwork into gallery exhibitions uninvited. The gallery's authority as an institution and the aura of the artworks mean that visitors are unlikely to challenge events or objects on display whose exact status is unknown to them. At the same time, Banksy appears less to be undermining the museum's special status than trying to appropriate it for himself.

In 1940, when Walter Benjamin fled from Nazi-occupied Paris, it was Georges Bataille who took Benjamin's manuscripts into the safe-keeping of the French National Library (Benjamin and Arendt 1999, 23).

Unlike the artefacts and objects in museums and galleries, original archival material has to be taken out of the protection of the store room by archives staff and brought directly to visitors in the reading room. Researchers have to handle vulnerable material, touching it with their own hands. This of course increases the risk of damage or disorder, unintentional or otherwise, and increases the risk of theft. With this exposure to direct handling, extra, practical steps need to be taken, which may range from providing pencils to researchers for their note-taking to formal requirements for visitors, such as obligatory registration for a reader's card before approval and any access to archival material is granted.

Museums often have special 'handling collections' to provide opportunities for interaction, but these tend to be collections of duplicate items which would perhaps otherwise be disposed of. Museums also often have extensive research collections, with many items in store rooms or work areas, not displayed to the general public perhaps for practical reasons, but made available to academic researchers by arrangement.

Museums, Archives and Identity

Museums and galleries are often closely linked with national, regional or cultural identity. The general public does not seem to make such an association when it comes to archives. The two written documents seen as part of the 'British' identity are the Domesday Book and Magna Carta, a copy of the first being held at The National Archives and a copy of the second at the British Library, institutions quite clearly identified as British. But the 'Britishness' of those two documents may be the subject of debate[23] and their content and significance may be poorly understood by the general public.

British Lawnmower Museum

The British Lawnmower Museum[24] is located in Southport, Lancashire. The Museum is situated above a hardware shop and is open to casual visitors. As well as the machinery, the Museum also has a collection of printed ephemera and offers an archival research service.

The Museum has been described as a 'very British' tourist attraction, 'celebrating part of our national heritage' (Halstead et al. 2005, 7–12).

National Museum of Iraq

With artefacts and manuscripts dating back thousands of years, the Baghdad Archaeological Museum (now the National Museum of Iraq) was established in 1923 by the British archaeologist Gertrude Bell (1868–1926). Bell was Honorary Director of Antiquities for the new government of Iraq, and also president of Iraq's first public library. Bell had been recruited by British military intelligence in 1915 and shortly thereafter joined the Mesopotamian Expeditionary Force in Basra and Baghdad (Winstone 1978). Bell went on to figuratively and literally draw the map for the new country of Iraq (Wallach 1997).

During the invasion of Iraq in 2003 the National Museum and many archaeological sites were damaged, an inevitable consequence of war perhaps. When Baghdad was occupied by US forces the Museum was not protected from looters. This apparently wilful negligence was widely condemned by international heritage organizations. The Museum had been closed during the Gulf War of 1991, and it was reopened in 2000 on the occasion of Saddam Hussein's birthday (Crawford 2005): 'the emotive or unifying power of the past … is something that Saddam Hussein understood well. In a country such as Iraq, which has a diverse population of different ethnic, linguistic and religious traditions, it is pride in the achievements of the past that unites them.'

Unlike museums, archives seem to be associated with individual rather than national identity, and of course many archives users are there to research their own individual family history.

Learning to read and write requires a great deal of time and effort. At least a small amount of work has to be put into reading a written document. Such efforts may not always be made and such skills may not always be valued.

---

23 See for example 'Magna Carta tops British day poll', BBC News website, 30 May 2006, at <http://news.bbc.co.uk/1/hi/uk/5028496.stm>, accessed May 2006.

24 British Lawnmower Museum website, at <http://www.lawnmowerworld.co.uk/> (home page), accessed July 2007.

Around 5,000 years ago the Sumerian people invented writing, in Mesopotamia, in what is now Iraq (Martin and Cochrane 1994). The Iraq National Library and Archives was burnt down in 2003.[25]

As We Dream, Alone

Public museums might be considered as a form of mass medium. Mozambique's new government in the late 1970s consulted the French film-maker Jean-Luc Godard and the production company Sonimage on the creation of a national television broadcasting service. Godard and Sonimage suggested that individual television viewers were joined together into a mass audience by all receiving the same message through their TV aerials, whereas an individual who has chosen to visit the cinema may have made the same choice to visit as others, but essentially watches alone (MacCabe 1980, 138–40).

Reading and writing are solitary pursuits (Manguel 1997, 43; Ong 2002, 100), demanding a certain degree of concentration. Libraries are commonly associated with the words 'Silence' and 'Shush!'. Archival repositories cannot be said to have the same place in popular consciousness, otherwise no doubt they too would also have a proverbial association with an enforced silence. Researchers in archival repositories need to concentrate on studying, reading and writing notes, and therefore prefer a quiet reading room. Archival researchers can expect this to be made a condition of their access to the reading room, and are more than likely to be grateful for this particular restriction.

Museums encourage group visits, whether from school groups, families, special-interest groups or coach parties of tourists. A visit to a museum as part of a group can be enjoyable and rewarding. Museums do not demand silence, although their 'aura' may mean that conversation is carried out in quieter, more reverent tones. But anyone who has visited a museum at the same time as a school group will know just how noisy this may be, particularly if the display itself includes its own audio elements.

Sensations

Museum visitors do not necessarily have to do any reading. A 'casual' visitor to a museum may still enjoy their visit without reading any of the text panels or labels there as part of a display. Museum displays are primarily visual, and may address other senses with a wide range of supplementary material such as commentary, music or sound effects. They may even address the sense of smell. The displays at the Jorvik Viking Centre in York include synthetic olfactory stimulation supplied by Dale Air, a company which creates 'designer aromas' including 'Pencil/Wood shavings' and 'Cloisters'. Visitors to the Centre 'have the opportunity to see, hear,

---

25 See 'Diary of Saad Eskander, Director of the Iraq National Library and Archive', hosted by the British Library website, at <http://www.bl.uk/iraqdiary.html>. Attempts at reconstruction are underway.

touch and even smell the Vikings'.[26] Visitors to archives and libraries are used to such physical sensations generated by the documents there, and may well even develop a fondness for such things (Wood 2000, 20–48).

In the mid-1970s the UN defined a museum as 'a building to house collections of objects for inspection, study and enjoyment' (MacCannell 1976, 78). The Museums Association's Code of Ethics uses similar language: museums should '[e]ncourage people to explore collections for inspiration, learning and enjoyment'.[27] The enjoyment of undertaking our own research, of reading, of handling original documents, is not often openly acknowledged, and if it is at all, it is likely to be perceived as trivial or somehow salacious (Manguel 1997, 21; Wood 2000).

'It is an Exhibition, Not a Book'

Museums displays almost always include written textual elements, such as introductory subject panels and explanatory object labels. Curators, exhibition designers and other museum professionals may at times find these textual elements problematic. 'Modern science has yet to find a cure for the number-one museum killer: death by verbiage,' one museum professional has commented; 'It is an exhibition, not a book' (Calder 2006, 40).

Visitors can make their way through exhibitions without reading any of the textual material that supports it: 'throughout an entire museum visit, visitors read about 18 per cent of the labels they encountered' (Punt et al. 1989, 49). One potential problem has been identified for carrying out research into how visitors read text labels: 'Even if visitors look in the direction of a label for an extended time, you can't be sure that they are reading it. They may also be daydreaming' (Punt et al. 1989, 50).

In the reading room of an archival repository, visitors can sit down at a table and take as much time as necessary to read the documents they have selected and requested, unlike the museum, where visitors 'are usually reading exhibition text while they are standing. This means that visitors are subject to crowding and fatigue as they read the words – not sitting comfortably reading at a time of their choosing' (Spencer 2002, 397).

Few amongst the general public who visit museums or other heritage institutions open to the public will have the skills required to read the ancient documents on display, whether papyri or the Magna Carta. It is enough for most museum visitors just to *see*. Here, very particular written documents may have developed an aura almost akin to that of sacred texts: 'illiterates profit from rubbing books on their foreheads, or from whirling prayer-wheels bearing texts they cannot read' (Ong 2002, 92).

When a medieval Book of Psalms was accidentally unearthed from an Irish bog in July 2006, it was taken into safe-keeping by the National Museum of Ireland.

---

26 'Case study – JORVIK Viking Centre', Dale Air designer aromas website, at <http://www.daleair.com/casestudies/jorvik.html>, accessed 13 July 2007.

27 'Code of ethics', Museums Association website, dated 2002, at <http://www.museumsassociation.org/ma/10937>, accessed 27 July 2006.

Within a very short time, the Museum felt obliged to issue a public disclaimer that the document was without any eschatological significance.[28]

Interpretations

Visitors to museums are used to seeing artefacts organized by curators according to a particular theme or forming a narrative of some kind. Museum displays are the result of an interpretation of the past, although this might not necessarily be made obvious to the visitor. Perhaps such a thought might not even occur to the visitor.

However, visitors to archives have to make a conscious effort, and probably expect to make such an effort. Some interpretation may be supplied through the historical notes within finding aids. The finding aid itself simply represents one interpretation, of course. Within the museum, artefacts and objects have been removed from their original environment and require contextual information, usually provided by display text.

When the British Lawnmower Museum's curator, Brian Radam, is available, he will talk visitors through the development of individual machines and their provenance as he guides them through the displays. Visitors without detailed knowledge of mechanical engineering, industrial heritage or horticulture will appreciate the curator's commentary, aiding the interpretation of the collection, which might otherwise even just appear as an extension of the hardware shop. Fortunately, Brian is an entertaining storyteller.

The Smithsonian displayed the *Enola Gay* with the very minimum of interpretative text – almost as if it were a photograph of the aircraft within an archival collection. This in itself nevertheless made a strong political statement, because this was a *public* statement.

The provision of descriptive and interpretative text is an important task for museums. When the Brooklyn Children's Museum undertook visitor research to prepare guidelines on exhibition text, they found some unexpected results: 'To our surprise, we found out that visitors come to our museum with a lot less prior knowledge than we thought' (Punt et al. 1989, 66). This is despite the fact that museums generally try not to make too many demands of their visitors. One manual advises: 'Write all text and narrated components at a level of understanding commensurate with completion of primary school; don't assume secondary or tertiary levels of education' and 'Text should be made accessible to persons without secondary education' (McManus 2000, 14).

Furthermore, museums do not expect a high level of literacy from their visitors: 'Many text writers use a test for an age range of 14 to 15 years – this is about the reading age of a tabloid newspaper' (McManus 2000, 14).

---

28 'Clarification re Psalm 83 in ancient Book of Psalms', National Museum of Ireland website, 27 July 2006, at <http://www.museum.ie/news/details_news.asp?sPressType=1&ne wsid=231>.

Literacy

Lack of reading skills is a problem that is often underestimated. Yet the UN estimates that 860 million adults are illiterate worldwide and state furthermore that 'countless children, youth and adults who attend school or other education programmes fall short of the required level to be considered literate in today's complex world'.[29]

In the UK, recent front-page newspaper headlines have included '12m workers have reading age of children' (Smithers 2006, 1), and 'Firms told: Teach the staff to read' (Austin 2005, 1). These were prompted by government reports into standards of education. The Director-General of the Confederation of British Industry, Sir Digby Jones, had told a conference not many years earlier: 'One in five adults cannot read a fish-and-chip shop menu and 3.5 million adults are paid to go to work every day, yet do not have the functional literacy of an 11-year-old'.[30] This was indeed borne out by the statistics.

The Nobel prize-winning writer José Saramago, sitting on a panel for the Portuguese government's literacy programme, has said 'Reading was and always will be something for the minority. We aren't going to demand a passion for reading from everybody' (Reuters Lisbon 2006, 19).

A passion for reading is apparently lacking in the UK. The National Literacy Trust is an independent charity 'dedicated to building a literate nation'.[31] The Trust recently collated the results of a number of surveys which showed, for example, that more than a third of adults do not read books, with one in five stating that they do not enjoy reading. And more than half feel they do not have a good reason to visit a library.[32] Literacy is a basic minimum skill required for users of archives. This is not a case of archival repositories restricting access or acting in a 'socially exclusive' manner.

Visitors to archives have to make a request to access quite specific documents, and they have to interpret these documents themselves. They have to spend time reading written documents, even when visiting a film or sound archive. At the very least, a researcher has to start with reading the rules and requirements of the reading room. A researcher then has to spend time searching catalogues, reading finding aids, examining any accompanying documentation, perhaps reading transcripts of the recorded spoken word or other supplementary texts.

Written text is linear, sequential, ordered (Büchler et al. 1990, 14). It takes time to read. There is no way around that. The great bulk of material in archival collections consists of text documents. The original material held in an archival repository is therefore at greater risk than that held in a museum, because only a small proportion of archival material is available in facsimile. The text of the original

---

29 United Nations Literacy Decade website, 18 November 2005, at <http://www.unesco.org/education/litdecade/> (home page).

30 'Enterprise in action 2000', National Federation of Enterprise Agencies website, at <http://tinyurl.com/ynoj8r>, accessed 13 July 2007.

31 National Literary Trust website, at <http://www.literacytrust.org.uk/> (home page), accessed 25 July 2007.

32 'Statistics on library use and reading habits', National Literary Trust website, at <http://www.nationalliteracytrust.org.uk/Database/stats/readingstats.html>, accessed 25 July 2007.

documents themselves has to be read, and in order to be read, the documents have to be handled.

Where facsimiles are available, researchers may perhaps be reluctant to make use of them, but few really need more than a reproduction of the original text to meet their information requirements. Only very specialist research demands handling and investigation of the medium of an original document.[33]

There are important resources for researchers, such as the Liddle Collection at the University of Leeds[34] or the Scott Polar Research Institute collection at the University of Cambridge,[35] where a large part of the material is in microfilm or photocopy form. The National Nuclear Archives will be providing access to facsimile documents in these forms.

Facsimiles in turn allow opportunities for outreach. The Museum of London's Roman Boxes project combined surplus genuine Roman artefacts with replica artefacts and introductory text in a 'mini-museum', packed in metal toolboxes, designed to be supplied to 2,000 London schools (Hall and Swain 2000). The World Wide Web, of course, has provided a tremendous outreach opportunity, making digital facsimiles available to a worldwide public.

The World Wide Web

From the late 1940s André Malraux wrote of 'le musée imaginaire'. This title was originally translated by Malraux's US publishers as 'the museum without walls', and it is in this form that the phrase has since entered the lexicon. Malraux wrote of the museum without walls bringing together widely dispersed artworks in different media to a far wider public, making artworks more accessible through the publication of photographic reproductions. Real museums can only display objects and artefacts which are portable, but the museum without walls can display photographic reproductions of tapestries, stained-glass windows, colossal statues or entire buildings (Malraux 1967).

This might perhaps serve as an analogy for the World Wide Web, and Malraux's original phrase might well be translated today as 'the virtual museum'.[36] 'A museum without walls has been opened to us, and it will carry infinitely farther that limited revelation of the world of art which the real museums offer us within their walls' (Malraux 1967, 12).

Gathering documents together in this way also allows many opportunities for creating links of all kinds. For example, the Special Collections division of the John Rylands University Library of Manchester is assembling a digitized collection of

---

33 See Wood 2000, p. 35, to read of some ingenious research by biologists into the work of Geoffrey Chaucer.

34 'Liddle Collection – special collections', Leeds University Library website, at <http://www.leeds.ac.uk/library/spcoll/liddle/index.htm> (home page).

35 Scott Polar Research Institute website, at <http://www.spri.cam.ac.uk/> (home page).

36 With apologies to the 24 Hour Museum website, at <http://www.24hourmuseum.org.uk/> (home page). Established in 1999, and funded by the Museums, Libraries and Archives Council, this has the strap-line 'The National Virtual Museum'; accessed July 2007.

around 11,000 fragments from the document depository (or document cemetery) of an Egyptian synagogue, making them available together online.[37] This material on this project's website can then be easily compared with that displayed on the websites for similar projects at Cambridge University Library and the British Library.

In many cases, the Archives Hub has published for the very first time finding aids that had previously been languishing as typewritten foolscap sheets in filing cabinets in the basements of libraries somewhere in the middle of university campuses: 'It may take generations to evaluate and understand some of these things. It is unfortunate that they must remain here in this inaccessible place, for it will take a concentrated effort by numerous scholars to make meaning of them' (Miller 1993, 224).

Publishing on the Web brings its own challenges. We know that visitors to the Archives Hub want to see more than collection-level descriptions. Some visitors to the website are disappointed not to see digital images and transcripts of the complete contents of collections. The National Archives' online *Domesday Book* will surely raise public expectations even higher.

The Web presents its own issues of physical accessibility, and for digital documents there is still the question of physical preservation. For at least a decade now there has been concern over the threat of a 'digital Dark Ages' (Kuny 1998), with archivists having to take on a new role protecting and preserving electronic resources and maintaining access to these resources. We have seen how the National Nuclear Archive views digital documents at risk of degeneration or loss of accessibility and therefore plans to embark on converting digital documents to physical, analogue forms.

At the same time, of course, for the International Council on Archives the Web presents new opportunities for interlinking information resources, managing and exchanging data and transmitting information to large, dispersed audiences (Macarthy and Upshall 2006, 14).

The presentation of digitized documents on the Web provides opportunities for display and interpretation of the kind perhaps previously only available in museums. The online version of the Domesday Book made available by The National Archives does much more than provide reproductions of the original document, also providing transcripts, translations and information about the document's historical context.[38] Sitting down at the computer at home, at school or in the library, visitors to the website have the chance to read as much or as little of this material as they wish. They could even access such websites when on the move, thanks to the many portable Internet devices that are becoming increasingly available. Many other important documents or even complete collections have been digitized in recent years; for example, the photographs, letters and diaries of Gertrude Bell held at the University of Newcastle have all been made available to view and read on the Web.[39]

---

37 Rylands Genizah website, at <http://rylibweb.man.ac.uk/insight/genizah.htm> (home page), accessed July 2007.

38 'Domesday Book: Britain's finest treasure', The National Archives website, at <http://www.nationalarchives.gov.uk/domesday/> (home page), accessed July 2007.

39 Gertrude Bell Project website, at <http://www.gerty.ncl.ac.uk> (home page), accessed July 2007.

Documents and readers

The Web is a public space, and a predominantly visual environment, like the museum. Yet at the same time the World Wide Web is predicated on the written word, like archives.

The Archives Hub sometimes receives direct enquiries via telephone or e-mail from Web users who clearly have failed to understand what they have been looking at. When the Archives Hub publishes a finding aid for the records of a corporate body such as a commercial company, visitors who have reached the finding aid directly from a search engine such as Google will have little context in which to interpret this document. Such users may completely fail to recognize this very particular genre of document and therefore assume that they have reached the company's own corporate website, even mistaking the Archives Hub's helpline telephone number and e-mail address for those of the company whose records are being described.

This is a common example of a distinct disadvantage in accessing documents this way. In the early days of the Web, the Australian author and Internet advocate Dale Spender observed, 'in comparison to the sophisticated way that we are alerted to what is in books (so that we usually know at a glance whether or not we are interested), the packaging on the Internet has not got to first base' (Spender 1995, 60). At around the same time, the information scientist David M. Levy, of the Xerox Palo Alto Research Center, had noted how when reading documents in long-established analogue media we can 'recognize the intended purpose and institutional role of a document from the form alone' and remarked that 'one does not need a user manual to read a newspaper' (Levy 1994, 25). Malraux had noted this disadvantage of the museum without walls: 'In an album or an art book, objects are generally reproduced in more or less the same format. The limitations of the printed page are such that a reclining Buddha over sixty feet in length may appear four times the size of a Tangara figurine' (Malraux 1967, 82). This applies just as much to the many transformations undergone by documents published on the Web. Very recently Spender has said: 'Where we once needed print literacy – now we need digital literacies'.[40]

There is great scope for user education, whether it comes to accessing archives in a repository or to accessing facsimiles online. Archivists can have a role to play in general education as intermediaries working with education professionals, with archives as an educational resource, as demonstrated by the West Midlands 'pay&power' archives project. This included both workshops for teachers and training for archivists (McCourt 2006). Bringing an awareness of archives in this way to new audiences, and especially to younger audiences, may well enhance understanding of archives and would certainly encourage a public *perception* of archives.

---

40 Dale Spender website, 15 July 2007, at <http://www.dalespender.com.au/> (home page).

Whose History? Permitted Use and Users

> The drama of the civilization of the century of machines is not to have lost the gods, for they are less lost than people say; it is to have lost all sense of a profound notion of Man (André Malraux, in Cate 1997, 377).

> We are who we are because of the strides and accomplishments of our ancestors. To that end, we must call to task the caretakers of our heritage when they no longer safeguard that inheritance. Who owns the past? We all do (International Committee for the Preservation of Lascaux).[41]

Just how 'inevitable' or 'unavoidable' are restrictions on access? Are some restrictions merely due to tradition, inertia, or prejudice? Of course, there are circumstances where lack of access may be due to a lack of resources. Nevertheless, we should always ask ourselves what we can do to improve access.

Visitors to archives have already begun their own personal journey into the past. They will now perhaps require some guidance in identifying and locating documents, but beyond that they will have to do some work of their own; they will have to spend time reading and thinking, alone.

In light of all this, can we really talk of a 'casual' visitor to an archives? Should we ever restrict access to 'serious' researchers? Family historians are somewhat maligned and visitors may have very personal reasons for their research (Etherton 2006). Nevertheless, surely all visitors to archives are serious researchers? Jean-Luc Godard has commented on the distinction between 'amateur' and 'serious': 'It's not division of labour but division of love and labour. … And if they were together it would be a multiplication not a division' (MacCabe 1980, 157).

There are situations where access has to be restricted in order to protect unique, original material. Digital technologies, especially the World Wide Web, mean that it is becoming easier to create and publish facsimiles, and therefore more difficult to justify restricting access when it comes to the *content* of those documents.

However, the creation and provision of facsimile documents, in digital or other forms, may of course be too expensive an operation for the many archival repositories struggling for financial resources. Researchers will almost certainly have to handle original documents for quite some time yet.

The slogan for the pay&power project was 'Archives, a bridge between the past and the future'. We need to preserve records of the past for many reasons. We need access to the past to understand the present. The past needs a future. The past needs us.

Let's try to preserve the future.

---

41 'The heritage of Lascaux: to whom does the past belong?', International Committee for the Preservation of Lascaux website, at <http://savelascaux.org/crisis_past.php>, accessed 25 July 2007.

References

Ascherson, N. (1995), 'Modernism and the Nazis: a Nightmare', in Büchler, P. and Papastergiadis, N. (eds), pp. 69–83.

Austin, S. (2005), 'Firms told: Teach the staff to read', *Metro*, 14 December, 1.

Bataille, G. (1955), *Lascaux: or, The Birth of Art: Prehistoric Painting* (Lausanne: Skira).

Benford, G. (1999), *Deep Time: How Humanity Communicates Across Millennia* (New York: Avon).

Benjamin, W. and Arendt, H. (1999), *Illuminations* (London: Pimlico).

Büchler, P., Kolář, J. and Lingwood, J. (1990), *Jiří Kolář: the End of Words: Selected Works 1947–1970* (London: Institute of Contemporary Arts in association with the Albemarle Gallery).

Büchler, P. and Papastergiadis, N. (eds) (1995), *Random Access: On Crisis and Its Metaphor* (London: Rivers Oram).

Buckland, M.K. (1997), 'What is a "document"?', *Journal of the American Society for Information Science*, 48(9), 804–8.

Calder, P.R. (2006), 'The right type', *Museum Practice*, 35, 40–41.

Cate, C. (1997), *André Malraux: a Biography* (New York: Fromm International).

Chernow, B. (2002), *Christo and Jeanne-Claude: a Biography* (New York: St. Martin's Press).

Christo's Valley Curtain (2004), DVD. Film directed by Albert Maysles, David Maysles and Charlotte Zwerin, 1974. Additional audio commentary by Christo, Jeanne-Claude and Albert Maysles recorded 2004. Disc 1 of *5 Films about Christo & Jeanne-Claude: a Maysles Films Production* (2004) DVD. USA. Plexifilm. Available as commercially published DVD.

Clute, J. and Nicholls, P. (1993), *The Encyclopedia of Science Fiction*, new edn (London: Orbit).

Connor, S. (2006), 'Prehistoric "Sistine Chapel" under threat from fungus', *The Independent*, 10 May, 3.

Crawford, H. (2005), 'Turning a blind eye', *Museums Journal*, 105 (2), 6–7.

Croall, S. and Sempler, K. (1980), *Nuclear Power for Beginners*, rev. edn (London: Writers and Readers).

Dubin, S.C. (1999), *Displays of Power: Memory and Amnesia in the American Museum* (New York and London: New York University Press).

Edwards, R. (2005), 'Politics left UK nuclear waste plans in disarray', *New Scientist*, 186, 12.

Eshleman, C. (2003), *Juniper Fuse: Upper Paleolithic Imagination and the Construction of the Underworld* (Middletown CT: Wesleyan University Press).

Etherton, J. (2006), 'The role of archives in the perception of self', *Journal of the Society of Archivists*, 27 (2), 227–46.

Hall, J. and Swain, H. (2000), 'Roman Boxes for London's Schools: an Outreach Service by the Museum of London', in McManus, P.M. (ed.).

Halstead, R., Hazeley, J., Morris, A. and Morris, J. (2005), *Bollocks to Alton Towers: Uncommonly British Days Out* (London: Michael Joseph).

Hapgood, D. and Richardson, D. (2002), *Monte Cassino: the Story of the Most Controversial Battle of World War II* (Cambridge MA: Da Capo).

Kuny, T. (1998), 'A digital Dark Ages? Challenges in the preservation of electronic information', *International Preservation News*, 17, 8–13.

Levy, D.M. (1994), 'Fixed or fluid? Document stability and new media', in European Conference on Hypermedia Technology, *Echt '94: 1994 Proceedings, Edinburgh* (New York: ACM), pp. 24–31.

Lord, B. and Lord, G.D. (eds) (2000), *The Manual of Museum Exhibitions* (Walnut Creek CA: AltaMira Press).

Macarthy, G. and Upshall, I. (2006), *ICA Study 18: Radioactive Waste Information: Meeting our Obligations to Future Generations with regard to the Safety of Waste Disposal Facilities* (Paris: International Council on Archives).

MacCabe, C. (1980), *Godard: Images, Sounds, Politics* (London: Macmillan).

MacCannell, D. (1976), *The Tourist: a New Theory of the Leisure Class* (New York: Schocken Books).

McCourt, K. (2006), 'Industry and politics in the West Midlands: the pay&power project', *ARC (Archives, Records Management & Conservation)*, 197, 28–9.

McManus, P.M. (ed.) (2000), *Archaeological Displays and the Public: Museology and Interpretation*, 2nd edn (London: Archetype Publications).

McManus, P.M. (2000), 'Written Communications for Museums and Heritage Sites', in McManus, P.M. (ed.), pp. 7–22.

Malraux, A. (1967), *Museum Without Walls* (London: Secker & Warburg).

Manguel, A. (1997), *A History of Reading* (London: Flamingo).

Martin, H. and Cochrane, L.G. (1994), *The History and Power of Writing* (Chicago IL and London: University of Chicago Press).

Miller, W.M. (1993), *A Canticle for Leibowitz* (London: Orbit).

'Nuclear Future' (2005), *Museum Practice*, Winter, 8.

Ong, W.J. (2002), *Orality and Literacy* (London: Routledge).

Palmer, S. (2006), 'Look out! Nuclear waste below', *New Scientist*, 191 (2568), 44–5.

Procter, M. and Lewis, C.P. (eds) (2000), *New Directions in Archival Research* (Liverpool: Liverpool University Centre for Archive Studies).

Punt, B., Ratcliffe, S. and Stern, S. (1989), *Doing It Right: a Workbook for Improving Exhibit Labels* (Brooklyn NY: Brooklyn Children's Museum).

Reuters Lisbon (2006), 'Nobel-winning author criticises reading plan', *The Guardian*, 2 June, 19.

Simpson, M. (2005), 'Standing on ceremony', *Museums Journal*, 105 (10), 14–15.

Smithers, R. (2006), '12m workers have reading age of children', *The Guardian*, 24 January, 1.

Spencer, H.A.D. (2002), 'Exhibition Text', in Lord, B. and Lord, G.D. (eds) *The Manual of Museum Exhibitions* (Walnut Creek CA: AltaMira Press), 393–404.

Spender, D. (1995), *Nattering on the Net: Women, Power and Cyberspace* (North Melbourne: Spinifex).

Trask, R.L. (1999), *Language: the Basics*, 2nd edn (London: Routledge).

'A Very British Burial' (2005), *New Scientist*, 186 (2504), 3.

Wallach, J. (1997), *Desert Queen: the Extraordinary Life of Gertrude Bell, Adventurer, Adviser to Kings, Ally of Lawrence Of Arabia* (London: Phoenix Giant).

Winstone, H.V.F. (1978), *Gertrude Bell* (London: Cape).

Wise, M., Gray, D. and Upshall, I. (2005), 'For the record ...', *Nuclear Engineering International*, 50 (616), 24–7.

Wood, H. (2000), 'The Fetish of the Document: an Exploration of Attitudes Toward Archives', in Procter and Lewis (eds), pp. 20–48.

Supplementary bibliography

Although not cited here, the following works provided inspiration and some initial guidance for the original conference presentation and this subsequent essay. A transcript of the presentation with illustrations is available online at <http://www.archiveshub.ac.uk/fallout.shtml>.

Fischer, S.R. (2001), *A History of Writing* (London: Reaktion Books).

Hoban, R. (1982), *Riddley Walker* (London: Picador).

Hoban, R. (1975), *Turtle Diary* (London: Jonathan Cape).

Morville, P. (2005), *Ambient Findability* (Sebastapol CA and Farnham, UK: O'Reilly).

Saramago, J. (1999), *All the Names* (London: Harvill).

Spalding, J. (2005), *The Art of Wonder: a History of Seeing* (Munich and London: Prestel).

Index